*Praise for*

# NEW YORK ART DECO

"Anthony Robins's *New York Art Deco* fills a void in the design library of New York. Well organized by itineraries that begin at the very tip of Manhattan and work their way into the other four boroughs, it is filled with invaluable information on the monuments of Art Deco and French *moderne* structures whose design perfectly expresses the streamlined era when speed and movement were celebrated. This is a must-have book for every lover of Art Deco, whether you are a New Yorker or a visitor from New Zealand."

— David Garrard Lowe, author of *Art Deco New York*

"The Art Deco style fits New York like a glove, from the skyscraping Chrysler Building to the little, eye-popping Lane Theater on Staten Island, and nobody knows it like Anthony Robins. If you thought you knew Art Deco—as I did, before I read his *New York Art Deco*—then buy this book and be surprised."

— Christopher Gray, author of the former
*New York Times* Streetscapes column

"Buy this book, take a few wonderful walks around the entire city (discovering some fine New York neighborhoods you probably have never been to), from the Grand Concourse and Washington Heights' treasure trove of Deco to the Chrysler Building to Flatbush in Brooklyn, and ask yourself, do all those new glass towers in Manhattan leave you as delighted as Art Deco's confections, whether seven stories or seventy? That generation knew how to make buildings that you really want to live in, work in, and walk by. Thank you, Anthony Robins, for giving us the keys to that kingdom."

— Barry Lewis, architectural historian

"With the publication of *New York Art Deco* everyone, from the city explorer to the armchair reader, can now experience Anthony Robins's dynamic Art Deco walking tours. Robins not only discusses the city's famed Deco skyscrapers, but also identifies the spectacular but little-known Deco gems spread across the city. This book is a must for those who love New York and thrill to Art Deco architecture."

— Andrew Scott Dolkart, author of *The Row House Reborn: Architecture and Neighborhoods in New York City, 1908–1929*

# NEW YORK ART DECO

Silhouette of the Empire State Building superimposed over a map of New York State, designed by Oscar Bach, and located in the Fifth Avenue lobby of the Empire State Building. *Photograph by Meghan Weatherby*

# NEW YORK ART DECO

## A Guide to Gotham's Jazz Age Architecture

Anthony W. Robins

COLOR PLATES BY RANDY JUSTER

MAPS BY JOHN TAURANAC

excelsior editions

AN IMPRINT OF THE STATE UNIVERSITY OF NEW YORK PRESS

*Frontispiece photograph by Meghan Weatherby*
*Photographs in gallery by Randy Juster*
*Author photo by Joyce Ravid*
*All additional photographs by the author*

Published by
State University of New York Press, Albany



Printed in the United States of America



Excelsior Editions is an imprint of State University of New York Press

For information, contact State University of New York Press, Albany, NY
www.sunypress.edu

Production, Laurie D. Searl
Marketing, Kate R. Seburyamo

**Library of Congress Cataloging-in-Publication Data**

Names: Robins, Anthony, author.
Title: New York art deco : a guide to Gotham's jazz age architecture / Anthony W. Robins.
Description: Albany : State University of New York Press, 2017. | Series: Excelsior editions | Includes bibliographical references and index.
Identifiers: LCCN 2016031440 (print) | LCCN 2016032159 (ebook) | ISBN 9781438463964 (pbk. : alk. paper) | ISBN 9781438463988 (e-book)
Subjects: LCSH: Art deco (Architecture)—New York (State)—New York—Guidebooks. | New York (N.Y.)—Buildings, structures, etc. | New York (N.Y.)—Tours.
Classification: LCC NA735.N5 R63 2017 (print) | LCC NA735.N5 (ebook) | DDC 720.9747—dc23
LC record available at https://lccn.loc.gov/2016031440

10 9 8 7 6 5 4 3 2 1

*To the Art Deco Society of New York*

*Educating New Yorkers about their city's Art Deco wonders for thirty years.*

ART DECO: A name coined by the curators of a 1966 Paris exhibition looking back at 1920s design. The curators derived the name from the title of an enormously influential Paris exposition of 1925 devoted to contemporary trends in all the visual arts: *Exposition Internationale des Arts Décoratifs et Industriels Modernes* (International Exposition of Modern Industrial and Decorative Arts). Though Art Deco can be found around the world—in North and South America, Europe, parts of Asia and Africa, and Australia and New Zealand—in New York City it has a particular flavor, developed in the city's great skyscrapers.

Though the term "Art Deco" can refer to all kinds of architectural design trends from the 1920s to the 1940s, it's often used specifically to refer to the "vertical style" of late-1920s skyscrapers. The term "Moderne"—a shortening of the term "Style Moderne"—generally refers to buildings from the 1930s and '40s with a horizontal rather than a vertical orientation, and noticeably streamlined curves. "WPA Moderne" refers to government buildings commissioned by the Works Progress Administration during the Great Depression; such buildings often combine Moderne styling with a stripped-down version of Classical columns and arches. During the 1930s, the style became known as "Modern Classic." For the most part, this guidebook focuses on the earlier buildings, but does include several notable later examples.

# CONTENTS

# ACKNOWLEDGMENTS

Photographer Randy Juster contributed the exquisite color plates that capture the beauty of New York's Deco treasures.

Legendary New York cartographer John Tauranac drew the maps that accompany each of the Manhattan itineraries.

Rob Schaffer walked the itineraries and drove with me on photo safaris through the Bronx and Brooklyn.

My wife, Susan Leicher, who has explored countless blocks of the city with me, has been urging me to write this book for thirty years.

Thanks to them all!

# INTRODUCTION—ART DECO NEW YORK

Art Deco today is the fashionable name for all the various modernistic architectural styles, current between the two World Wars, that helped redefine New York City as the world's modern metropolis. The style is readily recognizable, but its substance is sometimes hard to pin down. Its sources can be found in European decorative arts, but also in New York's zoning regulations. Its practitioners range from socially prominent architects with sophisticated European training to immigrant builders who were largely self-taught. Its monuments include major Midtown skyscrapers and modest Bronx apartment houses. It is flowery and it is zigzag; it is intimate and it is monolithic; it is abstract and it is figurative; it is Roaring Twenties extravagant and it is Depression-era cheap. In all, Art Deco has become the collective name for all the brash, polychromatic, geometric, whiz-bang effects that could make a neighborhood diner or a multimillion-dollar skyscraper somehow suggest a skimpy dress, a rakish look, and a glass of champagne.

## New York in the Jazz Age

Art Deco coalesced as a distinct manner of architecture at a time of massive growth in the great metropolis of the New World. New York emerged at the end of the First World War as one of the world's great cities. Its population was increasing by the millions, spilling into new residential districts in the Bronx, Brooklyn, and Queens, while its dense Wall Street business district grew denser and spread to Midtown, which sprouted the city's second skyline. As it grew, the city characterized in the nineteenth century as one of sunshine and shadow—of the very rich and the very poor—developed a massive middle-class population, and with it a mass culture made possible by the technical marvels of the new century. This was the Jazz Age, defined by one writer as a modern era of skyscrapers, the World Series, tabloids, radio, and the movies.

This new city—dense, modern, and a citadel of mass culture—found its built expression in skyscrapers, apartment houses, movie palaces, lunch counters, and bus terminals, all serving the anonymous millions of the metropolis, particularly those on their way up from immigrant poverty to middle-class comfort. In the first years of the century, architects draped such buildings in exotic styles, extravagant if imprecise versions of the past glories of foreign places. But in the late 1920s, and on through the '30s and into the '40s, the glories of the past gave way to the fantasies of the future, in the explosion of exotic modern styles we now call Art Deco.

## The Skyscraper Architects

Art Deco drew on many disparate sources, and ultimately touched every modern building type, but in New York it took shape first as a fashion for skyscrapers. Two dozen major monuments, conceived or completed inside nine years (from 1923 to 1932), designed by a handful of architects—several of whom regularly lunched together—created the new modern style that soon spread to thousands of buildings of all sizes designed by dozens of other architects over the better part of three decades.

The handful of Deco pioneers included four very different architects, of varying output, who were associated with the style from its beginnings: Raymond Hood, Ralph Walker, William Van Alen, and Ely Jacques Kahn.

Hood took the limelight by winning, together with John Mead Howells, the influential 1922 Chicago Tribune Building competition, and then designing four major Manhattan towers: the American Radiator (5.7), Daily News (5.1), McGraw-Hill (5.8/5.12), and RCA Buildings—the last as the seventy-story centerpiece of Rockefeller Center (6.10). Hood adopted the pose of a no-nonsense, businesslike architect manufacturing shelter, writing that "there has been entirely too much talk about the collaboration of architect, painter and sculptor; nowadays, the collaborators are the architects, the engineer, and the plumber." And: "Beauty is utility, developed in a manner to which the eye is accustomed by habit, in so far as this development does not detract from its quality of usefulness." Yet while writing about design as a series of effects clustered to give the greatest impact for the dollar, Hood produced some of the most imaginatively theatrical architecture of his day: the red-and-white-striped tapered stacked masses of the Daily News Building, the greenish-blue-tiled McGraw-Hill Building, and the soaring RCA tower. In the words of a 1931 *New Yorker* architectural critic, "Raymond Hood possesses the position in architecture that he wants. He is its brilliant bad boy."

Walker, later voted "architect of the century" by the American Institute of Architects, emerged in 1923 as the enfant terrible of architecture with his Barclay-Vesey Telephone headquarters (2.4) in lower Manhattan. This was the first of a chain of Walker-designed Art Deco phone company skyscrapers based on behemoth massing, expressionistic brickwork, and huge lobbies, many with grand pictorial schemes illustrating some facet of modern telecommunications. Most extraordinary of all Walker's work was No. 1 Wall Street, the Irving Trust Company building (1.3), a monolithic fifty-story Gothic Modern tower, with undulating brick walls, zigzag windows, and a gold-and-red mosaic-lined two-story Reception Hall.

Van Alen, once called "the Ziegfeld of his profession," produced only one major Art Deco monument before moving on to other pursuits, but it proved to be the best known of them all: the Chrysler Building (5.4). While Florenz Ziegfeld, the great showman, dazzled audiences on West 42nd Street with his Follies, over on East 42nd Van Alen dazzled the world with the first skyscraper to rise above the thousand-foot mark set by the Eiffel Tower. From setbacks marked by giant metal replicas of winged Chrysler hood ornaments, Van Alen's tower rose to a brilliantly shiny, tapering steel crown and spire visible for miles around.

Kahn, perhaps least familiar of the four, is best known for his high-profile office building at Two Park Avenue (3.4)—one of the city's earliest Art Deco skyscrapers—with its speckled, multicolored, terra-cotta façade, and for several idiosyncratic lobby designs, like the Film Center Building (5.11), which draw on a strong decorative arts aesthetic. Yet Kahn was by far the most prolific of the original group, producing dozens of loft buildings for the garment industry, the printing trade, and manufacturing businesses throughout downtown and Midtown Manhattan. Hood and Walker developed the style, Van Alen created its best-known icon, but Kahn filled up Manhattan's business precincts with solid, serviceable, workaday products.

Older, established firms soon found their way to the new modernistic styles. Schultze & Weaver, designers of such elegant, Beaux-Arts Classic-inspired Fifth Avenue hotels as the Pierre and the Sherry-Netherland, turned to Art Deco for the new Waldorf-Astoria (6.5/6.7). Walker & Gillette (no relation to Ralph Walker), known for houses and estates in a variety of traditional styles—Tudor Revival, Mission Revival, neo-Georgian, neo-Federal—produced the geometric Fuller Building (7.2). Cross & Cross, authors of sober, academically styled office buildings, turned out the wildly exuberant General Electric tower (6.4/6.6). Shreve & Lamb, formerly partners with Carrére & Hastings, masters of Beaux-Arts classicism, produced the Empire State Building (3.3/3.6). And dozens of smaller firms brought the style to buildings of every kind throughout the five boroughs.

## The Art Deco Look

The great Art Deco skyscrapers owe certain of their decorative motifs to the Exposition for which they were later named, especially to the stylized floral fashions of early-twentieth-century France. Other European sources include the French Art Nouveau, the Austrian Sezession and German Expressionism, among a host of early Modern design movements. Much of the formal conception of the skyscrapers—the internal planning of their public spaces, their external expression as major urban monuments—marks them as heirs to the grand Classical tradition of the École des Beaux-Arts in Paris. Their ornamental forms often reflect the influence of Aztec, Mayan, and African art.

The modern American buildings owe just as much, however, to the circumstances of their own time and place. The influence on the skyscrapers of New York's revolutionary 1916 zoning resolution can scarcely be overstated. Designed to ensure adequate light and air for surrounding streets and buildings, the new law helped shape skyscraper bulk for half a century, virtually mandating buildings that fill half a city block at their base, then taper inward via mathematically calculated setbacks, rising into the skyline as slender towers. An influential set of studies in the early 1920s by Hugh Ferriss, the famed architectural renderer of the period, explored the potential of skyscraper design under the new regulations. Thanks to the new zoning laws, three-dimensionally-designed building mass, like a piece of abstract sculpture, became a chief characteristic of the new Art Deco architectural manner.

Another hallmark, on the other hand, goes straight back through the genealogical skyscraper line to Louis Sullivan in Chicago: the organization of a building's hundreds of windows in long, vertical columns. It was Sullivan who wrote that a skyscraper should be "a proud and soaring thing, rising in sheer exultation." Rather than organizing windows as horizontal rows, suggesting floors of offices stacked one on top of another, he arranged them vertically, as tall, uninterrupted bays of windows recessed behind and between tall, uninterrupted vertical stripes of brick wall, suggesting uninterrupted upward motion. The same arrangement became typical of Art Deco towers—and architects at the time, lacking a better name, often described their buildings as in the "vertical style."

The most publicly visible part of any skyscraper, of course, is its presence on the skyline. From neo-Gothic towers to International Style boxtops, all skyscrapers have skyline value of one kind or another. The Art Deco skyscrapers meet the sky in a variety of razzle-dazzle concoctions, ranging from the Chrysler Building's elegant steel spire to the General Electric Building's Gothic Modern crown to the Empire State Building's dirigible-mooring mast. Perhaps most telling of all is the disingenuously flat top of the Daily News Building. Raymond Hood later wrote that he decided to let the building simply stop when it reached its top. In fact, however, he did no such thing—he continued the walls of the façade many feet higher than the building's roof, to hide such ugly utilities as elevator shafts and water towers. He wanted to add to the skyline a building with the dramatic effect of stopping at the top, not the messy reality. But perhaps the most remarkable aspect of the Art Deco skyline is that it can appear on six-story apartment houses as easily as on seventy-story skyscrapers, witness the skyline treatment of elevator buildings on the Grand Concourse in the Bronx or Ocean Avenue in Brooklyn.

Standard Art Deco ornament certainly helps identify the buildings from the period—zigzags, stylized floral patterns, striking geometries, and later, streamlined curves and speed lines. But perhaps more telling than the mold from which the forms are cut are their materials and color. The Art Deco period saw the development and use of such modern synthetic materials as Vitrolite and Bakelite for decorative use. For buildings, a major new material proved to be Nirosta, a rustproof, nickel-chrome-steel alloy that allowed the use of metal on the exterior of skyscrapers, most extravagantly on the tower and spire of the Chrysler Building. The ornamental use of metal, brick, and terra cotta, and especially the application of a variety of colors, became the decorative hallmark of Art Deco buildings, replacing in large measure a reliance on carved stone ornament based on historical styles. Hood's American Radiator Building is black and gold. His Daily News Building relies almost entirely on the contrast between red and white brick for its decorative effects, including red and white brick spandrels set between the windows—the few metal zigzags at the building's base hardly matter at all.

## The Art of Advertising

An architectural critic writing about the Daily News Building in 1930 shrewdly observed that Hood had come to understand architecture as a variant of advertising art. And indeed, the great Art Deco skyscrapers are nothing if not giant advertisements for their clients. Exotic grand entrances, dramatic vertical towers, and long tapering spires made for buildings that could hardly help becoming corporate symbols.

But the architects went further, incorporating corporate imagery into the building's ornamental schemes, especially at main entrances and inside grand lobbies. To the Chrysler Building's winged radiator caps Van Alen added brick tracery suggesting a Chrysler's tires, hubcaps, and running board, and, in the lobby, a ceiling mural showing the building's very construction, but also suggesting the history of transportation—which culminated, of course, in the Chrysler automobile. The elevator doors at Walker & Gillette's Fuller Building, headquarters of the Fuller Construction Company, sport metal images of men at work building the metropolis of the future, while mosaic portraits of major Fuller projects are set into the floor. Hood's grand, three-story entrance to the Daily News Building centers on an enormous bas-relief showing the denizens of a busy modern metropolis buying newspapers, while inside, a lobby conceived as a gigantic popular science display helped educate the masses that the paper considered its core audience. Perhaps the most elaborate program was concocted for Rockefeller Center, where the symbols of John D. Rockefeller, Jr.'s, cherished hopes for international understanding and technological advancement covered the buildings inside and out.

The most unusual aspect of such ornamental programs may have been the glorification of the very buildings in question. The grand bas-relief over the Daily News entrance rises to a dazzling image of the great striped building itself. The ceiling mural of transportation inside the Chrysler Building's lobby metamorphoses into a tall portrait of Chrysler's skyscraper, its tip touching the top of the main entrance on Lexington Avenue. On the far wall of the Empire State Building's Fifth Avenue entrance lobby rises a silhouette of the world's tallest building. Perched above the main entrance of the Cities Service Building at 70 Pine Street (1.6) is an enormous sculpted replica of that seventy-story tower—with a duplicate over the entrance on Cedar Street thrown in for good measure.

## Filtering Out and Down Across the Metropolis

The Depression put an end to the building of skyscrapers—the last ones opened in 1932—but the great towers had already transformed the skyline, and their impact was felt across the metropolis. Art Deco, firmly launched, continued into the 1930s and 1940s in building types of all kinds throughout the five boroughs.

Among the first to show the influence of the skyscraper style were Manhattan apartment buildings. Late-nineteenth-century apartment houses—accepted by New York's well-to-do only reluctantly—had early on turned to the glories of Europe for respectable architectural models. The Dakota on West 72nd Street, built in the 1880s, suggested a grand, German Renaissance palace fit for, if not a German prince, then several hundred fortunate American families. Fifty years later, the designers of the Majestic Apartments (8.3) directly across the street abandoned the European palaces of centuries past in favor of the American skyscrapers of the new century to come—creating one of three strikingly vertical twin-towered Art Deco apartment skyscrapers prominently silhouetted in the residential skyline of Central Park West. At the same time and in the same way, the new

Waldorf-Astoria, successor to the old Victorian pile that once occupied the site of the Empire State Building, was brought up to date as a twin-towered Art Deco skyscraper hotel on Park Avenue.

More unexpected perhaps was the creation of a residential skyline not of thirty-story apartment towers in Manhattan but of six-story elevator apartment houses in Brooklyn and the Bronx. Dozens of architects—many of them immigrants whose training ranged from sophisticated to rudimentary—brought the color and vitality of Midtown skyscrapers to the Grand Concourse, Ocean Avenue, and the side streets of Brighton Beach where Brooklyn meets the Atlantic Ocean. How did the high-class skyscraper style make its way to the middle-class precincts of the outer boroughs? Marvin Fine, of the firm of Horace Ginsbern & Associates, watched both the Daily News and Chrysler Buildings rise in 1930 from the ringside seat of his East 42nd Street office; he later recalled telling his boss that those red and white brick spandrels on the Daily News would make a terrific trademark for their new apartment blocks on the Grand Concourse.

By the 1930s, builders and architects throughout the city had caught on to the new style. Sedate department stores expanded into raffish modern additions, as at Bloomingdale's (7.1) in Manhattan, or commissioned brand-new Deco buildings, like J. Kurtz & Sons (14.8) in Jamaica, Queens. The exotic eclecticism of movie palaces gave way to an exotic modernism, whether in small Depression-era neighborhood houses like the Lane (15.5) in New Dorp, Staten Island, or in the grand fantasy of Radio City Music Hall in the heart of Midtown Manhattan. Parking garages and filling stations, banks, restaurants, nightclubs, airport terminals, even churches found their way to the style of the modern metropolis.

## The Fall and Rise of Art Deco

Economics undoubtedly played a part in the appeal of the Art Deco style. In hard times, what could be more attractive than a simple and affordable design, in which a change in color or a geometric pattern in the brickwork could make a cheap building seem stylish and up-to-date? Perhaps inevitably, the various modernisms of Art Deco became associated with the Great Depression in the minds of the people who lived through it. By the 1960s, shortly before its name was coined, Art Deco had fallen into almost total disrepute, a depressing relic of the past, condemned as a misinformed modernism whose practitioners had been unable to comprehend the austere, pristine purity of the International Style, the True Modern.

Over the past four decades, as part of the general reappraisal of all historic architecture, Art Deco has been rediscovered, reconsidered, and re-embraced. It appeals to us as stylish and romantic. Perhaps we see it, wistfully, as the modern road not taken, and wish it could take the place of the dreary banality that passed for modern in the decades following World War II. We have, in short, adopted it as a usable modern past. The rediscovery of Art Deco may have seemed a passing fad at times—witness a *New Yorker* cartoon captioned, "Do you realize we are living through the second time people got tired of Art Deco?" Deco lovers may note with pleasure, however, that the cartoon in question appeared in 1984, and in the decades since then the national and international passion for Art Deco has only grown.

Today, Art Deco New York survives and flourishes. Ninety years after Art Deco's introduction to the city, its great monuments have evolved from brash modern upstarts to historic landmarks. Many have been lovingly restored, from the world-famous spire of the Chrysler Building to the lobbies of Bronx apartment buildings. And they're waiting impatiently for you to visit and discover their many charms.

# A NOTE ON ITINERARIES

I developed many of the itineraries in this guidebook—beginning in 1982—as programs for the Art Deco Society of New York. The first eleven are in Manhattan, arranged roughly from south to north, and each is meant to be walked. The sites in the other boroughs, too widely scattered to be organized as walking tours, are simply grouped by neighborhood, and best visited by car, bus, or subway.

Each building is numbered to indicate both itself and its itinerary; for example, the first building in the first itinerary is 1.1 (actually, since that entry has two buildings, it's numbered 1.1a). "See" references will always use that numbering system. In a few instances, of very tall skyscrapers, the entry is split in two—for example, the Empire State Building, seen first from afar (3.3), and later from closer up (3.6); the "see" reference will be (3.3/3.6).

Directions rely on the convention that in Manhattan—which does not lie on a true north-south axis—"north" means uptown, "south" downtown, "east" toward the East River, and "west" toward the Hudson River.

The itineraries are designed to be easy to follow. But tours can sometimes feel like scavenger hunts. Feel free to break away from any itinerary if you see something interesting, to stop for coffee, or just to look around.

Please note that this is a guidebook, organized into itineraries, and not an exhaustive survey of every Art Deco building in the city. The Art Deco Society of New York has undertaken an Art Deco Registry, and may one day have a complete list, but it will include hundreds, if not thousands, of buildings. If your favorite Art Deco building in Manhattan hasn't made it into this guide book, it's most likely beyond the reach of any of the walking-tour itineraries. Among my own favorites that couldn't be included: the 369th Regiment Armory on Fifth Avenue in Harlem and the Salvation Army headquarters on West 14th Street, as well as several of Ralph Walker's telephone-company buildings. The itineraries for the boroughs outside Manhattan include a dozen or so of the most interesting buildings, but much has had to be omitted. The eleven WPA-era pools and play centers are wonderful structures, and the single examples in the Bronx, Queens, and Staten Island are included, but the remaining eight, divided between Brooklyn and Manhattan, are not, for reasons of space.

Please also note that, with the exception of government-owned buildings, all the sites in this tour are private property. Most hotels, and some office buildings, normally allow visitors to enter at least their lobbies, but inclusion in this book does not of itself grant permission to enter any building.

Many of the buildings in this guide are either individually designated New York City landmarks, or included within a designated New York City historic district, and so noted in the text as follows: each entry for an individually designated landmark is marked with an asterisk★; if it is also an interior landmark, with two asterisks★★; if exclusively an interior landmark, with three asterisks★★★. Buildings located within historic districts are marked (HD); a few are both individual landmarks and within historic districts and marked ★(HD). Several of the buildings, while not local landmarks or included within local historic districts, are nevertheless listed in the National Register of Historic Places, or included within National Register historic districts; these are marked (NR) or (NR HD) but only if they are not also local landmarks. All landmarks and historic districts, whether locally designated or listed in the National Register, have official research reports available online (see "A Note on Sources" for information on how to access those reports).

# ITINERARY NO. 1
# FROM BOWLING GREEN TO WALL STREET

Downtown Deco includes more than a dozen major skyscrapers and midrange office buildings rising from Manhattan's bedrock. Unrivaled skyscraper designs include Ralph Walker's Gothic Modern fantasy of the Irving Trust tower (1.3), and the Art Deco–encrusted Cities Service headquarters (1.6). A new insurance district on John Street created opportunities for architects better represented in other parts of town: Ely Jacques Kahn (1.8, 1.11), better known in the Garment Center; Shreve, Lamb & Harmon (1.9), architects of the Empire State Building; and Louis Allen Abramson (1.7), designer of automats, hospitals, and synagogues. Tucked in and around the sides of the financial district, smaller but equally stylish Deco survivors include a pair of buildings on West Street by Starrett & Van Vleck (1.1).

*The walk begins at the steps of the former U.S. Custom House facing onto Bowling Green at the foot of Broadway.*

Visitors approaching New York City across the harbor—whether on million-dollar ocean liners or the Staten Island ferry—can still find themselves mesmerized by the fairytale skyline of Downtown Manhattan. That view has changed over the decades, but a careful observer can still pick out the romantic spires of an earlier age that made the skyline the symbol of New York, the world's first modern metropolis. And of those spires, the most romantic of all are the great Art Deco towers.

Unlike Midtown Manhattan, which grew its original skyline in the 1920s just as Deco was coming into fashion, Downtown had already sprouted some of the country's very first skyscrapers back in the late nineteenth century, leaving fewer plots available for post–World War I redevelopment. But towering here and there above the narrow streets—bequeathed to the city by the seventeenth-century Dutch colony of Nieuw Amsterdam—are some of the country's finest zigzag and streamlined delights, glittering pinnacles of Wall Street prosperity, monuments to the high-flying corporations of 1920s banking, oil, and telecommunications.

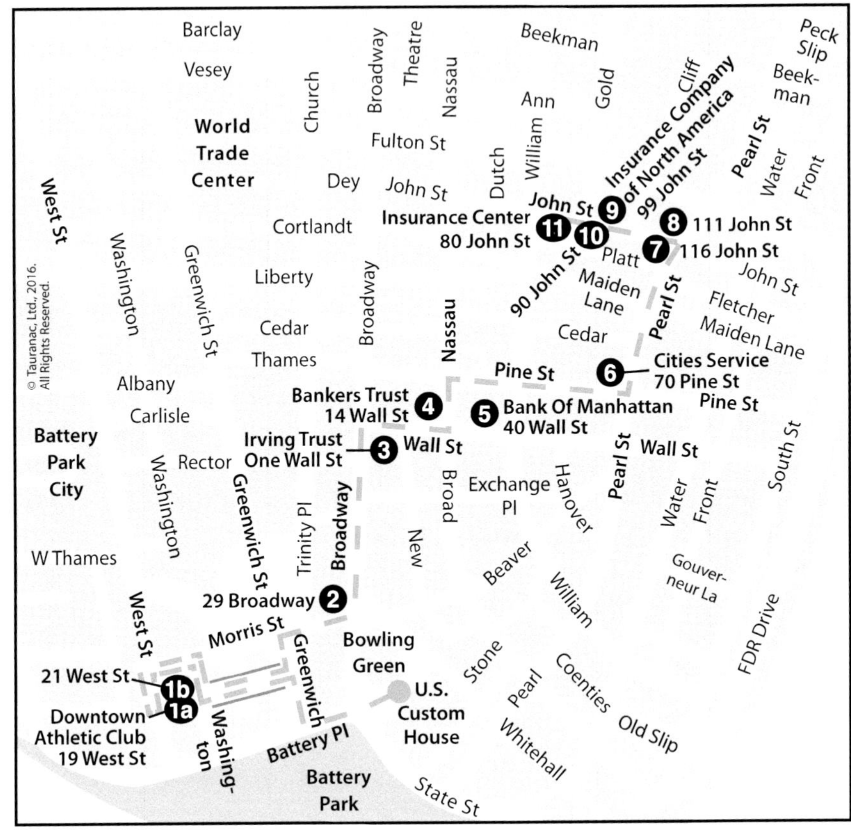


# MAP 1

Surprisingly, quite a few of the largest towers rose into the sky in the months following the great stock market crash of 1929. The *Wall Street Journal*, in June 1930, reported that "probably at no previous time in Wall Street history has lower Manhattan been involved in more important and extensive real estate and building operations than have recently been consummated or are currently under way or planned." Of the buildings visited on this walk, the Bank of the Manhattan Company (1.5), Irving Trust Company (1.3), No. 29 Broadway (1.2), No. 21 West Street (1.1b), the adjoining Downtown Athletic Club (1.1a), Nos. 90 and 116 John Street (1.10, 1.7) in the insurance district, and perhaps half a dozen more major towers, date from 1930, as do the initial plans of No. 70 Pine Street (1.6). And—at least as of June in that year—they were filling up quickly, the *Journal* reporting that One Wall "is nearly all rented from plans." These new modernistic towers transformed the downtown skyline more or less overnight.

*From Bowling Green, cross Broadway to the northwest corner of Broadway and Battery Place, opposite the north side of Battery Park, and continue west one block to Greenwich Street. Turn right on Greenwich Street and walk north halfway up the block to the pedestrian footbridge that crosses over the entrance to the Brooklyn-Battery Tunnel. Standing on the footbridge, you can enjoy a modernistic panorama: two late '40s Moderne buildings flank the Brooklyn-Battery Tunnel's approach road (the road passing beneath the footbridge), while straight ahead, to the west, stand two slender towers designed in 1929. The two Moderne structures—the Brooklyn-Battery Tunnel Ventilation Building (1947–49) to your left and the Battery Parking Garage (1948–50) to your right—were designed by Norwegian immigrant Ole Singstad; their stark exteriors, and especially the curve of the Parking Garage, take them out of the realm of Art Deco. We're here to see the two slender towers rising to the west, at the other end of the bridge.*

## 1.1a. ⋆Downtown Athletic Club, 19 West Street
Starrett & Van Vleck, 1929–30

## 1.1b. ⋆21 West Street
Starrett & Van Vleck, 1929–31

At the far end of the pedestrian bridge, at the southwest corner of Morris Street, stand two lonely Deco outposts on the western edge of the island. Side-by-side tall slender towers, designed in the same year by the same firm, they nevertheless do not look alike, because they were commissioned by different owners for different purposes. The Downtown Athletic Club—home of the Heisman Trophy—built the darker tower on the left (south); No. 21 on the right (north), today residential apartments, began life as a speculative office building. You're looking at the Washington Street façades of both buildings; the formal address of each is on West Street, as both buildings extend westward completely through the narrow block.

Though something of a second-string firm, Starrett & Van Vleck produced excellent work, perhaps more derivative than original, but expertly carried out. Goldwin Starrett (1876–1918) was one of the five Starrett brothers from Lawrence, Kansas, who formed major construction companies in Chicago and New York: the Thompson-Starrett Construction Co. and Starrett Brothers Construction Co. (later Starrett Brothers & Eken). Goldwin started in Daniel Burnham's Chicago office, joined his brothers in forming Thompson-Starrett in 1901, but in 1907 went into partnership with Ernest Alan Van Vleck (1875–1956). The firm specialized in public buildings and schools, and also commercial work, including such top department stores as Lord & Taylor and Saks Fifth Avenue. Though initially partial to a modest Renaissance Revival approach, in the late 1920s and early 1930s, like almost everybody else, they turned modernistic. Their Deco productions include, besides these two West Street towers, the American Stock Exchange (2.1) and the 1930 addition to Bloomingdale's (7.1) on Lexington Avenue at East 59th Street in Midtown.

The posh Downtown Athletic Club, founded by lawyers and bankers in 1926, found itself hemmed in by high land prices, and had to make do with a small plot. Instead of spreading out its facilities—swimming pool, gym, tennis and squash courts, even a miniature golf course, as well as dining rooms and bedrooms—like a traditional country club, the club stacked them into a skyscraper. The building's profile reflects those varied uses—the four-story projection at the bottom encloses the public reception rooms and offices, and several game rooms. The setback portion directly above houses the athletic facilities. Several of those floors have no windows—interrupting the flow of what could have been an elegantly continuous tower—because they house squash courts and other facilities that don't do well with glass or daylight.

Neighboring 21 West Street, simply an office building, gave the architects more scope for a uniform design—no pesky, windowless squash courts to deal with—and they obliged by turning out one of the area's handsomer Art Deco towers. The slender, tapering façade sets back from all sides—watch the resulting diagonal setbacks at the corners—while the windows rise in vertical pairs. Cross to the west side of the bridge for a closer look at the materials. The façade is simply clad in brick—but what brick! Different colors—tan, orange, purple.

Different patterns, some smooth, some angled. Different textures, marking the setbacks. Note the corner windows—all glass, no columns. Such windows became standard on later buildings, especially on apartment houses on Central Park West and in the Bronx.

The ground-floor arcade, which extends along two of the building's three façades, shelters shoppers and, on the Morris Street side, people entering and leaving the building. Walk into the arcade to see the geometrically patterned mosaic ceiling, the metal grilles on windows at the south end of the Washington Street façade, and the multicolored metal bands in the storefronts. Follow the arcade around to the Morris Street façade to see the building's main entrance. The lobby survives remarkably intact, including a mosaic map showing lower Manhattan in 1776. Continue around to the far side to see the West Street façades of both buildings, then return to Washington Street.

***Walk halfway back across the pedestrian bridge, stopping in the middle, and look east.***

## 1.2. (NR HD) 29 Broadway Sloan & Robertson, 1929–31; Broadway addition, Boak & Raad, 1962–64

At the northeast corner of Morris and Greenwich Streets rises the rear façade of No. 29 Broadway. Completed at almost the same time as 21 West Street, 29 Broadway offers a different take on the same basic building—a tall, slender tower with façades on three sides. Planned for use by banks, brokers, and lawyers, it was built by Abe Adelson, a milliner who got started in real estate in the garment district and went on to commission some of Ely Jacques Kahn's finest work, including Two Park Avenue (3.4) and the Film Center Building (5.11). In 1929 Adelson hired Sloan & Robertson (for Sloan & Robertson, see 10.4) for two downtown projects: 80 Broad Street and 29 Broadway. Given Adelson's earlier buildings, it's not surprising that the design for 29 Broadway would be announced in the *New York Times* in November of 1929 as a "modern expression of classic motifs." Adelson also announced that the

exterior would be "of natural stone giving the impression of a tower structure, in keeping with" its neighbors on Broadway.

A completely stone-faced building would likely have been too expensive, so the architects did use some brick, but stone is the most noticeable material. From across Greenwich Street, the building's rear has a three-story stone-faced base, unfortunately altered at the ground floor, but with geometric window frames and spandrels above the second story. The central portion sports horizontal rows of white brick and vertical columns of black and red brick—similar to the color scheme of the Daily News Building (5.1)—framed at either side by fanciful, heavily molded stonework, rather like an enormous abstract sculpture, strictly symmetrical and geometric, unlike anything else in the city.

***Walk east along Morris Street toward Broadway, stopping halfway up the block.***

What on Greenwich Street forms a single composition—the wide brick bands and windows in the center flanked by stone sculpture—on Morris Street becomes a single element repeated three times. Other buildings with secondary façades facing onto less important streets often leave them unadorned, but not here. The façade on Morris Street—so narrow it's difficult to look up at the building—gets the full treatment.

***Follow Morris Street east to Broadway; cross Broadway and look back at the building's Broadway façade.***

The massive, 180-foot-long Morris Street side and the more modest, 84-foot-wide Greenwich Street façade give no hint of the narrow sliver of a main façade, just 30 feet wide, on Broadway—the most expensive frontage. Here, with only two bays available, the façade becomes asymmetrical—with white, red, and black brick on the left (south), and abstract stone sculpture on the right. That stone explodes into a floral fantasy framing the open entrance vestibule. Step inside the vestibule to admire the unusual curving walls, ornamental metalwork and chandelier, and mosaic ceiling.

The six-story wing directly north of the tower uses the same white, red, and black brick as No. 29, but it's not part of the original building. In the early 1960s, the building's owners annexed the adjoining six-story building and arranged to give it a matching façade. With Sloan & Robertson no longer available, the owners hired the firm of Boak & Raad—successors to Boak & Paris, who knew something about the "modern expression of classic motifs" (for Boak & Paris, see 11.6).

*Walk north along the west side of Broadway. The strips of paving in the sidewalk list, in chronological order, the names and dates of some two hundred ticker-tape parades—New York's official welcome to visiting dignitaries and heroes. The parades named here date from the 1930s. Continue north on Broadway, past Exchange Place and Rector Street to Wall Street and Trinity Church; continue past Trinity Church until next to the church yard, then turn around for a view of One Wall Street, at the southeast corner of Broadway.*

## 1.3. *Irving Trust Company (later Bank of New York, currently being converted to residential use), One Wall Street Ralph Walker, 1929–31

Barely eighty-five years, just one lifetime, separate the enormous modern skyscraper at One Wall Street from Trinity Church across the street, and yet the distance between them is vast—from the churches of the pre–Civil War horse-and-buggy era to the mammoth skyscrapers of the Roaring Twenties.

One Wall Street opened in 1931 as the home of the Irving Trust Company—whose purchase of this site was billed at the time as the most expensive such real-estate transaction in world history. Ralph Walker, once voted "architect of the century," produced dazzling Art Deco skyscrapers in the late 1920s and early '30s. His tower at One Wall Street, with its tall, jagged windows and curving limestone walls, could be described as Gothic Modern—a skyscraper reflection of Trinity Church. That connection might not be entirely accidental. Walker's firm was founded in the mid–nineteenth century by Cyrus Eidlitz, whose father, Leopold, once

worked for Richard Upjohn, Trinity's architect. Even without that connection, Walker would have been aware of his skyscraper's famous neighbor, and perhaps drew inspiration from its design—he later wrote, in his office monograph, that "the building does relate well to Trinity Church."

Walker described the enormous limestone walls of his tower as a "curtain wall." That phrase is generally understood to mean a wall of plate glass, hung on the steel frame of a modern skyscraper. But Walker had other ideas—he called it a "rippled" wall, designed to look like a curtain, ringing down on Broadway.

*Walk back to Wall Street, and cross to the Broadway side of the building.*

From closer up, you can see that the vertical rows of windows are actually set in concave curves. To get that effect, Walker had to set the wall back a few inches from the property line. But doing so caused a problem—in a tradition going back to English common law, private property adjoining the public way, but not clearly marked, eventually becomes part of the public way. Irving Trust risked losing those few inches to the City of New York. But square inches on Wall Street are worth an awful lot of money. So if you look down at the sidewalk, you'll see a thin brass line just a few inches away from the building marking the property's boundary. Walker described this as the first such marker in New York—since his day they've become fairly common.

*Walk east along Wall Street, halfway down the block, to see the skyscraper's entrance.*

A tall, jagged entranceway matches the building's tall, jagged windows. Looking through the windows or doors, you can just make out the three-story-tall Reception Hall, thirty-seven feet high, whose walls and ceiling are lined with nine thousand square feet of sparkling mosaics in red, orange, and gold designed by Hildreth Meière. The mosaic colors shade from dark red to a lighter orange, while both are gradually overtaken by abstract geometric patterns in gold; because the walls appear to lighten in color as they rise, they lift your eyes up toward the ceiling.

*Continue east to the corner of Wall Street and New Street*

Security fences make it difficult to get close to the New Street façade, but if you look carefully you may be able to see the firm's signature on this building in a cursive script: Voorhees Gmelin & Walker.

*Walk east to the end of the block at Nassau Street, turn left onto Nassau Street and walk north half a block.*

## 1.4. *Bankers Trust, 14 Wall Street<br>Nassau Street extension: Shreve, Lamb & Harmon, 1931–33

Twenty years after opening, the neo-Classical tower at the corner of Wall and Nassau Streets, built in 1910–12 for Bankers Trust, got a twenty-five-story L-shaped extension, faced in limestone and granite, designed by the architects of the Empire State Building (3.3/3.6). Shreve, Lamb & Harmon produced a Modern Classic façade—a modernistic version of Bankers Trust's neo-Classicism—that turned tall classical piers into ribbed modernistic verticals. Abstract, geometrically patterned entrance gates and window grilles in wrought iron and polished bronze join zigzag window spandrels in the tower and geometric stonework at the entrance—which includes a stylized eagle with outspread wings over the entrance. Inside, the architects created a twenty-seven-foot-tall modernist banking hall.

*Continue north half a block to Pine Street. Turn right on Pine Street, walk east down the block toward William Street, but stop halfway, at the steps leading up to Chase Manhattan Plaza. Walk up the steps to the plaza, stopping at the sunken fountain. To the east, the slender tower of 70 Pine Street rises into the sky. To the south is the Pine Street façade of 40 Wall Street.*

## 1.5. ★Bank of the Manhattan Company, 40 Wall Street (Pine Street façade) H. Craig Severance; Yasuo Matsui, associate architect; 1929–30

For a building famous for its competition with the Chrysler Building (for the competition, see 5.4) in the "world's tallest building" category, 40 Wall Street has remarkably modest Art Deco detailing. It certainly relies on the usual vertical window bands, and the tall flat columns in the lower floors qualify as Modern Classic in style—but compared to its rival on 42nd Street this is a very quiet design. Contemporary accounts, in fact, described it as "modernized French Gothic," suggesting a stripped down version of the older style.

And its reign as tallest building, if not in the world then at least in the financial district, ended within a couple of years, thanks to one of the truly astonishing Art Deco towers downtown, the Cities Service Building (1.6).

*Turn east to look at 70 Pine Street.*

## 1.6. ★★Cities Service Building, 70 Pine Street (formerly 60 Wall Tower) (Plate 1) Clinton & Russell, Holton & George, 1930–32

The last enormous Downtown tower completed before the Depression put an end to such extravagance, 70 Pine Street—planned, at sixty-six stories and 952 feet high, to accommodate between seven and eight thousand office workers—briefly held the title of world's third-tallest building. Chartered originally in 1910, by 1930 Henry Doherty's Cities Service corporation (later known as CITGO) had become one of the nation's largest, incorporating some two hundred energy companies spread across the country.

Cities Service had offices at 60 Wall Street, and Doherty hoped to build a skyscraper there, but couldn't get approval from the City's Buildings Department. Determined to build his tower, Doherty acquired $2 million worth of property one block to the north, along Pine Street. Not one to have his ambitions thwarted by mere geography, he connected the new Pine Street skyscraper to the old headquarters at 60 Wall Street by an aerial bridge, naming his new aerie "60 Wall Tower." When the bridge eventually came down in 1976, following the building's sale, 60 Wall Tower became 70 Pine Street. (The current bridge, added in 1979, connects to 72 Wall Street.)

The old established firm of Clinton & Russell had long turned out solid, conservatively styled towers for Wall Street firms, but in 1930, with the original principals deceased, the firm, led by partner Thomas George, designed a modernist fantasy for Doherty's corporation. Still one of the city's tallest skyscrapers, it rises in subtle setbacks like an elaborate, elongated faceted jewel of Indiana limestone and white brick to a glass-enclosed solarium with an illuminated lantern (said to be visible from twenty miles away) and a stainless-steel spire. Doherty initially planned to live in the top three stories, but instead converted the solarium into a (formerly) publicly accessible observatory.

***Walk east along Pine Street, cross William Street, and walk up to the main entrance to 70 Pine Street.***

The enormous series of windows and entrances along Pine Street sport remarkable ornamental details. Aluminum panels in the windows include elaborate stylized floral patterns backed by sunbursts, while over the doors what seems like an abstract pattern turns out, on closer inspection, to represent butterflies supping on sunflowers. Landmarks Preservation Commission staff have identified these panels as the work of Cliff Parkhurst, who wrote, in a November 1930 issue of *Metalcraft*: "Today, the skyline of many of our great cities bears evidence of our collaborative work and although our part is relatively minor, we really get a thrill out of our work."

Going beyond the typical inclusion of ornament suggesting the client's business, the stone ornament here includes a triangle inscribed within a trefoil—the Cities Service logo (which appears again in the lobby, in the form of annunciator lights above the elevator doors). Even more extraordinary, tall limestone scale models of the building itself stand above the main entryways on both Pine and Cedar Streets—the height of Art Deco vanity.

The building has two main entrances on Pine Street, reflecting the existence of two lobby floors—in turn reflecting the original use of double-decker elevators. For odd-numbered floors, use the entrance to the odd lobby, for even-numbered floors use the entrance to the even lobby. (One syndicated columnist feared that this arrangement would "cut the possibility of elevator flirtations exactly in half." Perhaps that's why the double-deckers eventually went out of use.) The vast lobby spaces are jammed with polychromatic marble, rippling marble walls, beamed plaster ceilings, and gorgeous, abstract geometric Art Deco aluminum metalwork on everything from elevator doors to mailboxes—all polished and shining in splendor. Even the elevator cabs survive intact.

*Continue east on Pine Street to the corner of Pearl Street. Turn left on Pearl and walk north to the northeast corner of Fletcher Street. (If you duck left—west—on Cedar Street for a moment, you will see the other entrance to Cities Service with a second statue of the building.) Further to the north stand five buildings on John Street, forming the insurance district.*

## 1.7. 116 John Street<br>Louis Allen Abramson, 1930–31

The insurance industry in New York City dates back to the eighteenth century. In the late 1920s, as the financial district grew, the industry moved north into John Street, just as Art Deco came into fashion—hence this cluster of buildings.

The tall, white brick building closing the vista on Pearl Street, at the southwest corner of John Street, is the back of 116 John Street, facing Platt Street (Louis Allen Abramson, 1930). To the left (west) along Platt Street, separated from No. 116 by low buildings, is the rear of No. 90 John Street (1.10; Springsteen & Goldhammer, 1930). Slightly further west are the rear and side of No. 80 John Street (1.11; Buchman & Kahn, 1925–27). Peering out between No. 90 and No. 166, over the intervening lower buildings, is the front of No. 99 John Street (1.9; Shreve, Lamb & Harmon, 1932–33). And just visible further north on Pearl Street, beyond No. 116 John, is the edge of No. 111 John Street (1.8; Buchman & Kahn, 1928–29) at the northeast corner of John and Pearl.

*Walk north along Pearl Street to John Street. Cross to the north side of John Street, and turn around to see the front of No. 116.*

Louis Allen Abramson (1887–1985) had a long architectural career stretching from the turn of the twentieth century through the late 1960s. Beginning as an office boy and then draftsman in the turn-of-the-century office of John Duncan, he worked in and around Seattle for several years before returning to New York to establish an independent practice. Abramson specialized in hospitals, nursing homes, synagogues, office buildings, and restaurants. Many of those restaurants, including Horn & Hardart Automats on West 33rd and West 181st Streets, six Longchamps restaurants in Manhattan, restaurants for the Brass Rail including the outlets for the 1939 World's Fair, and Ben Marden's Riviera night club and restaurant perched on the Palisades, were elegant Art Deco and Art Moderne creations designed in the 1930s and '40s—most, sadly, no longer stand.

At thirty-five stories, No. 116 John Street is by far Abramson's tallest building. On its completion, the *Times* described it as "one of the dominating structures in the insurance district." It rises straight from the sidewalk for its first twenty-two stories, then tapers gracefully through a series of terraced setbacks, carefully disrupting the monotony of all those brick stories by having the center bays break forward from the rest. The modest detail, nothing like the fantasies of Abramson's restaurants and nightclub, and the muted color—white-glazed brick and white terra-cotta—create an elegant, if restrained, midrise tower. Abramson saved his decorative flourishes and vivid colors for the lobby, which the *Times* described, a little stuffily, as "unusual in appearance, being done in black and green marble, with indirect lighting." Despite the deepening Depression, 116 John quickly rented up with insurance companies.

***Turn around to see No. 111 John Street, directly across the street from No. 116.***

## 1.8. 111 John Street
## Buchman & Kahn, 1928–29

The announced construction of No. 111 John Street—intended to provide offices for insurance and indemnity companies—was taken, according to the *Times* in February 1930, as "evidence of the demand for office space in a location once far removed from the financial district but apparently to be the goal of the northerly expansion of the section."

The insurance district is just another of those clusters of commercial buildings in which Ely Jacques Kahn (for Kahn, see 3.4) shows up—not so different, really, from the garment district or the printing district. Indeed, one of Kahn's Garment Center clients gave Kahn his first commission here, the Insurance Center building at 80 John (1.11).

The details of No. 111 are unmistakably Kahn—the woven metal patterns in the windows at the second and third stories, the accordion-like folds of stone at the fourth story, and the plainer but equally geometric patterning in the spandrels and the horizontal striations at the corners. Kahn's pragmatic approach to architecture must have meshed nicely with the record-setting speed for erecting the building's steel structure—just six-and-a-half weeks.

*Walk west along John Street to the corner of Cliff Street.*

## 1.9. Insurance Company of North America Building (later American International Company), 99 John Street Shreve, Lamb & Harmon, 1932–33

Originally a tenant at 111 John Street, the Insurance Company of North America—one of the country's oldest—moved out and built itself a new headquarters just across the street at No. 99, at the northwest corner of Cliff Street. Designed by Shreve, Lamb & Harmon just two years after the firm's Empire State Building (3.3/3.6), No. 99 John Street brings something of the look of that firm's signature skyscraper to this much smaller building in the insurance district.

No. 99 marks a particularly important moment in skyscraper development in New York: not only the tail-end of skyscraper building in the pre–World War II era, but also, perhaps, the last of its kind before the complete victory of the International Style. No. 99 inspired *The New Yorker*'s architecture critic, Lewis Mumford, to see it as combining "the best points of the Empire State Building and the [Daily] News Building." He admired its "beautiful directness" and declared that "the building as a whole is both honest and handsome; there is nothing left to be done in the design of business buildings but repeat this fundamental pattern."

The contrast with Kahn's approach at No. 111, just across Cliff Street, is striking, and illustrates Mumford's observation: Kahn's rippling façades versus Shreve, Lamb & Harmon's flat walls; Kahn's bright colors versus plain stone and aluminum spandrels; even the setbacks are handled differently.

## 1.10. 90 John Street
## Springsteen & Goldhammer, 1930

Springsteen & Goldhammer, much better known for apartment buildings in Manhattan and the Bronx, found their way down to John Street the same way that Kahn did: thanks to a commission from a client, Samuel Friedenberg, for whom they'd earlier designed a couple of Midtown loft buildings. The design includes cascading setbacks, angled corners, and geometric brick spandrels, along with interesting brick patterning at the setbacks.

## 1.11. Insurance Center Building, 80 John Street
## Buchman & Kahn, 1925–26

The earliest of these five buildings, full of inventive detailing, is one of Kahn's first modernistic designs. Kahn's biographer, Jewel Stern, considers 80 John the prototype for much of his newly modernistic approach to office-building design, particularly massing and setbacks.

As you look up the building's façades, watch for the proliferation of geometric ornament—a bandcourse of zigzags at the fourth story, where the stone-faced base gives way to the brick tower; window spandrels with oddly projecting brick patterns suggesting an optical illusion.

Even as the building rose on John Street, Kahn published an article in the *New York Times*, in May 1926, called "Our Skyscrapers Take Simple Forms," in which, commenting on the direction of New York architecture, he wrote:

> Almost unknown to the New Yorker himself, a new style of architecture is being created that is so characteristic of New York that it would be more logical, by far, to call it a New York Style. . . . As buildings have reached toward the sky they have sloughed off, by a natural process of refinement, the cluttered detail of the past. . . . Decoration becomes a far more precious thing than a collection of dead leaves, swags, bull's heads and cartouches. It becomes a means of enriching the surface with a play of light and shade, voids and solids. . . . [Today's ornamental forms] respond to the bulk and simplicity of the skyscraper itself.

When the building changed hands in April 1928, the *Times* noted:

> If there is any pessimism in the real estate business it is not sighted in the neighborhood of William and John Streets, where first-quality space rarely comes in the market except when a new building is constructed, in which case tenants are promptly secured.

# ITINERARY NO. 2
# CIVIC CENTER AND TRIBECA

Though this tour begins at the edge of the financial district with Starrett & Van Vleck's new façade for the American Stock Exchange (2.1), followed by the former East River Savings Bank (2.2), a late Moderne design by Walker & Gillette, it continues into the Civic Center with the Federal Post Office (2.3), a WPA product of the Modern Classic, and three remarkable municipal buildings at the northern tip of the Foley Square courts district: the New York State Building (2.7) at 80 Centre Street; the Health, Hospitals and Sanitation Building (2.8) across the street at 125 Worth Street; and the Manhattan Criminal Courthouse (2.9) at 100 Centre Street. But the star architect of the walk is Ralph Walker, designer of three communications-related behemoths: the delightfully decorative New York Telephone Company headquarters (2.4) downtown, and in TriBeCa the ponderously massive Western Union Building (2.6) as well as the Long Lines Building (2.10), which is both massive and decorative.

*The walk begins in front of the American Stock Exchange, at 86 Trinity Place, directly opposite the rear of Trinity Church, between Rector Street and Thames Street.*

Most skyscrapers in Lower Manhattan stand east of Broadway, where the bedrock comes closest to the surface. Broadway runs near the original shoreline—early on, the Dutch colonists began a long tradition of reclaiming land from the water. As a result, west of Broadway bedrock can be seventy feet below ground—which is why so few older skyscrapers will be found there. The first few buildings on this walk do not rise too far above the ground. Once we reach the Civic Center, the city and state office buildings remain low for a similar reason—they sit atop the filled-in Collect Pond. Only in TriBeCa will we find a couple of true skyscrapers.

Canal
Grand
Varick
Sullivan
Thomp-son
W Bway
Wooster
Greene
Mercer
Broadway
Howard
Lafayette
Grand
Mott
Hester
Canal
Watts
Desbrosses
Washington
Greenwich St
Vestry
Laight
Hubert
Beach
Collister
St. John
York
6 Av
Canal
Long Lines Building
32 Sixth Avenue
10
Lispen-ard
Walker
Ericsson Pl
Varick
6 Av
West Broadway
Franklin Al
White
Cortlandt Al
Lafayette
Centre St
Baxter
Mulberry
Bayard
Franklin
Manhattan Criminal Courthouse
100 Centre Street
9
Pell
N. Moore
Franklin
Leonard
Health, Hospitals & Sanitation Building
125 Worth Street
8
7
Worth
Western Union Building
60 Hudson Street
6
Worth St
West St
Harrison
Jay
Staple
Hudson St
Thomas
Duane
Reade
West Broadway
Church
Broadway
New York State Building
80 Centre Street
Centre St
Pearl
Bertrand Building
157 Chambers Street
(Now Artisan Lofts,
143 Reade Street)
5
Chambers
Elk
Chambers
Police Plaza
City Hall
Brooklyn Bridge
Warren
Battery Park City
West St
Murray
Greenwich St
Murray
Frankfort
Broadway
Park Row
Spruce
Park Place
New York Telephone
(Barclay-Vesey
Building)
140 West Street
4
Federal Post Office
90 Church Street
3
Barclay
Vesey
Theatre
Nassau
Beekman
Vesey
West St
World Trade Center
Fulton St
Dutch
William
Ann
Gold
Brookfield Place
(World Finncial
Center)
Church St
Dey
East River Savings Bank
22 Cortlandt Street
2
John St
Cort-landt
Maiden Lane
Platt
Washington
Greenwich St
Liberty
Cedar
Thames
Cedar
Broadway
Pine
Nassau
William
Pine St
Pearl St
Albany
American Stock Exchange
86 Trinity Place
1
Carlisle
Trinity Pl
Wall St
New
Broad
Rector
West St
Washington
Greenwich St
Hanover
Beaver
Battery Park City
W Thames
© Tauranac, Ltd., 2016.
All Rights Reserved.

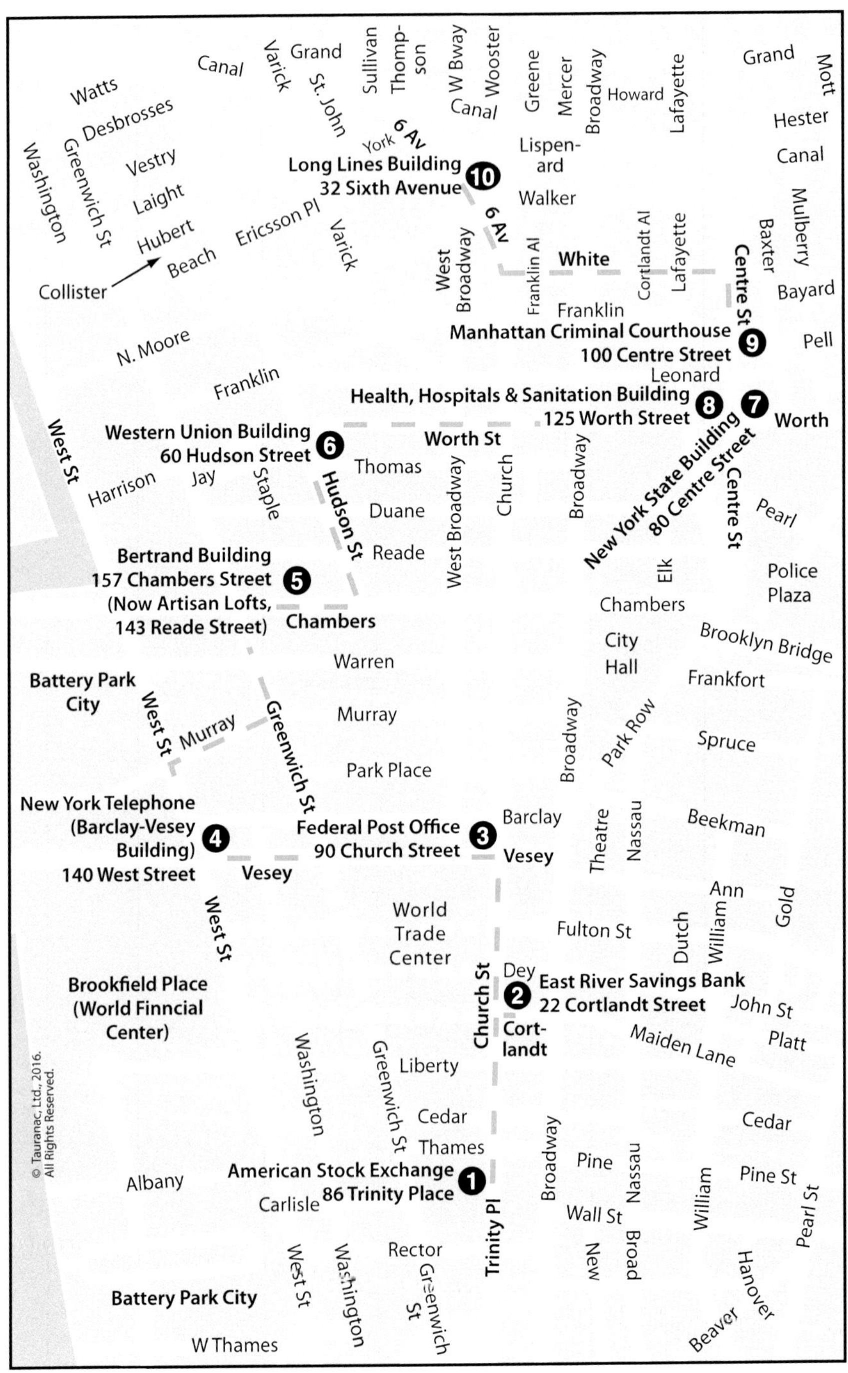

MAP 2

## 2.1 ★American Stock Exchange, 86 Trinity Place Starrett & Van Vleck, original building 1921, expansion to Trinity Place 1929–31.

The American Stock Exchange began life as the Curb Exchange or Curb Market, so-called because its brokers actually did their jobs standing on the curb—in the street—yelling and signaling back and forth, right up until 1921 when they opened their first home on Trinity Place. Just eight years later, as reported in the *Wall Street Journal*, "the volume of business transacted by the Curb Market has expanded so rapidly that larger quarters are necessary." To the original six-story building, set back somewhat from the street, the Exchange attached a fourteen-story addition in front of and rising above the original, with a five-story-tall trading room. As described in the *Journal*, "The Trinity Place façade will be of carved stone of modernistic design, with metal work of nickel bronze finish and steel windows."

Starrett & Van Vleck (for Starrett & Van Vleck, see 1.1) designed both the original building and the "modernistic" extension. Besides the usual vertical columns of windows, long ribbed piers, and modest setbacks, the building has two wonderful deep-relief panels, at either side of the façade, with stylized geometric renderings of the various industries traded on the floor inside, including oil wells, locomotives, ocean liners, tractors, and derricks.

*Walk north along Trinity Place—which, after crossing Liberty Street, becomes Church Street—as far as Cortlandt Street.*

## 2.2 East River Savings Bank (now Century 21), 22 Cortlandt Street Walker & Gillette, 1934

This two-story bank building—a "taxpayer," just big enough to produce the necessary income to pay the assessed real-estate taxes on the property until better times come along—replaced the fifteen-story Havemeyer Building, said to have been among the tallest office buildings downtown when built in the 1890s. Under the headline, "Erect Taxpayer on $3,000,000 Plot," the *New York Times* called this development "perhaps the most striking illustration of the changed conditions in building operations in New York City" resulting from the Great Depression. "If it is not the largest [taxpayer] in Manhattan it at least has the unique distinction of occupying the most valuable piece of New York real estate for a taxpayer in the city."

Despite being a taxpayer, the building housed the new main office of the East River Savings Bank, hence Walker & Gillette's design, much more elaborate than the typical taxpayer. A. Stewart Walker (no relation to Ralph Walker) and Leon Gillette formed their partnership in 1906. Walker had studied at Harvard, while Gillette had attended the École des Beaux-Arts in Paris, and later worked for the firm of Warren & Wetmore (architects of Grand Central Terminal). Initially the firm designed in conservative styles: estates, apartment houses, hospitals, yacht and steamship interiors, clubs, museums, hotels, banks, the Playland amusement park in Rye, N.Y., and the entire city of Venice, Florida. By the late 1920s, however, Walker & Gillette had mastered the modernistic, their best-known Deco work being the Fuller Building on East 57th Street (7.2).

The East River Savings Bank now serves as an annex of the Century 21 retail emporium, its interior full of shoppers and clothing racks, but its exterior remains practically unchanged from the 1930s. Walker & Gillette's design treats the two-story building (the equivalent in height of four or five stories) like a robust piece of sculpture. Its narrow façades on Cortlandt and Dey Streets each frame massive gates within a polished stone surround, topped by stern Moderne eagles, all set within a curving stone frame. The Cortlandt Street entrance includes a defunct night depository (note the slot for a nickel fee)—the ancestor of the ATM.

The entrance on Church Street leads to the two-story-tall former bank interior, where the upper story survives intact, with black and red marble and remarkable modernistic metal chandeliers. Unfortunately, the lower story has been completely renovated, resulting in the removal from view of a mural, by Dale Stetson, on the east wall—a canvas of three thousand square feet—that showed a birds-eye view of the East River.

***Continue north on Church Street to the southeast corner of Vesey Street, and look across the intersection.***

## 2.3 (NR) Federal Post Office, 90 Church Street Cross & Cross, with Pennington, Lewis and Mills; Louis A. Simon, Supervising Architect of the Treasury; 1933–37; top six floors added 1938

The design by Cross & Cross (for Cross & Cross, see 6.6) of the Post Office building at the northwest corner of Vesey and Church Streets mixes classical columns with abstract geometry—a good definition of Modern Classic. One of a series of post offices financed by the federal government as part of the larger effort to create employment during the Depression, 90 Church Street replaced the huge, mansard-roofed post office that once stood at the southern tip of City Hall Park, just a few blocks away. Larger than most such buildings, it was intended to house, besides the post office, the offices of various federal agencies, including the Post Office Department but also the departments of Commerce and Treasury, as well as the Federal Housing Authority.

On the building's exterior, the architects have crossed—so to speak—a Greek temple (the lower floors) with a modern skyscraper (the set-back tower above). The odd mix of metaphors continues in the ornament: Greek

decorative details alternating with stars and stripes and, at the corners of the main setback, giant stylized American eagles.

***Cross to the north side of Vesey Street, and then to the west side of Church Street.***

The building's three entrances on Church Street combine geometric aluminum grilles with a series of double-height "fasces"—a Roman motif of a bundle of sheaves tied together, symbolizing the strength achieved through unity. Here each fasces includes a set of stars and, at the top, an eagle, symbols of the United States government—though the fasces eventually became better known as a symbol of Italy's fascist party. Two enormous sculpted roundels by Paul Jennewein flank the three sets of doors—the lively male figure on the left symbolizes "Day," the sleepy female figure on the right "Night."

Inside, the building has hardly changed at all—a postman from the late 1930s entering the space today would notice almost nothing amiss. The large central lobby connects to the office space above, while the side lobbies lead to the post office. The lobby's materials are positively lush—terrazzo and marble floors set in geometric patterns, marble panels with sunbursts, and more stars and American eagles—marble, aluminum, and glass in every direction. Original metal teller cages and aluminum signs survive, as well as marble tables on which customers can address and stamp their letters.

***Walk back along Church Street to Vesey Street, turn right, and walk west, along the north side of Vesey Street, as far as Washington Street.***

## 2.4 **New York Telephone Company (Barclay-Vesey Building, undergoing conversion to residential use), 140 West Street (Plate 2) Ralph Walker of McKenzie, Voorhees & Gmelin, 1923–27

Ralph Walker designed three enormous downtown towers for the telecommunications industry—the Barclay-Vesey Building, the Western Union Building (2.6) at 60 Hudson Street, and the Long Lines Building (2.10) at Walker Street and Sixth Avenue. They are unmistakably siblings, sharing as they all do a hulking sculptural massing in dark brick.

The Barclay-Vesey Building helped propel Walker to a partnership in his firm, and on to the top of his profession. Designed in 1923, two years before the famous Paris Exposition—in fact, Walker may have been working on the project a year earlier, at the time of the Chicago Tribune Tower competition—the tower with its modernistic massing made an enormous impact on the American architectural scene. The firm's connection with the phone company dated back at least to 1885—by 1923 they had some thirty phone company buildings under their belts—but for this new headquarters the phone company and Walker struck out in a new direction, aiming for a self-consciously modern expression for a rapidly growing modern industry transforming twentieth-century life.

Occupying an entire, small, irregular downtown block near the Hudson River, this bulky ziggurat of an office building rises to a square tower set askew to its base—neatly demonstrating the paramount importance of skyline value to the designers of New York skyscrapers. Its ponderous sculptural massing and vertical rows of windows point firmly to the modernistic future. The muted color and ornamental patterns of animal and plant life don't yet fall into the standard Art Deco mold, yet the ornament is no longer early-twentieth-century eclectic. Walker, who had first considered the Gothic and Italian Renaissance for his scheme, opted in the end to make his building "as modern in conception as the telephone." Grapevines and seahorses cavort in metal and cast-stone across the lower stories of the building.

***Turn right on Washington Street, and walk north to the building's main entrance.***

The only suggestion on the building's exterior that it might house the New York City headquarters of New York Bell Telephone is a small but clearly sculpted bell above the main entrance.

Inside, however, telephone company imagery takes over completely, in a gently curving vaulted ceiling emblazoned with a dozen hand-painted scenes showing the development of communications across the ages. West African drums, Chinese carrier pigeons, Egyptian megaphones, and Native American smoke signals all converge from east and west onto a central painting that in earlier times might have been entitled *The Apotheosis of the Telephone*: a handsome, black standing phone with detachable earpiece (the kind on which reporters always frantically phone in their stories in 1930s movies), with the sun blazing forth behind it, surrounded by sun rays intertwined with the telephone cables of the modern world.

***Walk back south on Washington Street to Vesey Street, turn right, and walk west on Vesey to West Street. Turn right and walk north on West Street two blocks to Murray Street; turn right onto Murray and walk east one block to Greenwich Street; then turn left onto Greenwich and walk two blocks north to Chambers Street. Turn right onto Chambers Street and walk east to the middle of the block.***

## 2.5 Bertrand Building, 157 Chambers Street (now Artisan Lofts, 143 Reade Street) Victor Mayper, 1931

The modest commercial building on the north side of Chambers took the name "Bertrand Building" in memory of the son of the president of the Graham Chisolm Co., a printing company that leased the second through sixth floors while the building was still in the planning stages.

A modest commercial structure, not a corporate headquarters, the Bertrand Building illustrates the beauty of the Deco approach even for buildings on a tight budget. All it takes is some slender brick piers and geometrically patterned brick—it's just a matter of how the brick is laid. The most eye-catching feature is the entranceway, with molded and angled stone making a kind of modernistic cutaway on either side, and an arch formed by stepped slabs of stone each projecting out slightly from the next, adorned with chevrons and stepped profiles and various other geometric fancies. A metal band zigzags across the entrance, interlaced with alternating diamond patterns, above which rises a metal screen of slender staircase motifs.

Recent conversion to residential use has left the building's exterior largely intact. Unfortunately, the conversion included revamping what had been an intact Deco lobby, with echoes of the Chrysler Building, into a nondescript store.

***Continue walking east on Chambers Street to the intersection of Chambers, Hudson Street, and West Broadway; turn left (north) onto Hudson.***

## 2.6 ★★Western Union Building, 60 Hudson Street Voorhees, Gmelin & Walker, 1928-30

That squat brick building hulking in the distance once housed all the operations of the Western Union Telegraph Company, making it "the heart of a nerve system of wires and cables reaching to every corner of the nation and the world."

***Walk north on Hudson Street to the southwest corner of Hudson and Duane Streets.***

Brickwork in this building comes alive in a dozen different ways. It rises into the sky in vertical piers, it forms piers behind piers within piers at ground level, it zigzags and ripples like a curtain drawn back from a stage over windows and grand entrances. Though the building's bulk follows the ziggurat massing of Walker's seminal Barclay-Vesey Building of five years earlier, by now the master has abandoned all interest in anything other than pure form—no application of cast-stone ornament, no grand pictorial schemes showing the history of the telegraph. It's all in the patterns, in the geometric shape, in the golden effects possible with nineteen different shades of brick, that gradually lighten toward the sky. A renovation of thirty years ago obscured some of the color-change effect, but look carefully and you can still find some of it.

*Continue north on Hudson Street to the southwest corner of Jay Street.*

From closer up, you can see the zigzag brick spandrels at the first and second stories, and modernistic brick piers rising above. Responding to criticism of the skewed angles of the Barclay-Vesey Building—originally dictated by the irregular site of that building—here at Western Union Walker insulates his massive tower from its own irregular site with a two-story projecting brick screen, which permits the rest of the building a rectangular profile, and also brings it to a more human scale at the sidewalk. Note the geometric layering of the projecting screen—shallow layer upon shallow layer.

*Cross to the east side of Hudson Street, turn left, and walk north to the end of the block at Worth Street; then turn right and walk east along Worth Street.*

The two-story entrance screen continues around the corner onto Worth Street, but flattened out. As you walk east along the Worth Street side of the building, see how many different brick patterns you can find. Note how the smaller metal triangles in the window frames became larger brick versions to the west. At the second-story level you can clearly see a change in the brick color. At the corner of Worth and West Broadway, look to your left (north)—that third hulking brick building is the Long Lines Building (2.10), to which we will return.

The building's surface positively ripples, but its lobby takes that rippling to an even greater degree. Stretching from Hudson to Greenwich Streets, it counts among the most unusual in New York. Showing the influence of Dutch and German Expressionism, the lobby relies almost entirely for its dramatic effect on undulating brick walls and a curving vaulted ceiling supported on multifaceted brick piers, all lit indirectly by wall sconces and floor lamps.

*From the corner of West Broadway and Worth Street, cross to the east side of West Broadway and continue east along Worth Street four blocks to the corner of Centre Street.*

## 2.7 New York State Building, 80 Centre Street Sullivan W. Jones and William E. Haugaard, 1928–30.

Worth Street leads into the northern section of Manhattan's Civic Center, the nerve center of New York's municipal government. From the days of City Hall (1811), two blocks south in City Hall Park, government buildings—whether offices or courthouses—hewed to the classical ideal. Still, by the late 1920s, modernism infiltrated even here, first in versions of the Modern Classic, eventually in all-out Deco or Moderne. Three buildings clustered around Centre Street north of Worth Street neatly illustrate the evolution: No. 80 Centre Street (at the northeast corner of Worth Street), generally classic in flavor but with a geometric edge; No. 125 Worth Street (2.8), similar, but a little less classic and a little more modernistic; and No. 100 Centre Street (2.9), thoroughly Moderne.

Architects Jones (1878–1955) and Haugaard (1889–1948) did not work as a team on the New York State Office Building. Jones, the official New York State Architect, sketched out the initial design, but resigned suddenly from his position in February 1928 in a political dispute. According to the *New York Times*, Jones had only just begun what Governor Al Smith called "the largest architectural program in the United States"—everything from prisons to hospitals to armories—and his replacement, Haugaard, was "comparatively little known." Haugaard, nevertheless, completed the building's design, and remained State Architect until 1944, designing dozens of government buildings. And it was Haugaard who attended the December 1928 cornerstone laying, with Governor Smith—who brandished a "silver trowel"—and Mayor James "Gentleman Jimmy" Walker.

Just one year after completion of the new, grandly columned County Courthouse across the street at 60 Centre Street, Jones and Haugaard deliberately aimed for a modern version of classicism. Governor Smith personally assured Mayor Walker that the new State Building would be "monumental in character, so as to harmonize with the other buildings which are being planned by the city in the hope of making the civic centre

ultimately one of the most beautiful sections of Manhattan." The resulting building suggests classicism through its endless row of flattened fluted columns in the upper stories, but with the simplified profile of a more up-to-date modernism. The Moderne breaks through completely in the huge dark pylons supporting modernistic lanterns, framing the entrance on Centre Street.

***Walk west, back along Worth Street, to the southwest corner of Worth and Lafayette Streets, and enter the landscaped public area there for a view of 125 Worth Street, on the north side of Worth between Lafayette and Centre Streets.***

## 2.8 Health, Hospitals and Sanitation Building, 125 Worth Street (Plate 3) Charles B. Meyers, 1933–35; ornamental metalwork by Oscar Bach

Five years after completion of the New York State Office Building (2.7), architect Charles B. Meyers (1875–1958) designed a companion piece on the opposite side of Centre Street—a new home for New York City's Health, Hospitals, and Sanitation Departments. Even before Meyers got the job, the City announced that the new health headquarters would match the State Building—hence the matching inscriptions facing each other across Centre Street, "CITY OF NEW YORK" and "STATE OF NEW YORK."

The battle for public health has been a major municipal responsibility since the days of yellow fever epidemics. Early weapons in the city's arsenal ranged from imposing quarantines and draining swamps to forbidding New Yorkers to let hogs and goats run loose in the streets. With the development in the 1880s of antitoxins and vaccinations, the Department opened the world's first bacteriological laboratory conducting routine diagnoses of diseases. The City built 125 Worth Street to consolidate the offices of its three departments responsible for public health—Health, Hospitals, and Sanitation—under a single roof.

Meyers had long years of service on various City commissions, and worked on many government buildings (see 2.9, 3.10), including several hospitals. His design for 125 Worth Street mirrors and extends the State Building's Modern Classic style: faced in the identical gray granite, with five-story-tall square columns, a cornice, and a typically classical attic story—but all squared off, simplified, and streamlined. Typically modernistic details include a geometric wave pattern above the second story, and, at the Worth Street entrance, tall modern pylons bearing lamps and eagles, similar to those at the State Building.

Symbols of medicine adorn the building, including sculpted microscopes and chemist's beakers at the corners, flanked by American eagles, and the inscribed names of public health pioneers—from Hippocrates through Louis Pasteur—arrayed on all four sides of the building. Octagonal metal medallions above the third-story windows portray medically themed scenes, including a man mixing some kind of potion, a woman looking at a child's knee, and an experiment on a caged rat. Cast in duralumin—an alloy of aluminum, copper, and manganese that takes its name from the German town of Düren—they are the work of German-born and trained metallurgist and sculptor Oscar Bach (1884–1957), who emigrated to the United States in 1912. The journal *Iron Age* later pronounced Bach "probably the foremost metal craftsman of this country." His work includes similar duralumin panels in the lobby of the Empire State Building (3.6).

***Cross to the north side of Worth Street and then to the east side of Lafayette Street. Walk north along Lafayette to the building's Lafayette Street entrance in the middle of the block.***

Bach's work at 125 Worth Street extends to a variety of metal grilles inside and out. Among the most notable: the huge ornamental grilles and entrance gates, on Lafayette, Worth, and Centre Streets, done in a variety of metals in different colors, in abstract flowery motifs.

***Continue north on Lafayette Street to the corner of Leonard Street. Turn right at the corner and look east to see the hulking cubistic mass of the Manhattan Criminal Courthouse.***

## 2.9 Manhattan Criminal Courthouse, 100 Centre Street
Harvey Wiley Corbett and Charles B. Meyers, 1940–41

In 1936, the judges of General Sessions—described by the *New York Times* in August 1941 as "the oldest criminal tribunal in the country," dating back to the Dutch colony—asked the city to replace its deteriorating home. Five years later, the judges moved into the spanking new Manhattan Criminal Courthouse, the seventeen-story Moderne fortress at 100 Centre Street that still looms over neighboring buildings.

Harvey Wiley Corbett, a modernist architect on the team designing Rockefeller Center (6.10), collaborated with Charles B. Meyers (for Meyers, see 2.8), an experienced architect for municipal projects, to create this behemoth. Corbett (1873–1954), who had studied engineering at Berkeley and architecture in Paris at the École des Beaux-Arts, in 1912 started a partnership with Frank Helmle, in which he was joined in 1927 by his former student, Wallace K. Harrison. An early designer of setback towers, Corbett became an advocate for the new skyscraper form in his writing, lecturing, and building.

With this new courthouse, Civic Center classicism completely surrendered to the modern movement. The building gives the impression of a series of huge granite blocks seamlessly linked beneath a skin of limestone, interrupted only by endless vertical window columns sporting simple spandrels that give the illusion of rippling in the wind.

As Geoffrey Baker, architectural critic of the *New York Times*, wrote approvingly in June of 1941: "The new building assumes for the first time that the law courts and prisons require no more architectural mumbo-jumbo than any other modern business . . . the dominant impression is of a cleanly designed modern office building . . . stripped bare of historic trappings." Baker particularly admired the color of the materials: "Pale cream beige limestone alternates with gray, with unpolished black granite spandrels. . . . The color contrast is intensified by the contrast between the flat, simple texture of the limestone and the linenfold decoration of the granite, with the top panel in these gray strips given an elegantly formal open cresting." And he noted the architectural orthodoxy of 1941: "'verticalism' is a conscious style of our time. It is the romance of a Hugh Ferris [sic]rendering, a vast depression dream city cast in stone and steel."

The architects planned the enormous abstract granite pylons—standing guard at each entrance courtyard—as "gate posts and pedestals for bronze statuary" to "establish the majesty of the law." Given the absence of those gateposts and statues, that majesty appears elsewhere: in legal inscriptions, large and small, on the outside walls, and in faded murals of The Law high up inside the double-height lobby (adorned with geometric railings and ventilation grilles), near the ceiling.

*Walk north along Centre Street to the corner of White Street; turn left and walk west along White Street three blocks (five if counting narrow Cortlandt Alley and Franklin Alley) to Church Street. At the intersection of Church and White, Sixth Avenue branches off to the west from Church Street. Cross to the west side of Sixth Avenue for a view northward of the massive Long Lines Building, stretching along the east side of Sixth Avenue from Walker to Lispenard Streets.*

## 2.10 **Long Lines Building, 32 Sixth Avenue Voorhees, Gmelin & Walker, 1930–32 (expansion of original of 1911–14 and 1914–16)

Ralph Walker's last downtown skyscraper, another of his series for the phone company, incorporates one of the firm's earlier efforts, the Walker Lispenard Building, an original of 1911 with a seven-story addition. Built to house the Long Lines Department of AT&T, in its final form in 1932 this modernistic monolith served as the world's largest long-distance telephone complex, handling all long-distance calling in the Northeast and all overseas traffic.

Though apparently cast from the same mold as Walker's Barclay-Vesey (2.4) and Western Union (2.6) buildings, the Long Lines Building, last of the group, is the most geometrically organized, with massive cliff-like walls of brick piers and vertical windows that rise at competing angles and jut futuristically into the sky. (Two of those walls survive from the earlier building, but, relieved of their original eclectic ornament, they melt into the new

version.) The walls in turn are broken up into geometric patterns, with brick zigging and zagging so that almost no wall surface parallels the street.

The long lobby, snaking from Sixth Avenue to Church Street, has managed to survive with almost no alterations to its typically Deco ornamental materials, from green mosaic bands to frosted glass slat light fixtures. Like the Barclay-Vesey lobby, this one too is adorned with symbolic renderings of modern communications, by Hildreth Meière (designer of the mosaics at One Wall Street, 1.3). An enormous wall map shows long lines connecting the world, with a caption, "TELEPHONE WIRES AND RADIO UNITE TO MAKE NEIGHBORS OF NATIONS," while other long lines on the ceiling connect willowy female allegorical figures of four continents: Australia with sheep and kangaroo; Asia with tiger and elephant; Africa with lions and pyramids; and Europe with Roman aqueduct, the dome of St. Peter's, and the tower of Notre Dame in Paris. According to Meière's biographers, Catherine Brawer and Kathleen Skolnik, the artist originally proposed illustrating a day in the life of a young woman telephone operator, but the telephone company demurred. The work is done in silhouette mosaic—colored cement within an outline of glass mosaic tile—a cheaper, Depression-era alternative to a full mosaic. The result seems anything but cheap.

# ITINERARY NO. 3
# FROM MURRAY HILL TO GRAMERCY PARK

This walk through the east side of Midtown South includes an unusual collection of buildings, each different from the next. We have a surprising modernist apartment building (3.1) among the genteel town houses of Murray Hill; Ely Jacques Kahn's most impressive office building (3.4; and another Kahn building—3.7—that's no slouch); a work (3.5) by Edgar Brandt, the great French iron master; the iconic Empire State Building (3.3/3.6); an incomplete attempt by Metropolitan Life to capture the Empire State Building's "world's tallest" title (3.8); and George and Edward Blum's Gramercy House (3.11), with some of the most enjoyable Art Deco terra-cotta ornament in the city.

***The walk begins at the northeast corner of Park Avenue and East 38th Street, in Murray Hill.***

A low-scale residential neighborhood tucked in the shadows of Midtown skyscrapers, Murray Hill still shelters many of its residents in brownstones and town houses dating as far back as pre–Civil War days. It takes its name from the estate of Robert Murray, whose eighteenth-century mansion stood roughly at the corner of Park Avenue and East 37th Street. When Murray's descendants developed his estate, they included protective covenants with each sale to promote a pleasant residential enclave. Over the next century the fashionable new neighborhood attracted the prominent and the creative—from Admiral David Farragut, hero of the Civil War, to architects R. H. Robertson and William A. Delano, to newlyweds Franklin and Eleanor Roosevelt, to actors Hume Cronyn and Jessica Tandy—as well as the moneyed, most notably financier J. Pierpont Morgan. Single-family houses were the rule right up to the 1920s, when, inevitably, apartment buildings began springing up along Park Avenue. Further west and south, commercial development overtook the residential. Still, neighborhood residents—who banded together in 1914 as the Murray Hill Association—have fought valiantly to protect the neighborhood's character, and today, because

W 43
E 43
Grand Central
E 43
W 42
E 42
E 42
6 Avenue (Av of Americas)
Bryant Park
5 Av
E 41
Madison Av
Park Av
Lexington
3 Av
E 41
2 Av
W 40
E 40
E 40
Broadway
W 39
E 39
E 39
Tunnel Approach
E 38
W 38
E 38
1
New York Towne House
108 East 38 Street
E 38
W 37
E 37
Madison Av
E 37
W 36
E 36
Park Av
E 36
Sniffen Court
Tunnel Exit
Herald Sq
W 35
E 35
E 35
Hotel Ten Park Avenue
10 Park Avenue
2
W 34
E 34
Empire State Building
350 Fifth Avenue
3
6
5
Madison-Belmont Building
181 Madison Avenue
W 33
E 33
E 33
Two Park Avenue
4
Park Av
W 32
E 32
E 32
W 31
E 31
Park Av South
E 31
E 31
W 30
5 Av
E 30
E 30
E 30
W 29
W 29
E 29
E 29
7
261 Fifth Avenue
W 28
Broadway
E 28
E 28
E 28
W 27
5 Av
E 27
Park Av S
E 27
Lexington
3 Av
E 27
2 Av
W 26
E 26
E 26
E 26
W 25
W 25
Madison Sq
Madison Av
E 25
8
Metropolitan North Tower
11 Madison Avenue
E 25
W 24
E 24
New York Family Court
11 Lexington Av
(133 E 22 St)
E 24
W 23
E 23
Park Av S
E 23
E 23
W 22
5 Av
E 22
E 22
10
E 22
9
11
6 Avenue (Av of Americas)
W 21
Broadway
E 21
Gramercy Arms
102 East 22 Street
Gramercy Park
Gramercy House
235 East 22 Street
E 21
W 20
E 20
E 20
W 19
E 19
E 19
2 Av
W 18
5 Av
E 18
E 18
Park Av S
Irving Pl
E 18
3 Av
W 17
E 17
Union Square
E 17
Rutherford
Stuy-ve-sant
Perlman
W 16
E 16
E 16
© Tauranac, Ltd., 2016. All Rights Reserved.

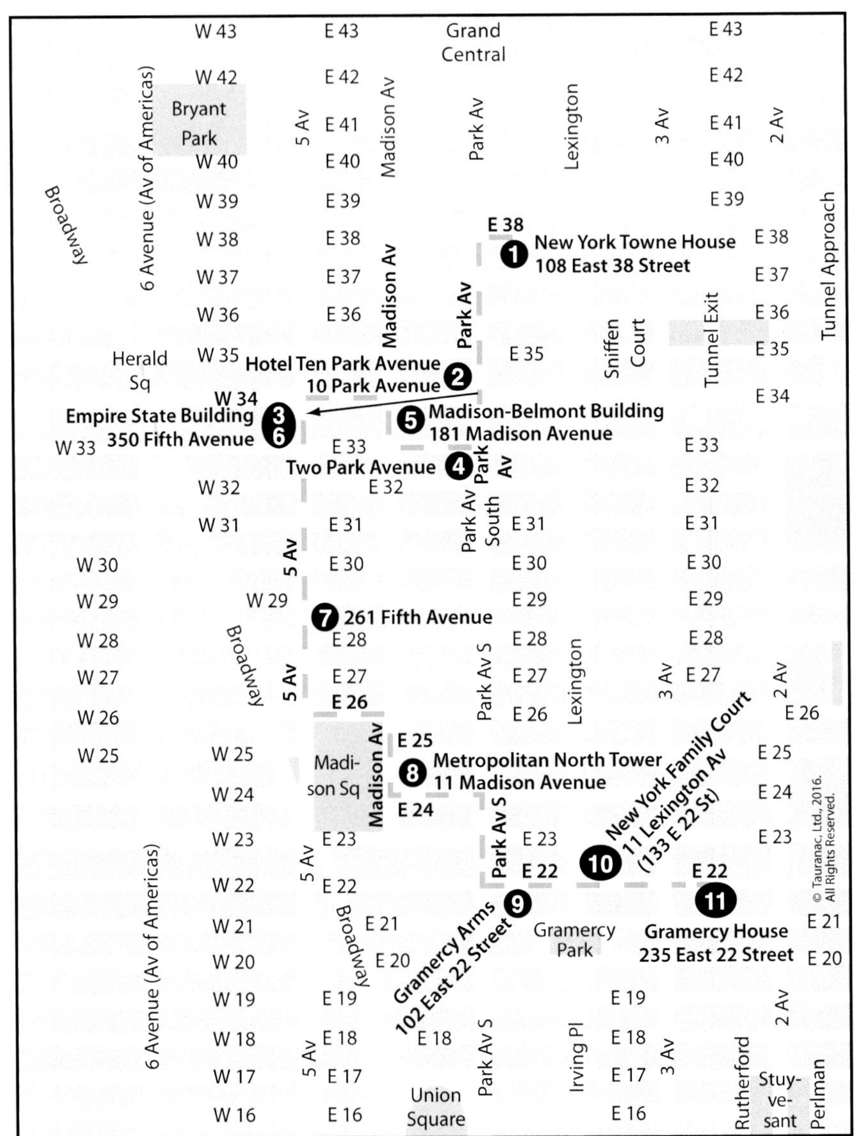

MAP 3

of the Association's efforts, zoning restrictions and Landmarks Commission designation protect much of the residential district.

***Walk east along the north side of East 38th Street halfway down the block, and look across the street.***

## 3.1 (HD) New York Towne House, 108 East 38th Street Bowden & Russell, with Emery Roth associate architect, 1929–30

Thanks to one of the Association's notable failures, Murray Hill today includes a most unusual Art Deco apartment tower midblock on East 38th Street, called—either ironically or cynically, as it replaced five actual town houses over the objection of the neighbors—the New York Towne House. Planned in 1928 as a thirty-one-story cooperative hotel, with each apartment a one-room pied-à-terre, it reached completion in 1930 as a twenty-four-story residential hotel. Initially meant to be a co-op, it converted almost immediately to rentals, but not before the top two floors could be sold as a duplex to lawyer William Edwards. Born in and still living at 108 East 38th Street, one of the five houses demolished to make way for the new building, Edwards didn't want to give up his address (talk about having your real-estate cake and eating it too).

Bowden & Russell (a short-lived partnership, 1930–36) designed an apartment building unlike most others in Manhattan. Towering above the Romanesque-inspired Church of Our Saviour at the corner of Park Avenue and East 38th Street (a much younger building, surprisingly, completed in 1957), its blocky silhouette rises through a series of setbacks to a slender but monolithic tower. Almost all its ornament depends on patterned brick—rippling brickwork in the window spandrels, brick ribbing at the setbacks. The wall above each window at the setbacks bows out and then effectively leans back into the building, leaving a series of vertical brick ribs protruding from the base.

The severely angular building may now be darker in color than originally intended. The *Times* described the brickwork as planned to be "in varied colors running from the deeper shade of reddish brown at the base to lighter shades of golden orange on the upper floors." The use of colors rising from darker to lighter found its way into a number of Deco buildings, from Raymond Hood's McGraw-Hill Building (5.8/5.12) to Ralph Walker's Western Union (2.6) and Schwartz & Gross's 55 Central Park West (8.2), all designed about 1930. Some of the Towne House colors may be hard to see today, but still quite visible are the brightly colored terra-cotta panels at the tower's very top. The tower itself was originally illuminated by light "shining through transparent panels of colored glass brick imported from Holland."

*Cross to the south side of the street for a closer look.*

Patterned brickwork at the lower floors includes what look like grilles of rounded brick separating the windows above the main entrance. Except for the marquee sheltering it, that entrance survives largely intact.

*Return to the corner of Park Avenue, turn left, and walk south on Park, staying on the east side, continuing halfway down the block toward East 37th Street.*

Pausing midway down the block, look west to see the top of the Empire State Building (3.3/3.6) poking its head above the surrounding buildings. We'll see it from closer up soon enough.

*Continue walking south on Park Avenue to the corner of East 34th Street, then look west across Park Avenue at the northwest corner of Park and East 34th.*

## 3.2 (NR HD) Hotel Ten Park Avenue, 10 Park Avenue
## Corbett, Harrison & MacMurray, 1929–31

One of the city's great modernist firms, led by Harvey Wiley Corbett (for Corbett, see 2.9) and Wallace K. Harrison, Corbett, Harrison & MacMurray designed this twenty-seven-story hotel about the same time the firm joined with Raymond Hood's firm to work on Rockefeller Center (6.10). The Community Church of New York owned the corner site and struck a deal with the hotel's developer permitting the demolition of the church in exchange for space within the new building for a church and community house—a not uncommon phenomenon for the times. Unfortunately, many such projects ran into financial difficulty. As reported in *The New Yorker* in December 1935 (in an article titled "Fiasco of the Church-Hotel"),

> Dr. John Haynes Holmes, of the Community Church, allowed himself to be persuaded that it would obscure the proposed new church to have it built into the apartment house at 10 Park Avenue in a style that would not impair the renting possibilities of the apartments. Four adjoining lots were purchased around the corner on Thirty-fifth Street for the promised church. . . . Dr. Holmes held out for a Park Avenue entrance for the church. He got it—a church door that is never opened and seldom noticed, in the front wall of 10 Park Avenue. Behind the door is a dusty lobby that is never used; the lobby stops at a bricked-up doorway in the back wall of the apartment house.

The congregation eventually did build a church on the lots on East 35th Street. In the meantime, the hotel had gone into foreclosure, victim of the Depression. But the building's design still reflects the original concept, and Dr. Holmes's Park Avenue front door.

For a hotel, Ten Park Avenue has a very commercial flavor—the enormous proportion of casement windows to brick, together with the modest amount of ornament, suggests a daylight factory more than a temporary residence. The stone facing at the first two stories offers some interesting ornament, but most of it is concentrated at the north end, at the would-be church entrance. The design here suggests a modernist take on a Gothic façade. The stone facing extends to the fifth and sixth stories, clearly marking off the planned church entrance from the hotel. The window width is cut in half, suggesting tall, narrow Gothic windows, while the plain stone area at the south, rising one story higher than the rest, suggests a church tower. The detailing has a Gothic flare, but a closer look reveals geometric patterns and stylized versions of Gothic motifs—a Gothic Modern church façade grafted onto a modernistic tower.

***Cross East 34th Street to the south side of the block, and walk to the middle of the block for a better view of the Empire State Building***

## 3.3 **Empire State Building, 350 Fifth Avenue (introduction, continued in 3.6) Shreve, Lamb & Harmon, 1929-31

The Empire State Building has become such an icon beyond its architectural design that its style seems almost beside the point. William Lamb, chief designer for the project, disliked the modernism now called Art Deco—according to his widow (in a 1981 interview with the author), his architectural preferences ran to the spare Romanesque of the cathedrals of southern France. Lamb thought of the elaborately modernistic Chrysler Building (5.4) as "the Little Nemo" school of architecture, referring to a fantasy comic strip, though he did admire the work of Raymond Hood, a close friend. But perhaps the main reason the Empire State Building doesn't spring to mind as an Art Deco monument is the addition of the enormously tall television mast at its top, which has altered the building's silhouette. To see the building's Deco profile, imagine it without the antenna—suddenly that silhouette seems stubbier, and more geometric.

The building has all the hallmarks of the Deco approach—vertical columns of windows, in this case paired windows set within aluminum frames, and setbacks leading to a slender tower. The stubby tower supporting the antenna is actually a gigantic mast, made of aluminum, nickel-chrome-steel, and glass, with overlapping metal wings and horizontal metal banding—all quite as much "Little Nemo" in flavor as the Chrysler Building, if somewhat less flamboyant. The building's developers famously intended this odd structure to serve as a mooring mast for dirigibles—theoretically, passengers would exit the dirigible at the building's top, 1,250 feet in the air, and be whisked by elevators down to Midtown's streets. It never happened. The rest of the building's ornamental treatment is better seen close-up, from Fifth Avenue (3.6).

***Walk south on Park Avenue one more block, staying on the east side of Park, and cross to the south side of East 33rd Street for a view of Two Park Avenue on the west side of Park between East 32nd and 33rd Streets.***

## 3.4 *Two Park Avenue Building (Plate 4) Buchman & Kahn, 1926–28

Ely Jacques Kahn designed this building in 1926, for developer Abe Adelson, just one year after visiting the 1925 Paris Exposition—making Two Park Avenue one of Manhattan's first Art Deco office buildings. Among the most prolific architects of his generation, during the 1920s Kahn designed more than seventy buildings of every kind, and found himself mentioned regularly with Ralph Walker and Raymond Hood. Kahn's work seems to reflect something of his family's interest in decorative arts—his father imported French and Belgian glass, and his sister kept a shop importing modern art objects from Germany and Austria. Kahn traveled unusually widely for the time—not just in Europe but also North Africa and the Middle East. He had connections to the Viennese Sezession, and admired the work of Josef Hoffman, but also the work of Frank Lloyd Wright. In contrast with his wide range of experience, contacts, and knowledge, Kahn found his clients among immigrant developers, self-made men with little formal education. He developed the pragmatic bent necessary to working with such businessmen, but also found them to be more open-minded about design.

Two Park Avenue shows both Kahn's pragmatism and his sense of decorative arts at work. On the one hand, he wrote that by designing the building as a square block with a rear light court he could produce the largest and most adaptable floor areas—just what his clients would want to hear. Uncertain about the direction new development on Park Avenue might take, they had asked Kahn to design something that could work either as offices and showrooms or as space for light manufacturing, and Kahn obliged. On the other hand, he abandoned what he called, in his unpublished autobiography, "the pompous sterility of 1900 with white lines of columns," turning instead to flat surfaces alive with color, which, he felt, could "replace the play of light and shadow of traditional ornament. . . . The possibilities of strong contrasts of colors eliminating futile carving and crockets, pinnacles and similar appendages of the early skyscraper are unlimited."

Kahn invested great effort in the building's colors. He worked with his friend Leon Victor Solon, a writer on color described by Kahn's biographer, Jewel Stern, as "the nation's leading authority on architectural polychromy." Together, Kahn and Solon chose the building's colors, and before installing the terra-cotta panels on the building had mock-ups fabricated and mounted at the correct height to assess their appearance from a distance. In a contemporary interview in the *New York World* unearthed by Stern, the architect announced, "In the past few days my own firm has decided to go still further in this experiment and use big masses of primary colors, three hundred feet up in the air, in the new building. . . . We are going to put on strong reds and blue, in big masses, and I think the effect will be wonderful." Kahn's clients apparently had doubts about the entire project, but consulted Raymond Hood, who reassured them that Kahn knew what he was doing.

The result is one of the city's most striking Art Deco façades. The large, bulky building rises to an explosion of bright colors, both in the terra-cotta and the brick—blue, ochre, red, black, and yellow. Brick and stone are set in geometric patterns. The façade feels almost woven—and indeed, Kahn wrote in his autobiography that he was "thinking of the texture of fabric."

***Cross Park Avenue to see the ground floor detailing, storefronts, and the entrance of Two Park Avenue.***

A restoration several years ago removed unsightly panels that had covered the ornamental, geometrically patterned cast-iron panels directly above the storefronts.

Walk into the open vestibule leading to the building's main entrance to see the marble walls and the wonderfully intricate patterned geometric ornament on the bronze door frames. If the building's façade suggests "the texture of fabric," the multicolored mosaic above your head feels positively like a grand tapestry spread out across the ceiling.

Beyond the doors lies one of Kahn's finest and most intact lobbies—bronze, marble, and mosaics in abstract geometric forms, in the light fixtures, radiator grilles, and even the postbox. Jewel Stern notes that it "became a permanent showcase for the firm when it moved its offices there in 1928."

***From the building's entrance, walk north up Park Avenue to the corner of East 33rd Street. Turn left and walk one block west on East 33rd Street to Madison Avenue; turn right on Madison and walk north to the southeast corner of Madison and East 34th Street.***

## 3.5 **Madison-Belmont Building (with the Cheney Brothers showroom), 181 Madison Avenue Building: Warren & Wetmore, 1924–25; Cheney Brothers storefront: Edgar Brandt of Ferrobrandt, 1925

Silk and iron—such different materials, and yet here they came together in an international collaboration. Edgar Brandt (1880–1960) reigned as the most prominent designer of ironwork in 1920s France. His early work partook of an Art Nouveau sensibility; by the early 1920s he'd moved toward Art Deco. At the 1925 Paris Exposition, he designed eighteen gateways, including the Porte d'Honneur, its main entrance, and mounted an entire display of his work.

Brandt's work attracted the attention of Henry Créange, art director for Cheney Brothers, America's largest silk mill. Historian Joan Kahr quotes Créange: "I saw his work in Paris . . . and I noticed in his work there was something new and something old. . . . He obtains his inspiration from the ancients and interprets them in forms that are more suggestive of the dynamic force of today."

In September 1924, Cheney Brothers created a collection called Prints Ferronière, which the *New York Times* later described as "thirty designs inspired by Edgar Brandt's work . . . embodied in 2,500 yards of printed silks, tinsels and cut velvets in a hundred colors. . . . the first textiles to show the influence of the modern master, M. Brandt." In February 1925, just a few months before the Paris Exposition opened, these went on display in Paris, at the Louvre. Later that same year, M. Brandt returned the favor, designing the entrance and exhibition hall of Cheney Brothers' new headquarters on Madison Avenue—sixty tons of ironwork inside and out.

Cheney Brothers chose the location because 34th Street and Madison Avenue had become the center of New York's silk district. At the showroom's official opening on October 14, architect Harvey Wiley Corbett presided, while congratulatory telegrams poured in from the likes of Herbert Hoover (then United States secretary of commerce), Louis Comfort Tiffany, and the French minister of commerce.

The three-story space no longer houses Cheney's quarters, but Brandt's exterior iron and gilded bronze gates survive, on both Madison Avenue and East 34th Street, as do his three-story-tall storefronts on the outside, and his metalwork inside the 34th Street lobby. Above the 34th Street entrance, a gilded fountain erupts over a background of vines, while the entrance gates below offer a lush fantasy of floral patterns and broad leaves.

The tall grille above the Madison Avenue entrance offers a different fantasy but still on floral themes. Though Decophiles can only imagine entering the 1925 Paris Exposition through Brandt's doors, walking through Brandt's New York gates remains an option.

*Cross Madison Avenue and walk west on East 34th Street to Fifth Avenue.*

## 3.6 **Empire State Building, 350 Fifth Avenue (continued from 3.3) Shreve, Lamb & Harmon, 1929–31

Among this building's most extraordinary characteristics is the way that a hundred-story skyscraper seems to fit comfortably on a Midtown Fifth Avenue block—thanks to the five-story base with storefronts and entrances that offers passers-by some human scale. At this level, Art Deco detail shows up in the ribbed stone piers, which create a more or less modernistic, stripped-down version of a classical order—basement, colonnade, attic story, with

monolithic stone eagles at the fifth story, flanking the words "EMPIRE STATE." The storefronts, almost all glass, are framed by black granite at the base, a black-granite panel set in molded aluminum bands at the top, and, at either side, molded aluminum mullions rising to a curling finial.

The Fifth Avenue entrance leads into a long, narrow hall, with gently curving side walls, that seems like nothing so much as a chapel—a shrine to the Empire State. John J. Raskob, the General Motors executive who built the skyscraper as a speculative venture, hired his childhood friend Al Smith, former governor of New York State, to serve as the building's president and figurehead—one of Smith's chief duties being to escort visiting dignitaries to the observatory. "Empire State" is another name for New York State—Al Smith's state. So the far end of this entrance "chapel" is devoted to an aluminum silhouette of the Empire State Building superimposed over the silhouette of the Empire State itself, all designed by Oscar Bach (for Bach, see 2.8), one of the great metal designers of the period. The ceiling, formerly hidden by a dropped ceiling, has been uncovered and its ornament beautifully recreated, with shining orbs suggesting stars and planets—orbiting, perhaps, around the Empire State. The long lobby corridors beyond the hall continue the newly visible ceiling, as well as a series of medallions cast in duralumin—an early alloy of aluminum—also designed by Bach; they represent the various building trades—electricity, masonry, heating—that made this building possible. The double-height hallways are crossed by strikingly modernistic mezzanine-level bridges.

*From the Fifth Avenue entrance continue south along Fifth Avenue to East 29th Street; look across the intersection at the southeast corner of Fifth and East 29th.*

## 3.7 (HD) 261 Fifth Avenue
## Buchman & Kahn, 1928–29

Rising well above its neighbors, this twenty-six-story loft building beckons with the multicolored terra-cotta bands of its setbacks. Begun the same year that Kahn completed Two Park Avenue (3.4), No. 261 Fifth housed offices, lofts, and showrooms, long occupied by houseware and carpet companies. The terra-cotta is particularly elaborate above the first and second stories, somewhat calmer above the third and fourth stories, then disappears, returning only at the tower setbacks. The wonderfully fine-grained detail, the sensibility of decorative objets-d'art, could only be by Kahn—no other architect produced anything like this. The same level of detail marks the lobby, one of Kahn's best surviving designs, with its multicolored wall mosaics, tiled floor, and plaster ceiling.

***Continue south on Fifth Avenue to Madison Square at East 26th Street, turn left, and walk one block east to Madison Avenue; turn right on Madison and walk one block south on Madison to East 25th Street; look across the street at the east side of Madison between East 24th and 25th Streets.***

## 3.8 Metropolitan Life North Tower, 11 Madison Avenue Corbett & Waid, 1931–33

The 1920s witnessed a very public competition to build the "world's tallest building." The Chrysler Building and Empire State Building both finally staked accepted claims, but over the decade quite a few other contenders announced plans. Most never got started, but in 1929 the Metropolitan Life Company—a former title holder with its 1909 tower at Madison Square—announced plans to recapture the glory with a hundred-story annex, and started construction. Insurance companies built quite a few of the country's early skyscrapers—they had to park all their capital somewhere. Harvey Wiley Corbett (for Corbett, see 2.9) and Dan Waid planned a vast telescope of a building, stepping back at each new level in conformance with the city's zoning regulations. By 1933, however, in the depths of the Great Depression, construction stopped, and today "Eleven Madison" sits like an enormous stump, fruitlessly awaiting its remaining telescopic extension—a huge building by any standard, but no taller than thirty-one stories.

The building's bulk, clad entirely in stone, rises in polygonal angles, its windows arranged in the standard vertical columns, and relieved by little if any ornamental treatment other than modest scalloped stonework above the windows at each setback. As the *Times* quoted Waid:

"The building is not fashioned after some predetermined architectural style but is essentially a creation of this age and time . . . a rational use of materials suitable for enclosing a steel frame structure. It stands as a modern interpretation of the American building problem, unhampered by archaeological precedent. The appearance of the building is secured entirely by a careful study of mass, silhouette, surface texture and form."

In the skyline, the building appears as a massive hulking—and unfinished—tower. At street level, however, the architects relaxed their stringent approach. At each corner, they created double-height arched porches, with tall ribbed piers rising past their arches to the third story and supporting stony baskets of flowers. The second story stretching along Madison Avenue between the two porches sports pairs of arched openings filled with stone screens based on floral patterns. Each porch rises to a vaulted stone dome, lined with illusionistic coffers, from the center of which hangs a handsome Moderne chandelier.

The richness of the marble entranceways, the elaborately stepped stone walls, and especially the huge, ornamental floral metal gates create an awe-inspiring space that elsewhere would be a grand ceremonial room but here just leads to the building's entrances.

***Walk east along the East 24th Street façade of the Tower to Park Avenue South, turn right and walk south on Park Avenue South to East 22nd Street, then turn left and walk just a few feet further east. Look across the street at the Gramercy Arms.***

## 3.9 Gramercy Arms, 102 East 22nd Street Sugarman & Berger, 1928

The Gramercy Arms (so called even though located one block north—and out of sight—of Gramercy Park) attracted little notice when it opened, with grander apartment buildings underway in the neighborhood at the time. But Sugarman & Berger's delightful design (for Sugarman & Berger, see 4.4) includes brick set in various geometric patterns, and sparkly terra-cotta ornament—double-height

fluted piers at the ground floor, rising to wild jungle floral patterns; flowery yet geometric spandrels below the windows at the second, fifth, seventh, and ninth stories; and a cast-stone entrance surround rising to a nifty decorative metal light fixture now partially hidden by an awning, but worth straining to see at least in a partial view.

***Continue walking east on East 22nd Street to the corner of Lexington Avenue; look across the intersection at the northeast corner of Lexington and East 22nd.***

## 3.10 New York Family Court Building (now Baruch College), 11 Lexington Avenue Charles B. Meyers, 1937–1939; aluminum reliefs by Harry Poole Camden

The ten-story stolid block on the northeast corner of the intersection of Lexington Avenue and East 22nd Street, today incorporated into the campus of Baruch College, originally housed a new Family Court meant to complement the earlier Children's Court adjoining it immediately to the east on East 22nd Street. Given Charles B. Meyers's experience in government classicism (for Meyers, see 2.8), it's hardly surprising that—in a nod to the classicism of the existing Children's Court—he designed the Family Court in a severe Modern Classic. In the words of the *Times* in December: "The building is simple in design and its decorations will follow classical lines with carved features over the Twenty-second Street entrance."

Those carved features turn out to be an aluminum relief of the Court's seal, including the State's motto, "Excelsior," the American eagle, and a figure of justice balancing her scales. Sculptor Harry Pool Camden had these cast in aluminum, along with a series of panels above the first-story windows showing families enjoying various activities. Camden—who balanced a military life with a sculptor's career, including an appointment as sculpture professor at Cornell University—had spent three years in Rome as a fellow at the American Academy, and then undertaken a number of government commissions. About the same time as his work on the Court, he

won the competition to design enormous sculptural figures for the Federal Building at the 1939 New York World's Fair. His work here displays that typically late 1930s muscular realism, producing human figures which seem totally unreal. In the ceremonial laying of the cornerstone in 1939, as reported in the *Christian Science Monitor*, Mayor La Guardia opined: "If our predecessors had had the social vision now accepted as a proper function of Government, we wouldn't need all the courthouses and jails today. I hope the time will come when I will be criticized for making this court as large as I have. I hope the time will come when people will wonder why we had such a large family court."

***Continue east on East 22nd Street; look across the street at the northwest corner of East 22nd and Second Avenue.***

## 3.11 Gramercy House, 235 East 22nd Street George & Edward Blum, 1930

George and Edward Blum designed some of New York's most imaginative apartment buildings in the early twentieth century. The brothers studied architecture at the École des Beaux-Arts, in Paris, like so many of their contemporaries, but, unlike most, they themselves came from a French family that moved back and forth between Paris and New York (George, 1870–1928, was born in New York; Edward, 1876–1944, in Paris), and they spent their youth in France. As a result, the Blums became more familiar with French contemporary architecture outside the École, and developed a style of brick ornament unlike anything being done in New York at the time. Toward the end of their practice, they turned to Art Deco, designing two large apartment houses in the style: No. 210 East 68th Street, in 1928 (10.7), and the Gramercy House in 1930—among the city's earliest Art Deco apartment houses.

As Andrew Dolkart and Susan Tunick note in their monograph on the Blums, Gramercy House and 210 East 68th Street "exhibit some of the most notable Art Deco terra cotta in New York." Instead of the typical geometric or stylized floral patterns, "the Blums created designs . . . by emphasizing the overlapping and weaving of elements, the interplay of positive and negative motifs, and the alternation of identical decorative elements to create varied patterns."

The Blums' terra-cotta here is just stunning—a wide multicolored band separating the second- and third-story windows mingles wavy lines, sharp angles, and oddly repeating circles and rectangles, all woven into a pattern unlike any other. While this band wraps around the entire building, at the main entrance on East 22nd Street it erupts into two stories' worth of horizontals and verticals surrounding windows and doors. At the corner, and around onto Second Avenue, terra-cotta bands light up the store fronts. But don't miss the other details on this building—patterned polychromatic brick bands marking the setbacks, and tiny angled brick couplets marking the corners in the upper stories—not to mention the wavy metal railings protecting small gardens within the building's recessed light courts.

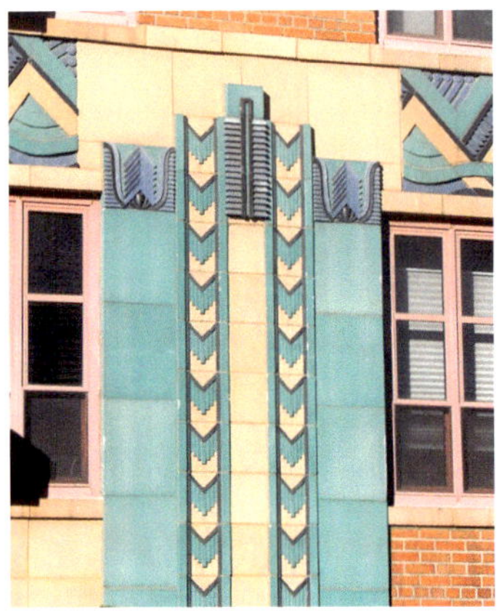

# ITINERARY NO. 4
# THE GARMENT DISTRICT

This walk takes us through Manhattan's fabled gritty district of clothing manufacturers—though the garment trade and fashion industry have long since begun to yield to higher-rent uses. Art Deco came late in the garment district's development—most of the buildings reflect the typical eclecticism of the 1920s—but modernistic gems lie scattered throughout. Ely Jacques Kahn is especially well represented here, both with earlier buildings and with Deco creations, including the Bricken Textile (4.1), Bricken Casino (4.3a), and Continental (4.2) buildings. Blum & Blum designed a handsome midblock loft building on West 36th Street (4.6). Other notables include H. Craig Severance's Nelson Tower (4.10), the district's tallest; Sugarman & Berger's Hotel New Yorker (4.8), in its day the city's largest hotel; and, at the other end of the spectrum, a tiny building for Bickford's Cafeteria (4.7), survivor of a venerable luncheonette chain.

***The walk begins at the northeast corner of Broadway and West 41st Street.***

> "Seventh Avenue in the city of New York, between 35th and 40th Streets, is not merely a geographic location. It's a legend. It's the birthplace of miracles. It's the fast-beating heart of an industry whose bloodstreams course through America."
>
> —Murray Sices, *Seventh Avenue*

The Garment District may be the only New York City district created largely by reform movements. Heart of the city's and the nation's garment industry, the district has a location and character that reflect, on the one hand, the economic forces of national markets, transportation (nearby Penn Station), and efficiencies of density, and, on the other hand, labor reform movements, building regulations, and the city's zoning resolution of 1916. Labor reform—especially following the deadly Triangle fire—led to requirements for safety, light, and air in new loft buildings. New regulations affecting the bulk and size of such buildings introduced the use of setbacks.

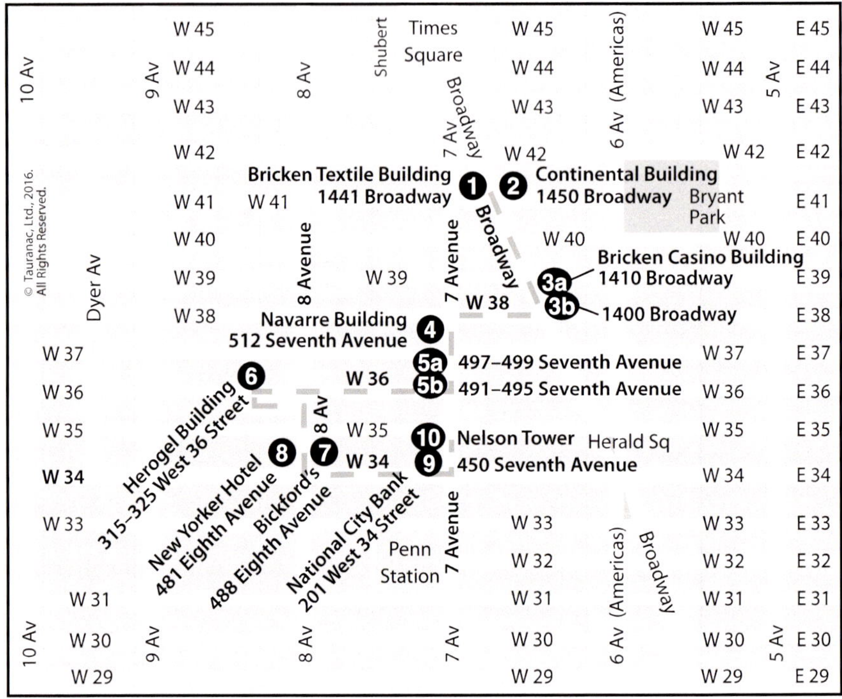


## MAP 4

Zoning regulations banned garment-industry lofts from the department store district along Fifth Avenue, specifically relocating the industry well to the west. The result: over a period of not much more than a decade, following the end of World War I, the blocks between Sixth and Ninth Avenues, from West 34th to West 42nd Streets, developed into a uniform cityscape of steep narrow canyons lined with setback buildings. Most of these new buildings adopted the standard eclectic styles of the 1920s, but at the end of the decade a dozen Art Deco designs brought light and color to the streets.

*Look at the northwest corner of Broadway and West 41st Street.*

### 4.1 (NR HD) Bricken Textile Building, 1441 Broadway Buchman & Kahn, 1929–30

Ely Jacques Kahn (for Kahn, see 3.4) designed more than a dozen buildings in the garment district, working with major developers including A. E. Lefcourt, Abraham Bricken, and Louis Adler. His four Art Deco contributions cluster here on Broadway between West 39th and West 41st Streets on what

might be called Kahn's Corners. He designed two of the four for Bricken, a Jewish immigrant from Kiev who started as a tailor on the Lower East Side, and rose to become one of the most active developers in the Garment District, constructing an estimated $50 million worth of lofts here between 1921 and 1927.

This stretch of Broadway south of Times Square once beckoned to New Yorkers as the "Rialto," the heart of New York's theater district. As the district moved north of 42nd Street, garment industry lofts and offices replaced the theaters and hotels. As the *Times* reported in July of 1929: "New York seldom has witnessed an era of destruction comparable to that through which the old metropolitan playhouses now are passing. . . . [C]urtains are being rung down for the last time in a dozen theatres closely linked with history; in their stead are rising greater structures, symbols of changing stagecraft and modern real estate methods."

The Bricken Textile Building replaced the former Broadway Theatre, built for James Bailey of Barnum & Bailey circus fame. The new building's name reflected its target market—the textile industry—but for office space, not manufacturing lofts. As advertised in the *New York Times* in 1930: "1441 Broadway gives new distinction to TIMES SQUARE OFFICES. Financial District quality and service . . . Grand Central Zone convenience and accessibility. . . . 1441 Broadway was built to supply a demand for the highest type office space in the Times Square Section." Initial tenants included Wall Street firms and the New York Telephone Company, as well as firms of "Textile Bankers."

Located on a short block of 41st Street between Broadway and Seventh Avenue—which cross just two blocks to the north—the Bricken Textile Building rises on three sides like a squat ziggurat to a series of shallow setbacks. Kahn uses brick and color to emphasize its vertical window arrangement—enormous angled piers of golden brick playing off against the darker buff brick at the corners, and contrasting with the gray stone of the first five stories. Typical Kahn details include the skinny metal window frames at the second through fourth stories, with ornamental spandrels that look like birds-eye views of an ancient temple compound, and the stone cupid's-bows separating the windows at the fifth story. Little survives of the building's original lobby.

***Look at the northeast corner of Broadway and West 41st Street.***

## 4.2 (NR HD) Continental Building, 1450 Broadway Ely Jacques Kahn, 1930–31

Two years later, Kahn designed the Continental Building for Louis Adler, a Jewish immigrant from Austria who started as a dressmaker and, like Bricken, moved into real estate. Adler commissioned three Garment District buildings from Kahn, all geared to high-level manufacturers of exclusive clothing.

The Continental—in a pattern typical of the district—took the name of the building it replaced, the old Continental Hotel, called by the *Times* "one of the last of the famous old hostelries that flourished in the vicinity before the [First World] war." Like the Bricken Textile Building across the street, the Continental offered offices rather than lofts. The *Times* described the forty-three-story tower as "the tallest high-class office building in the immediate Times Square area" and "the finest type of an office building of unusual architectural beauty that will tower 600 feet and be a credit to the Times Square section." The building would have stores on the ground floor, a bank on the mezzanine, and office suites—no loft spaces—above.

Like other office towers of the day, the Continental Building rises to a series of middling setbacks, from which emerges a slender tower—the entire building defined by its massing, its pairs of vertical window columns, and its stark white color. What a striking contrast to Kahn's earlier Bricken Textile Building just across the street—a tall, slender, white office tower compared to a short, squat, multicolored building. As the *Times* noted, "the height of the building practically insures light on all four sides and especially in the tower, which will have an illuminated crown and be surmounted by a 150-foot steel flag pole." Kahn made use of the setbacks to create balconied terraces for some of the office suites, prompting *Architecture and Building* to note that "the idea of a terrace just outside your office is a new one in New York." The finely sculpted abstract ornament typical of Kahn's buildings does show up here, but mostly just in the sixth-story window frames. The design relies instead on the sculpture of setbacks and tower. Look carefully at the top of the tower—it appears to be set at an angle to the rest of the building. That's because Broadway runs at an odd angle across the side streets; Kahn made the tower parallel to other buildings in the skyline, rather than to Broadway.

*Cross to the west side of Broadway, and walk south along Broadway to the plaza at the northwest corner of Broadway and West 39th Street. Look across the street to see 1410 Broadway at the southeast corner of West 39th Street, and immediately south of it 1400 Broadway at the northeast corner of West 38th Street.*

### 4.3a (NR HD) Bricken Casino Building, 1410 Broadway Ely Jacques Kahn, 1930–31

### 4.3b (NR HD) 1400 Broadway Buchman & Kahn, 1930–31

Broadway lost two theaters on this old Rialto block—the Casino Theatre, on the north end, which played light opera and musical comedy, and the Knickerbocker Theatre, on the south end, where Sarah Bernhardt once trod the boards. Describing the frantic building activity here in 1930, the *World* noted: "With [Abraham] Bricken tearing down the old Casino on the 39th corner and [Abraham] Gewirtz doing likewise to the old Knickerbocker Theatre adjoining at 38th Street, [Lewis] Adler will tackle the old Hotel Continental at the southeast corner of 41st Street to-morrow—all to rush up skyscrapers." Because Kahn filed plans for No. 1400 just before his partner, Buchman, retired, it's officially credited to Buchman & Kahn, while No. 1410 became the first building officially designed by the firm of Ely Jacques Kahn.

Though built for different clients, the Bricken Casino Building and the adjoining 1400 Broadway look like wings of the same building—similar in height, with similar setbacks and white brick facing. No. 1400 actually wraps around No. 1410, so that the two buildings have adjoining façades not just on Broadway but on West 39th Street. They differ, however, in their details. No. 1400 is somewhat starker in its whiteness, while No. 1410 uses white and black brick to create strong vertical stripes. Kahn's biographer,

Jewel Stern, quotes one of Kahn's staff, Ted Jacobsen, recalling the architect "coming into the drafting room to announce—now this one will be vertical lines in black & white (and with towering setbacks). . . . In those days the designers used to argue (over a couple of fast ones at lunch) the theory and merits of horizontal or vertical treatments of the spandrels and piers and which should be light or dark." Stern herself describes No. 1410 as "unique in Kahn's oeuvre" and "his most expressionistic design."

***Cross to the east side of Broadway, between West 39th and 38th Streets.***

Take a closer look at the details of each building. No. 1410 has a dramatic black stone base with elaborate, finely detailed bronze window frames. The base of No. 1400 has window frames in a similar spirit, but a completely different design.

From here, look across at the west side of Broadway, to see Kahn's past and his future. At the northwest corner of Broadway and West 37th Street, the Lefcourt-State Building (1927–28) shows Buchman & Kahn in their premodernistic mode. At the northwest corner of West 38th Street, by contrast, stretching all the way to West 39th, stands No. 1407 Broadway, a post–World War II work (1948–50), approaching the International Style, by Kahn's new firm of Kahn & Jacobs.

Cross back to the west side of Broadway, and walk west on West 38th Street one block to Seventh Avenue. Look across the street at the southwest corner of Seventh and West 38th.

## 4.4 (NR HD) Navarre Building, 512 Seventh Avenue Sugarman & Berger, 1928–30

Another tower taking its name from a demolished predecessor, the Navarre Building replaced the Hotel Navarre, one of a string of hotels built on Seventh Avenue following the completion of Penn Station. But just as the garment industry gradually replaced the theaters on the Rialto, so it also soon replaced most of the nearby hotels.

In a sense, it was the garment industry as a whole that redeveloped the Navarre site—the Garment Centre Capitol Company, led by Saul Singer. In

1919–20, Singer, formerly president of the Cloak, Suit and Skirt Manufacturers Protective Association, had joined developer Mack Kanner to build the Garment Centre Capitol, two buildings, at 488 and 500 Seventh Avenue, framing West 37th Street. They conceived of the project as a cooperative venture to house the showrooms and offices of the garment industry, then being ejected from precincts further east. As the *Times* explained: "This shift of the cloak and suit trade with its thousands of employees from Madison and Fifth Avenues to west of Seventh Avenue, marks the culmination of the work of the Save New York Committee, which was organized several years ago . . . to prevent further encroachments of manufacturing lofts in the new retail shopping zone and save Fifth Avenue from the blight of garment workers who at certain hours of the day crowded the streets." (Yes, the *Times* actually printed those words.) The Garment Centre Capitol buildings included, besides office and showroom space, an employers' club with a gym, squash courts, and billiard parlor, as well as a dining room and reading room, forming what the *Times* called "a city within a city."

The Garment Centre Capitol Company acquired the Hotel Navarre at the same time as its other sites, but went forward with the new tower only at the end of the decade—hence the striking contrast between the shorter and largely nondescript original Capitol buildings, and the forty-three-story Art Deco Navarre Building, designed to serve the same purpose as the originals. Sugarman & Berger (M. Henry Sugarman, 1888–1946, and Albert G. Berger, 1879–1940), the firm chosen to design the new tower, specialized in apartment houses and hotels, typically in designs inspired by medieval or classical sources. But by the end of the 1920s they too had turned to more modernistic notions.

A straightforward tower, the Navarre rises to the same height as its Capitol neighbor, and then sets back on both the avenue and the street fronts for the blocky tower portion. As Jacob Rapoport, one of the directors of the Garment Centre Capitol quoted by the *Times*, explained, "The building exhibits the modern tendency toward simple massing and stark vertical lines." Sugarman, interviewed by the *Times* in April 1928, "spoke of the project as one that has been studied throughout as a problem of masses, and the sculpturesque effect of the whole was the result of a most careful study of interior plan requirements, setbacks, restrictions and the demand for an impressive exterior. The plan of the tower which was finally adopted greatly accentuated the feeling of verticality in the mass and this expression was further developed in the treatment of the windows." Hence the paired vertical columns of windows, and the uninterrupted flat brick piers rising to the setbacks—standard Deco fare.

*Cross to the west side of Seventh Avenue*

What keeps the Navarre from being as nondescript as its neighbors is the treatment of its first five stories—divided into window bays by polished stone-faced piers with extravagantly ornamental tops, and window spandrels taking different modernistic forms from one story to the next. Most extraordinarily ornamental of all are two entrances on Seventh Avenue.

The northerly entrance originally led to the main office of the Industrial National Bank of New York, whose president, Max Weinstein, "thirty-seven years ago . . . sold candy for a living" on the building's site, according to the *Times*. Weinstein and the architects apparently put much thought into the bank's design, conducting "extensive research in this country and abroad, to adapt modern tendencies in interior decorating to a commercial building," earning a February 1930 *Times* article captioned "Artistic Banking Office." The former bank's entrance includes an elaborate pair of bronze doors which fold in to either side, topped by an ornamental panel with odd patterns focused on a central roundel with an eagle. The Navarre's main entrance, to the south, has lost some of its detail, but still has a handsome bronze frieze at the top, surrounded by modernistically detailed stonework.

***Walk south along Seventh Avenue to the corner of West 37th Street and look across the intersection at the southeast corner of Seventh and West 37th.***

### 4.5a (NR HD) 497–499 Seventh Avenue
### Schwartz & Gross, 1930–31

### 4.5b (NR HD) 491–495 Seventh Avenue
### George & Edward Blum, 1925–26

Across the street, at the southeast corner of Seventh Avenue and 37th Street, stand two buildings with one entrance. The corner building, No. 497–499,

is a Schwartz & Gross design of 1930–31; its fraternal twin, No. 491–495, is five years older, designed by George and Edward Blum (for the Blums, see 3.11; for Schwartz & Gross, see 8.2). As recounted in a *New York Times* article in December 1984, "To many people, the towers standing side by side on the corner of Seventh Avenue and 37th Street in the heart of New York's garment district were long known as the Bridal Buildings because they were occupied almost exclusively by wedding fashion showrooms." A new owner bought the buildings that year, but decided against combining them into one structure, instead joining them only at the base, with a common lobby and redesigned ground floor.

Above the storefronts, the buildings survive largely intact. In fact, they look as though they might have been one building, so similar are they in design—brick façades, vertical columns of windows separated by wider and narrower uninterrupted brick piers, each building rising to a series of dramatic setbacks. But a closer look shows a different approach to ornament. Where Schwartz & Gross make use of typically modernistic geometric brick patterns in the later building, the Blums' design has more of a medieval flavor. The Blums, in other words, in 1925 had moved toward the vertical organization and abstract massing now called Art Deco, but hadn't yet adopted the geometric ornament typical of the style, visible in its slightly younger neighbor. But they were almost there, as we will see in the next building on our walk, built by the Blums almost at the same time as No. 491–495.

***Walk south on Seventh Avenue to West 36th Street. Turn right and walk west on West 36th Street to Eighth Avenue. Cross to the west side of Eighth Avenue, and then to the south side of West 36th Street, then walk west on West 36th Street to the middle of the block, across the street from No. 315–325.***

## 4.6 (NR) Herogel Building, 315–325 West 36th Street George & Edward Blum, 1925–26

"Herogel" is an invented name combining the opening letters of the names of three partners: Paul Herring, Max Rosenfeld, and Isadore Geller, Jewish immigrants from Eastern Europe who made their way in New York's

construction industry. Sometimes together, sometimes separately, they built in the Garment District, the Upper West Side, the Upper East Side, Harlem, and Brooklyn. According to Rosenfeld's obituary, in 1928 alone "his firm started to build six twenty-five story buildings in the Garment District." Depending on the partners involved in a given project, they called their companies "Herogel" (Herring, Rosenfeld, and Geller), "Hero" (Herring and Rosenfeld), "Roher" (Rosenfeld and Herring), and "Rohegal" (Rosenfeld, Herring, and Geller), among others.

The Blums didn't develop fully Art Deco designs until their last three apartment buildings (including 3.11 and 10.7). Of all their Garment District buildings—more than a dozen—only one comes close: this loft building designed in 1925, the year of the Paris Exposition.

For the Herogel building, rather than simply following the zoning requirements with standard setbacks, the Blums varied the setbacks to create an arrangement along the lines of a French pavilion, with a central tower and slightly projecting wings at either end. Decorative metal spandrels with abstract floral designs, geometric patterns in light and dark brick at every setback topped by an abstract cast-stone molding, decorative stone panels with an eight-pointed star superimposed over a diamond form, rectangular stone panels with carefully carved swags of fruit and floral forms, panels with circular forms set within decorative surrounds—all combine to make this among the most architecturally interesting loft buildings in the district.

Following a conversion, the Herogel building now combines offices in the lower floors with residential lofts in the tower.

*Walk east back to Eighth Avenue, turn right and walk south on Eighth Avenue to the southwest corner of Eighth Avenue and West 35th Street. Look across the street at the east side of Eighth Avenue.*

## 4.7 (NR HD) Bickford's, 488 Eighth Avenue Stuckert & Company, 1929

Samuel L. Bickford founded a restaurant business in 1902 that eventually became a nationwide chain of cafeterias, including sixty outlets in New York, fifty in California, and eighteen in Boston. This one opened in 1929, as described in the *Times* in January 1929: "The Bickford Lunch System, Samuel L. Bickford, president, leased for sixty-three years the entire building at 488 Eighth Avenue. . . . The lessee plans to erect on the site a new building from plans by Stuckert & Co., architects. The entire ground floor is to be occupied by a branch of the Bickford chain of restaurants."

Closed sometime in the 1960s, this Bickford's had been thought lost, until the removal in 2000 of a deteriorating metal façade on the building. Its discovery led to a nostalgic *Times* article, in December 2000, by David Dunlap, who wrote: "If you lived in New York anytime from the 1930s through the 1960s, chances are you knew Bickford's. . . . 'Breakfast at Bickford's is an old New York custom,' a 1964 guidebook said. 'In these centrally located, speedy-service, modestly-priced restaurants a torrent of traffic is sustained for a generous span of hours with patrons who live so many different lives on so many different shifts.' To say the least. The best minds of Allen Ginsberg's generation 'sank all night in submarine light of Bickford's,' he wrote in 'Howl.'"

*Cross to the east side of Eighth Avenue.*

Though much altered, the three-story façade still retains some of its cast-stone zigzag ornament, as well as its name, "Bickford's," inscribed in cursive letters at the top.

*Turn around to look across Eighth Avenue at the Hotel New Yorker, on Eighth Avenue between West 34th and 35th Streets.*

## 4.8 (NR HD) Hotel New Yorker, 481 Eighth Avenue Sugarman & Berger, 1928–29

Mack Kanner, born in a tenement on the Lower East Side, built his first building in 1905, and eventually became one of the most important developers in the garment district, helping to get it started with the Garment Centre Capitol buildings on Seventh Avenue (for Kanner, see 4.4). Like so many other developers here, he also had a hand in the manufacturing of women's dresses.

At the same time that his Capitol company replaced the old Hotel Navarre with a forty-three-story tower designed by Sugarman & Berger (for Sugarman & Berger and the Navarre tower, see 4.4), Kanner hired that firm to design a new 2600-room hotel, the New Yorker. According to the *Times* in September 1929, he built here in the belief that West 34th Street was "destined to be the most important crosstown thoroughfare in the city," thanks to the subways and Penn Station.

Describing opening day, in January 1930, the *Times* wrote, "Hotel New Yorker Open. 800 Register in First Day and the Lobby is Thronged. The New Yorker, largest hotel in the city . . . was set into operation yesterday as a staff of 2,100 employees busied themselves in caring for almost 1,000 registered guests and hundreds of others who visited the forty-three story structure to promenade through its modernistic lobby."

Called "modern to the last degree," the Hotel New Yorker has the usual vertical windows and blocky setbacks. Its ornament, at the upper levels, includes cast-stone bands at each setback with multiplying diamonds and stylized floral patterns. Down at the sidewalk level, though geometry does rear its head occasionally, the most visible ornament is a set of cast-stone blocks inscribed with a low-relief basket of flowers.

*Walk south on Eighth Avenue to West 34th Street, cross to the south side of West 34th, then turn left and walk east along West 34th Street to Seventh Avenue; cross to the east side of Seventh. Look catty-corner across the intersection at the northwest corner of Seventh and West 34th.*

## 4.9 (NR HD) National City Bank, 201 West 34th Street Walker & Gillette, 1929–30

Walker & Gillette, architects of the skyscraping Fuller Building (7.2) on East 57th Street, found themselves designing smaller buildings thanks to the impact of the stock market crash (for Walker & Gillette, see 2.2). In 1929, still flush with the prosperity of the Roaring Twenties, National City Bank planned a sixteen-story building on this corner. By February of 1930, that plan had shrunk precipitously, and the bank opened this three-story branch, tucked into a corner of the Nelson Tower (4.10) erected at the same time—though Nelson suggested that he'd had a hand in keeping the bank low to protect his tower's access to natural light.

The bank shows the hallmarks of Modern Classic—a simplified, stylized version of traditional classic forms, in this case molded stone suggesting modernized columns framing the windows and entrances on both 34th Street and Seventh Avenue. At the top of either entrance, two stylized eagles flank a metal medallion of "The National City Bank of New York." More typically modernistic zigzags find their way into the metal window frames.

## 4.10 (NR HD) Nelson Tower, 450 Seventh Avenue H. Craig Severance, 1929–30

The walk ends with the Garment District's tallest building—the forty-five-story Nelson Tower. Another dress manufacturer turned real-estate developer, Julius Nelson, brought in H. Craig Severance to design his skyscraper, just as Severance's Bank of the Manhattan Company (1.5) at 40 Wall Street was competing with the Chrysler Building (5.4) in the race to the sky. With the Nelson Tower at Seventh Avenue and the forty-three-story Hotel New Yorker at Eighth Avenue, the block of West 34th Street just north of Penn Station now served as a skyscraper-flanked entrance to the garment district. Still, though Nelson built his tower specifically for the garment industry, he had doubts about the area's future. According to the *Times*, in November 1930, "while the structure is being prepared for rental to the garment industry for workrooms, showrooms and offices, Mr. Nelson believes that within ten years the character of the district will become more diversified and is having the building designed for conversion into general office space."

Severance pronounced the design of his building "modernized Greek," which would explain the four-story, flat, stylized piers supporting what in a Greek temple would be an attic story, all serving as a base for the building rising above it, through a series of setbacks, to a fifteen-story tower.

The ornament at the setbacks includes white stone pieces with three incised lines suggesting a Greek triglyph.

# ITINERARY NO. 5
# FORTY-SECOND STREET EAST TO WEST

Forty-Second Street is Midtown Manhattan's major boulevard of Art Deco skyscrapers, with some of the city's most famous monuments. Star architect of the walk is crusty modernist Raymond Hood. We visit three of his four skyscrapers—the Daily News (5.1), American Radiator (5.7), and old McGraw-Hill (5.8/5.12), as well as his Beaux-Arts Apartments (5.3). Star building, once the world's tallest, is the one and only Chrysler (5.4). Also visited: the Chanin (5.5), Paramount (5.9), and Film Center (5.11) buildings, and the Beaux-Arts Institute of Design (5.2), as well as 275 Madison Avenue (5.6)—a New York outpost of the Lone Star State—and the State Bank Building (5.10) on Eighth Avenue.

*Our walk begins on the southwest corner of East 41st Street and Tunnel Exit Street (halfway between 2nd and 3rd Avenues), facing the rear of the Daily News Building across 41st Street.*

New York, unlike most of the world's great cities, has not one, but two central business districts: Downtown from the Battery to Wall Street, the city's original center, and Midtown, which didn't develop as a business district until after 1900. The 1910s and '20s saw a major transformation of east Midtown thanks to the construction of Grand Central Terminal (opened in 1913) and the creation of sixteen blocks of pristine vacant real estate perched on steel girders over the newly sunken tracks of the New York Central. Massive office buildings transformed East 42nd Street into a skyscraper boulevard. Today, three major, late 1920s skyscrapers on East 42nd—the Daily News Building, the Chrysler Building, and the Chanin Building—stand just one block from each other. The west end of 42nd Street saw its own transformation, as nineteenth-century Long Acre Square—home mostly to stables—evolved into twentieth-century Times Square, the city's new theater district.

Film Center Building
630 Ninth Avenue
McGraw-Hill Building
330 West 42 Street
State Bank Building
681 Eighth Avenue
Paramount Building
1501 Broadway
American Radiator Building
(American Standard Bldg;
Bryant Park Hotel)
40 West 40 Street
275 Madison Avenue
Chanin Building
122 East 42nd Street
Chrysler Building
405 Lexington Avenue
Daily News Building
220 East 42nd Street
Beaux-Arts Institute of Design
304 East 44 Street
Beaux-Arts Apartments
307 & 310 East 44 Street
Penn Station
Times Sq
Herald Sq
Bryant Park
Rockefeller Plaza
Grand Central
Tunnel Exit
Tunnel Approach
Tudor City Pl
U N Plaza
Beekman Pl
Mitchell Pl
FDR Drive
© Tauranac, Ltd., 2016.
All Rights Reserved.

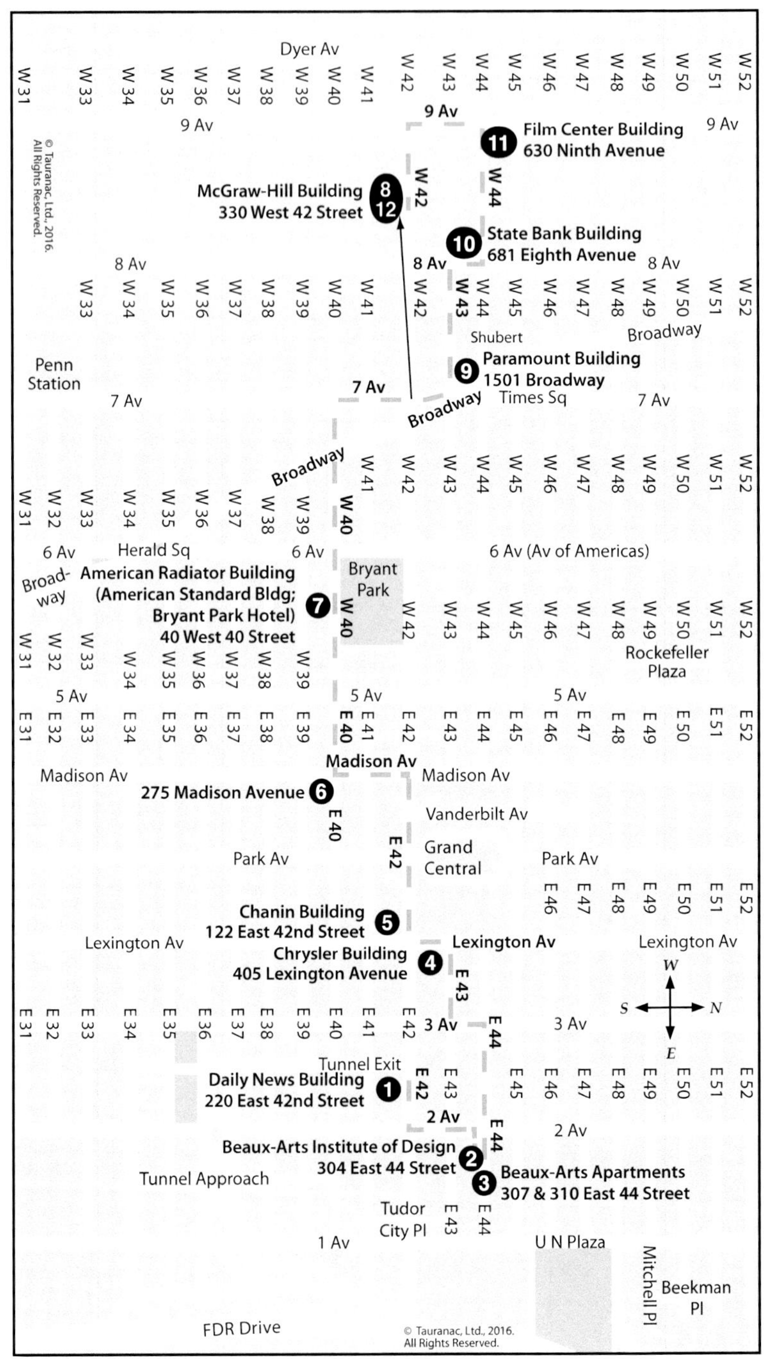

MAP 5

## 5.1 **Daily News Building, 220 East 42nd Street John Mead Howells, Raymond Hood, 1929–30

We start our walk here, at the rear of the Daily News Building, because in many ways it offers the most telling view. Raymond Hood's (for Hood, see the Introduction) dramatic, bulky, flat, red-and-white-striped Midtown headquarters for the great American tabloid is an early modern masterpiece that helped reshape the Midtown skyline and greatly influenced the architecture of the growing metropolis.

The story of Hood's battles with *News* owner Capt. Joseph Patterson over the building's design comes to us from Hood's biographer, Walter Kilham, a young architect in Hood's office at the time. According to Kilham's account, Hood actually talked the hard-boiled Patterson into commissioning a skyscraper, rather than just a printing plant with a few offices. Aside from any other consideration, a skyscraper commission offered Hood a chance to design a building visible in the round—in three dimensions. To Hood, much of Manhattan architecture seemed merely two-dimensional—just a façade—because the density of the city demanded buildings jammed together on the sidewalk, obscuring any view other than that of the front. Even in densely crowded Midtown Manhattan, a skyscraper that rises above its neighbors offers more than just one façade to the viewer. But look at the Daily News Building, and you'll notice another reason you can see two full façades—the open alley at the west façade. That alley was not there originally—Hood put it there, and it opens up a fuller view of the building.

Kilham also tells the story of Hood's hiring Rene Chambellan to create models showing the building shapes permissible under New York's then-current zoning regulations. One afternoon, Kilham found Hood standing in front of one of the models with a carving knife in his hand. In Kilham's telling, Hood said, "Do you mind if I do a little zoning myself?" as he sliced pieces off the model. "Somehow," Kilham continues, "arbitrary or not, the building now had a tapering effect: it began to look the way a modern skyscraper should in the new day of set-backs and towers—nothing that could be explained with a slide rule or a diagram." Hood created a free-standing skyscraper, treated like a piece of abstract sculpture, an asymmetric pile of tapered, stacked masses with a different profile on each façade.

Hood organized the building's windows as tall, uninterrupted vertical rows—the "vertical style"—by recessing them slightly behind tall, uninterrupted vertical rows of white brick (intended to be stone until economics reared its ugly head). He laid on almost no applied ornament, preferring instead to focus on starkly contrasting red and white brick stripes created by the window bays and intervening brick piers—originally accented by red window shades.

A contemporary critic quickly caught the aesthetic of Hood's building, describing it as "almost nothing but a series of stripes, nothing but surface pattern. Probably no building in America looks more like a huge backdrop, a sheet of awning, an enormous curtain, or a dazzling banner against the sky. . . . Even the window shades with their lighter hue of red are a part of this textile weave, and at night the lights shine through them merrily, as if the building were a sort of gigantic paper illumination on parade."

*Walk through the service alley to the 42nd Street façade.*

The grand two-story tall bas-relief over the building's main entrance is a classic icon of New York—the people of the busy metropolis walking briskly through a late 1920s urban landscape of flappers, capitalists in top hats, a boy and his dog, and a man selling newspapers (guess which one). Arcing across them is the legend, "He Made So Many Of Them," the second half of a quotation ascribed to Abraham Lincoln (the first half exists in two versions: "God must love the common people . . .," or "God must love common-looking people . . ."—some considered Lincoln a homely fellow) and a reference to the New York masses Patterson looked to serve with his paper. The figure in a top hat just below "He" appears to be Lincoln himself.

The Common People theme continues inside in the extraordinary lobby-as-planetarium, focusing on a giant globe sunken in a pit in the center of the space, rotating on its axis under a black faceted hemisphere, and surrounded by science and weather charts. In the original version, the black hemisphere continued down to the ground as a circular wall, but a 1950s expansion removed the wall and expanded the lower half of the lobby. Don't miss the pop-science inscriptions inside the pit, or the points of the compass under your feet—or the lines in all directions marked with the names of cities and their distance from the Daily News Building. Hood later wrote that he and Patterson agreed they should concentrate the decorating budget on the entrance and lobby to achieve the greatest "effect"—one of Hood's favorite words. And what an effect—there is no lobby like this anywhere else in New York, and possibly the world.

The building's modernistic urban look, incidentally, plus its newspaper history and the great globe, all made the *Daily News* a natural stand-in for the *Daily Planet* in the Superman movies.

***Walk east to Second Avenue, turn left, cross 42nd Street, and walk north along Second Avenue to East 44th Street. Cross to the north side of East 44th, then turn right, cross to the east side of Second Avenue, and continue walking east on East 44th Street to the middle of the block.***

## 5.2 ★Beaux-Arts Institute of Design, 304 East 44th Street Dennison & Hirons, 1928

This tiny building owes its name not to its style—clearly Art Deco—but to the École des Beaux-Arts in Paris, the school at which so many American architects of the late nineteenth and early twentieth centuries completed their education. A number of those architects founded the Society of Beaux-Arts Architects in 1893, and in 1916 chartered a New York school based on the educational principles of the Paris institution. The Institute offered free instruction, originally just in architecture but later also in mural painting, interior decoration, and sculpture. By the early 1930s, some twenty-five hundred students were studying at the Institute every year, following the classically inspired, competition-based curriculum of the École des Beaux-Arts—as practiced on East 44th Street.

Both Ethan Allen Dennison and Frederic Charles Hirons studied at the École in Paris. Hirons, one of the founders of the Beaux-Arts Institute of Design, served as president of the Beaux-Arts Society of Architects. No surprise, perhaps, that Dennison & Hirons secured the commission to design the Institute's new building—a commission they won, appropriately enough, in a Beaux-Arts-style competition, beating out such top-tier competitors as Raymond Hood, Ralph Walker, Harvey Wiley Corbett, and William Lamb of Shreve, Lamb & Harmon, architects of the Empire State Building (3.3/3.6). The judges found Hirons's competition entry to be "very simple, very architectural, and very appropriate."

Though the building reflects Beaux-Arts principles, it includes such clearly modernistic details as the stylized floral capitals of the two central piers in the upper stories, block lettering of the Institute's name, the polychromatic illusionistic piers of the double-height entrance topped by gilded abstract floral designs, and the wavy metal grille work flanking the doors. The building's true inspiration, however—its raison d'être—is summed up in three terra-cotta panels at the building's upper levels portraying three buildings: the Parthenon of classical Athens, St. Peter's Church in Rome, and, in the center, the École des Beaux-Arts in Paris.

## 5.3 ⋆Beaux-Arts Apartments, 307 and 310 East 44th Street Kenneth Murchison and Raymond Hood, 1929–30

The Beaux-Arts Institute, named for the École des Beaux-Arts in Paris, in turn passed on that name to a pair of apartment buildings directly next door and across the street, a spinoff of the school. The Institute's board created the Beaux-Arts Development Corporation to finance and build these two buildings specifically to provide housing and studios for artists and architects. Corporation board members included half a dozen major architects—among them, besides Murchison and Hood: Whitney Warren; Benjamin Wistar Morris; the firms of Delano & Aldrich and Voorhees, Gmelin & Walker; and John Cross of Cross & Cross—as well as artists, a real estate firm, and the Fuller Construction Company. As explained in a *Times* article in February,

"When the new building of the Beaux-Arts Institute of Design . . . was built the architects interested in the institute conceived the idea of buying up all the available property in the street and making of the street a sort of uptown artistic center. . . . This is probably the first time that such a group of architects and allied professions has ever gotten together to develop for their own account real estate in New York."

As described in the *Times* in January 1930, No. 310 originally included a "Café Bonaparte" (presumably after Rue Bonaparte, the address of the École), comprised of two rooms "decorated by Winold Reiss with ultra modernistic designs in blue, green and yellow." Opening night attendees included architects Hood, Murchison, Morris, Warren, Cross, with their wives, and such artists as cartoonist Peter Arno, muralist Ezra Winter, and illustrator Tony Sarg.

The Beaux-Arts Apartments make use of red and black brick stripes not unlike those on Hood's Daily News Building—but here Hood placed them within horizontal bands of casement windows, rather than within vertical window columns, taking a major step toward what would become the International Style version of modernism. Deco detailing nevertheless shows up in the zigzag metal window railings and the sculptural geometry of recessed levels at the entrances.

***Walk back to Second Avenue, cross to the west side, and continue west on East 44th Street to Third Avenue. At the corner of Third Avenue and East 44th, you will find an unobstructed view of the Chrysler Building.***

## 5.4 ★★Chrysler Building, 405 Lexington Avenue (Plate 5) William Van Alen, 1928–30

Built for an out-of-town automobile executive, designed by an architect whose other work is generally ignored, the tallest building in the world for barely twelve months before being eclipsed by the Empire State Building (3.3/3.6)—yet here it is, the Chrysler Building: one-of-a-kind, staggering, romantic, soaring, the embodiment of 1920s skyscraper pizzazz, the great symbol of Art Deco New York.

Self-made executive Walter Chrysler took on the building as a personal, rather than a corporate, project (in order, he wrote in his autobiography, to give his son something to be responsible for). Together with his architect, Chrysler got caught up in a one-upmanship battle with the Bank of Manhattan Company tower at 40 Wall Street (1.5) for the title of "world's tallest building." The proposed height of each tower grew repeatedly in a public back-and-forth, until finally Van Alen arranged for the Chrysler Building's slender, 185-foot, twenty-seven-ton steel spire to be secretly assembled inside the building and then hoisted by a derrick "from the top of the dome like a butterfly from its cocoon," raising Chrysler's height to 1,046 feet, leaving the Bank of Manhattan in the dust, and—in a skyscraper first—topping even the Eiffel Tower.

Rising into the Midtown skyline in tandem with the Daily News Building (5.1) a block to the east, the Chrysler Building includes many of its characteristics: vertical windows (with horizontal corner accents), a free-standing tower, three-dimensional massing as glorious urban statuary. In contrast to the flat, tapering striped masses of Hood's design, Van Alen draped the Chrysler Building in a romantic concoction of grand ornamental detail. An upper setback level of the tower is ringed by American architecture's most famous automotive symbols: gigantic winged figures modeled after Chrysler hood ornaments, connected by gray and white circles representing a Chrysler automobile's tires, metal circles within for hubcaps, and a line signifying its running board. White and light-gray brick, set in geometric patterns, add color to the tower, but the true color comes from the tapering steel spire glistening in the sun—one of the Manhattan skyline's best-loved icons. That spire—opening to the sky through enormous triangular windows—was made possible by the use of a nonrusting nickel-chrome-steel alloy, Nirosta, imported from Germany.

***Cross to the west side of Third Avenue, turn left, walk south on Third Avenue to East 43rd Street, turn right, and walk west along East 43rd Street halfway down the block toward Lexington Avenue.***

Here you can get a close-up look at the building's remarkably patterned lower walls, arranged in basket-weave fashion, with woof and warp of white stone and brick darting over and under each other to form a taut tapestry.

***Continue west along East 43rd Street to Lexington Avenue, turn left, cross to the south side of East 43rd Street, and walk south along Lexington to the bank entrance set in the building's base.***

The bank entrance, and surrounding lanterns, offer an up-close look at Nirosta, and also at a classic example of the two most common types of Art Deco ornament: abstract geometric patterns, and stylized floral forms.

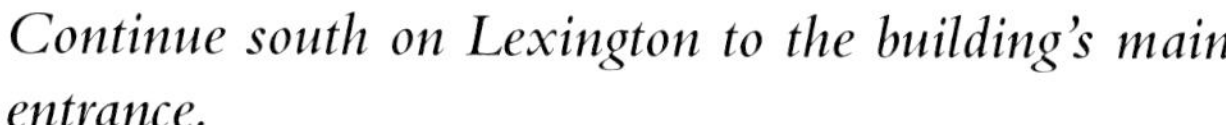

***Continue south on Lexington to the building's main entrance.***

The three-story-tall recessed entrance area has polished granite walls that step in toward the top—suggestive of skyscraper setbacks. Zigzags abound—in the polished metal above the doorways, in the pavement below your feet, and even in the walls themselves, which step in toward the entrance.

Inside, the Chrysler's geometric design extends to an unprecedented triangular skyscraper lobby. The original, low-level lighting is typically indirect, reflected from long, slender Nirosta fixtures off the pair of huge *rouge flamee* African marble piers supporting the ceiling. An extraordinary ceiling mural, painted by Edward Trumbull, radiates out in three bands from an image of Atlas. The first band includes abstract patterns apparently meant to represent natural forces; the third band is replete with images of industry and transportation; the second band includes scenes of the building's very construction and culminates in a long, slender painted image of the Chrysler Building, whose spire goes tip to tip with the top of the Lexington Avenue grand entrance. Many years ago, the building's owners punched downlights into the ceiling mural, to bring the lighting level up to contemporary standards of brightness, but a restoration has undone the damage. Just before the south and north exits to the street, stair halls lead up to a mezzanine and down to the basement and subway. The walls here seem to curve, but actually don't—they are, rather, faced in thin, flat marble strips set at very slight angles to each other, creating a curving illusion. Don't miss the wonderful zigzag Nirosta railings. Then turn around to face the elevator lobbies, with extraordinarily handsome inlaid wooden elevator doors and original cabs—as was only proper for what were originally the world's tallest elevator shafts.

***Walk south along Lexington to the northeast corner of East 42nd Street. Look across the intersection at the southwest corner of Lexington and East 42nd.***

## 5.5 ★Chanin Building, 122 East 42nd Street (Plate 6) Sloan & Robertson, 1927–29

Catty-corner from the Chrysler Building stands one of the East 42nd Street's very first skyscrapers, built by Irwin S. Chanin as headquarters for the Chanin Construction Company. Chanin's projects included the Century (8.1) and the Majestic (8.3), two of the twin-towered Art Deco apartment houses on Central Park West. Home to a cost-conscious construction company, rather than a publicity-conscious newspaper or the namesake of a major corporation, the Chanin Building has a simpler design than either the Daily News or the Chrysler Buildings, which followed Chanin to this rapidly redeveloping stretch of Midtown. The Chanin Building's tall, plain, rectangular tower rises out of a series of equally plain, symmetrically set-back lower blocks, marked by long vertical rows of windows. Its massing and setbacks inspired critic Matlack Price, in the May 1929 *Architectural Forum,* to call the building "an impressive realization of the most hopeful predictions" made at the time of the city's new zoning law: "At once it became necessary to design in masses rather than in façades."

***Cross to the south side of East 42nd Street, at the southeast corner of Lexington.***

Though the Chanin is not nearly as exuberant as its neighbors, it does sport modernistic detail, including a series of skyscraper-like buttresses on both the Lexington Avenue and the East 42nd Street fronts above the fourth story, matched by a dramatic set of buttresses in the crown of the tower.

A series of abstract reliefs designed jointly by architectural sculptor Rene Chambellan, Chanin's chief architect Jacques Delamarre,

and, apparently, Chanin himself, provide the building's chief ornamental work.

*Cross to the west side of Lexington Avenue.*

That ornament includes a terra-cotta band of stylized, abstract floral patterns—suggesting an exuberant, overgrown tropical jungle—wrapping around the building at the fourth story, and a bronze frieze wrapping around the building at the first story, said to illustrate the evolution of plant and animal life.

Inside, the small entrance foyer includes panels of overly muscular figures placed above four abstract bronze grilles, also designed by Chambellan and Delamarre, part of a series found throughout the lobby. These grilles portray "The City of Opportunity," the story of a city in which "an individual . . . may rise from a humble beginning to wealth and influence by the power of his own mind and hands." Meaning, of course, the Chanins. The foyer leads into the wonderfully restored lobby, which includes elaborate modernistic chandeliers, storefronts with geometrically ornamental metal grilles, and small diamond-shaped panels in the floor—much rubbed away by decades of pedestrian traffic—illustrating the building trades.

***Walk north along Lexington Avenue back to East 42nd Street, turn left, and walk west along East 42nd to Park Avenue. Cross Park Avenue (passing beneath the Pershing Square Viaduct that carries automobile traffic up over 42nd Street and around Grand Central Terminal), and continue walking west to Madison Avenue. Cross to the west side of Madison, then turn left and walk south along Madison to the northwest corner of East 40th Street. Look catty-corner across the intersection at No. 275 Madison Avenue, on the southeast corner of Madison and East 40th.***

## 5.6 ⋆275 Madison Avenue
## Kenneth Franzheim, 1930–31

The star forms that dot this building inside and out suggest the Lone Star State—reflecting its developer, Houston Properties, a New York company founded by Jesse Jones, Houston's major developer and skyscraper builder during the first half of the twentieth century. Kenneth Franzheim, who

moved his offices to the top three stories of No. 275, designed theaters in New York and Chicago, and also handled commissions for department stores. Beginning in the late 1920s, however, he designed many buildings for Houston Properties, and himself eventually moved to Houston in the late 1930s, where he earned a reputation as one of that city's most influential architects.

In his Madison Avenue skyscraper, Franzheim, according to the *New York Times* in December 1930, "has avoided entablatures, architraves, pediments, cornices and other conventional ornamental devices. He has used polished black granite, black terra-cotta and white enameled brick, set in parallels, to emphasize the structure's terraced vertical lines and its massive base. He believes that the offices in the building will be virtually 'shadowless.'"

The building's massive, three-story tall base of polished black granite—reminiscent of the base of the Chrysler Building (5.4)—supports a white and black brick tower rising through shallow setbacks not unlike those of the Daily News Building (5.1). But instead of the red and black brick spandrels of the Daily News, Franzheim's building separates windows with spandrels of black terra-cotta tiles.

***Cross to the southeast corner of Madison and East 40th Street.***

Though the tower seems largely devoid of applied ornament, the entrance and first floor positively drip in silver and black geometry. The Lone Star stars show up just above the first-story windows—half-stars here, atop what looks like a skyscraper silhouette—and again over the main entrance on East 40th Street.

***Walk east on East 40th Street to the building's main entrance.***

Metal grilles to the left and right of the entrance expand the half-stars into full stars. The entrance includes indirect lighting hidden behind modernistic half-shells. Inside, a full Lone-Star star forms the centerpiece of the floor of the lobby, which sports wonderful modernistic grilles and door panels throughout.

*Cross back to the northwest corner of Madison and East 40th, and continue walking west along East 40th Street to Fifth Avenue. Cross Fifth Avenue and continue walking west along what is now West 40th Street (Fifth Avenue is the dividing line between Manhattan's "east" and "west" streets), stopping not quite halfway down the block to look across the street.*

## 5.7 ★American Radiator Building (later American Standard Building, now Bryant Park Hotel), 40 West 40th Street Raymond Hood, 1923–24

Raymond Hood's first big New York commission, the American Radiator Building followed his triumph in the 1922 Chicago Tribune Tower competition (for Hood, see the Introduction). Completed one year before the 1925 Paris exposition that gave Art Deco its name, the Radiator Building still reflects an eclectic, early-1920s approach, with spires and niches and gargoyles that might feel at home on the back door of a French country church, and a Gothic crown descended from the crown of the Chicago Tribune Tower (itself modeled on the Butter Tower of Rouen Cathedral).

But look again: the façade's paired windows rise vertically in uninterrupted recessed lines. And again: Hood swathed his building in blazing color, black and gold. As the *Times* described it in January 1924, "Unlike any office building in the country, the new structure is faced entirely with black brick with golden colored stone trimming, worked together to give a rich black and gold decorative effect." Some suggested that black and gold recalled a glowing coal, symbolic of radiators, but Hood said no, the black was meant to create a solid block of color in which normally dark window openings would disappear from sight. In 1926, architectural historian Talbot Hamlin called this scheme "the most daring experiment in color in modern buildings yet made in America."

Though a modest midblock office building, the American Radiator rises like a free-standing tower, visible on three sides, thanks to a low wing on the west (with a matching façade added later by Hood's office), which keeps the side view open. And that free-standing, three-dimensional midblock tower is molded like a piece of sculpture, with angled corners effectively leading your eye from the front around to the sides. In five years' time Hood would jettison the French country Gothic; in the meantime, much of the 1929 modernism of the Daily News Building (5.1) was already budding here in 1924.

Hood's first venture into 1920s modernism attracted enormous attention, from editorials in architectural journals, to dramatic nocturnal photography by Samuel Gottscho, to Georgia O'Keeffe's 1927 painting *Radiator Building—Night New York*, which saw and celebrated only the modernist geometry and pitch-black color of the building. Both Gottscho's photos and O'Keeffe's painting showed night-time views because of the building's dramatic night-time floodlighting, which attracted what *The American Architect* described as "vast throngs" of people "who ordinarily give little heed to street architecture," even "blocking traffic as they stand to contemplate the lacy effect as shown in the brilliantly lighted gilded top."

***Cross to the south side of West 40th Street.***

Hood maintained his architectural office in this building until his untimely death in 1934, ten years after its completion. Stand next to the western edge of the central entrance portal—taking a closer look at the ornamental bronze Gothic Modern details—and look down toward the building's base, and you will see that Hood signed and dated his building. A four-leaf clover once sat directly above the date—sadly it disappeared some years ago.

***Continue walking west along West 40th Street to Sixth Avenue (also called Avenue of the Americas). Cross to the west side of Sixth Avenue, and continue walking west on West 40th Street, crossing Broadway, to Seventh Avenue. Turn right, and walk north on Seventh Avenue, crossing West 41st Street, then West 42nd. On the north side of West 42nd Street, look left (west) along***

*42nd Street to see the setback profile of the blue-green terra-cotta-sheathed McGraw-Hill Building, just west of Eighth Avenue.*

## 5.8 ★McGraw-Hill Building, 330 West 42nd Street (introduction, continued in 5.12) Raymond Hood, Godley & Fouilhoux, 1930–31

Stop just long enough to appreciate the east front of the McGraw-Hill Building—Raymond Hood's shiny blue-green headquarters for the publishing giant McGraw-Hill—appearing here in its Art Deco guise. At the end of the walk (5.12), you will see a very different silhouette—a prototypical International Style slab, with horizontal ribbons of windows and no setbacks, that within two years of its completion had earned the building a place as the only New York skyscraper in the Museum of Modern Art's seminal *International Architecture* exhibition, which gave the International Style its name.

Yet from this angle, it appears that the sleek slab is all illusion—another Hood "effect." The view from east or west reveals the dramatic setbacks that create a zigzag, vertical, pyramidal outline that has nothing to do with the International Style. Hood's design ties horizontal window bands together with a strong vertical line of windows in the center, which rises to a gigantic ribbed crown (suggestive of the German Expressionism of Erich Mendelsohn). On the north or south side, that crown includes hand-made terra-cotta blocks spelling out McGRAW-HILL in eleven-foot-high letters (though these have been painted out)—Hood's terra-cotta version of the giant electric advertising signs lighting the sky above buildings throughout 1930s New York. We will see more of this building soon.

*Turn around and walk east on West 42nd Street to Broadway, which is now a pedestrian mall; turn left and walk north along the mall to West 43rd Street. Broadway here crosses Seventh Avenue to create Times Square. Directly across the intersection, on the west side of Times Square between West 43rd and 44th, rises the Paramount Building.*

## 5.9 ★Paramount Building, 1501 Broadway
## Rapp & Rapp, 1926–27

The Paramount Building, today dwarfed by more recent skyscrapers, once towered over the surrounding theaters of Times Square. Though the legitimate stage dominated the Broadway theater district during the first decades of the twentieth century, it couldn't stave off invasion by the upstart movie industry. When Paramount Pictures decided to build its eastern headquarters here, the corporation brought in midwestern movie-palace architects Rapp & Rapp, who specialized in over-the-top French-inspired concoctions. The Rapp brothers designed a typically opulent French interior for the thirty-six-hundred-seat movie palace that once shared this building (until its conversion to office space in 1964) in the lower wing on West 43rd Street, and naturally extended French detailing to the office tower, but they couldn't entirely avoid the modernistic skyscraper flavor beginning to make its appearance in New York.

So this brick- and stone-faced office building—adorned with delicate French Renaissance scrolls and urns and theatrical masks—rises to a series of cascading setbacks, topped by a rectangular tower supporting four huge clock faces, and above them an enormous glass globe. Floodlights behind the parapets once dramatically lit up each setback; the clock faces mimic the Paramount logo of five-pointed stars ringing a mountain peak. The chimes of the clocks once synchronized with the illuminated globe, which, following a restoration, once again flashes on the quarter-hour.

***Walk north along the pedestrian mall until standing across Broadway from the main entrance.***

Take a closer look at the grand bronze two-story entrance, with its plethora of ornamental patterns—theatrical masks, crossed musical instruments, leafy branches, all intertwined with traditional classical forms. Inside the building's lobby, the rich detail maintains that traditional spirit. Rapp & Rapp haven't yet brought in Deco ornamental patterns—but in just a few years they will, as in the Paramount Theater (15.2) of 1930 on Staten Island.

***Walk south back along Seventh Avenue to the corner of West 43rd Street, turn right, and walk west along West 43rd to Eighth Avenue; look across the street at the northwest corner of West 43rd and Eighth.***

## 5.10 State Bank Building, 681 Eighth Avenue Dennison & Hirons, 1927–28

As the building of the new Independent subway line beneath Eighth Avenue during the late 1920s spurred construction up and down the avenue, the *Times* in December 1928 noted "the marked increase in banking facilities" in "the Times Square vicinity." In particular, "early in the new year one of the most artistic of the smaller banking structures in the city will be opened on the northwest corner of Eighth Avenue and Forty-third Street—that of the State Bank and Trust Company."

Though Dennison & Hirons (for Denison & Hirons, see 5.2) had recently completed the Beaux-Arts Institute of Design (5.2) on East 44th Street, the firm actually specialized in banks—by one count, designing more than a hundred during the 1920s. Their early work—like so many other banks of the day—mimicked Classical temples, complete with ranks of columns. For the new State Bank, they took that model and streamlined its forms, turning a classical temple into an Art Deco jewel box. Classical columns became ribbed piers; Corinthian capitals became multicolored ornamental terra-cotta panels.

Even in the building's current neglected state, the terra-cotta sparkles—brightly colored glazed panels with wildly imaginative abstract Deco floral patterns, almost identical to the capitals at the Beaux-Arts Institute but in living color. The Atlantic Terra-Cotta Company and Dennison & Hirons often worked together—in June

1928 the Atlantic Company published a special issue of its magazine devoted to its collaboration with the firm, describing the process by which one-quarter-scale painted models were mounted on the building, and then the colors adjusted for the local light conditions.

Don't let the terra-cotta keep you from noticing the rest of the building's ornament—especially the dark spandrel panels just below the top-story windows, with more abstract floral patterns surrounding the image of an ancient sailing vessel, and also a wonderfully geometric metal grille half-hidden behind the current advertising signs at the west end of the 43rd Street façade.

*Walk north up Eighth Avenue to West 44th Street; cross to the north side of the street, turn left on West 44th, and continue west roughly a third of the way down the block toward Ninth Avenue. Look south, over a group of low buildings on the south side of West 44th Street, to see the top of the McGraw-Hill Building (5.8/5.12) with the company's name spelled out in gigantic terra-cotta letters. Continue walking west to Ninth Avenue; cross to the west side of Ninth, then turn around and look back across the avenue at the Film Center Building, on the northeast corner of Ninth and West 44th.*

## 5.11 ★★★Film Center Building, 630 Ninth Avenue (Plate 7) Ely Jacques Kahn of Buchman & Kahn, 1928–29

Occupying the entire eastern block front of Ninth Avenue from West 44th to 45th Streets, facing the (now demolished) noisy, sooty, and sun-blocking Ninth Avenue El—and two long blocks from the pricey real estate of the Times Square theater district—the Film Center Building sprang up to house the film distribution companies servicing movie theaters both on Times Square and throughout the city. It joined a cluster of motion-picture-industry buildings that once shared the same block of West 44th Street—Twentieth Century Fox, Paramount Pictures, and Warner Brothers' Vitaphone Building. Ely Jacques Kahn (for Kahn, see 3.4) designed No. 630 for developer Abe Adelson, who had earlier commissioned Two Park Avenue (3.4) from Kahn, as well as 29 Broadway (1.2) from Sloan & Robertson.

Like so many of the modest Art Deco office and loft buildings that Kahn designed for modest manufacturing clients throughout Manhattan, the Film Center presents a somewhat muted exterior (though a good cleaning could change that), with patterned brick spandrels running beneath the windows (no longer original), as well as slender, patterned brick piers in the upper stories and a geometrically patterned brick roofline. Typically, Kahn reserved his liveliest treatment for the first and second stories, and especially the main entrance on Ninth Avenue.

***Cross back to the east side of Ninth Avenue and walk to the middle of the block to the main entrance.***

Blocks of oddly curving geometric patterns, set in three receding levels, flank the entranceway, and the second-story windows above it. The metal grille work above the doors displays the fineness of detail so typical of Kahn, a reminder of his fine-arts background.

The true joy of this building, however, is its lobby, which Kahn transformed into an abstract fantasy. His design treats the walls and ceiling of the small vestibule like woven plaster tapestries, accompanied by elaborate cast-metal grilles on either side and a patterned floor comingling jagged edges and curving figures. Beyond, in the lobby proper, he bathes the entire space in multicolored, abstract decorative detail, from broad horizontal stripes against the far wall of the elevator lobby, to wild orange, blue, and yellow mosaics, to tiled floors, to cast-metal grilles, to floor-to-ceiling stylized movie cameras flanking the elevator lobby. Watch for the red marble cylinders—suggestive perhaps of lollipops—that show up in various forms throughout the space, from the floor to the directory board.

*Walk south on Ninth Avenue, crossing West 44th and 43rd Streets. Turn left on West 42nd Street and walk east half-way down the block back towards Eighth Avenue. Look across the street at the south side of West 42nd.*

## 5.12 *McGraw-Hill Building, 330 West 42nd Street (continued from 5.8) Raymond Hood, Godley & Fouilhoux, 1930–31

As you approach the McGraw-Hill Building, you'll see its setbacks seeming to disappear. By limiting them to the east and west façades, Hood effectively created the illusion of a flat slab (see 5.8) on the north and south. The central vertical column of windows on the east and west façades disappears as well, leaving the north and south façades just with the continuous horizontal window bands that caught the eye of the International Architecture show curators. But those continuous bands prove to be as much an illusion as the flat slab, an approximation created by groups of four double-hung windows set closely together, with a painted line at the top helping to trick the eye into seeing them as one.

The building's startling blue-green color—following on the gold and black of the Radiator Building (5.7) and the red and white stripes of the Daily News (5.1)—derives from a façade covered entirely in glazed machine-made terra-cotta tiles. Hood, interestingly, always called the color blue, while McGraw-Hill always called it green. Hood supposedly offered McGraw a choice of color including yellow, orange, gray, and red. According to company lore, when McGraw saw the finished product, he asked an aide to tell him who had chosen the color. Informed that he himself had made the choice, McGraw replied that he must have been sick that day. To Hood, however, the

color was a critical part of the design; he described it as "Dutch blue at the base, with sea green window bands, the blue gradually shading off to a lighter tone the higher the building goes, till it finally blends off into the azure blue of the sky. The final effect is a shimmery, satin finish, somewhat on the order of the body of an automobile."

***Cross to the south side of 42nd Street to see the entrance.***

The idea of automobile imagery fits nicely with the Machine Age sensibility of the times, and appears again in descriptions of the main entrance. At the ground floor, blue and green enameled steel bands and silver and gold metal tubes shoot around the curves of the main entrance into the long green lobby. The editor of the *McGraw-Hill News*—an internal office newsletter—described the steel bands as "lacquered like the body of a motor car," and declared that in the future they would be "simonized, just like the old car." The lacquered steel continues inside the lobby, but here the color leans decidedly toward green. Even the elevator cabs were originally finished in green baked enamel on steel.

Though parts of the McGraw-Hill design do suggest the International Style, the building is clearly rooted in Hood's propensity for architectural effects relying on color, three-dimensional outline, and an extraordinary skyline treatment.

# ITINERARY NO. 6
# FROM BEEKMAN PLACE TO ROCKEFELLER CENTER TO THE BRILL BUILDING

Starting on the far east side of Midtown at posh Beekman Place, we visit a handful of modernistic residences ranging from the fabulously wealthy River House (6.3) to the more modestly middle-class Southgate apartments (6.2) to the former Panhellenic Tower (6.1a), a redoubt for young professional women taking on the big city in the 1920s. Pushing westward into the commercial heart of Midtown we visit the spectacular but lesser-known General Electric Building (6.4)—like so many Deco towers, built for a modern, twentieth-century enterprise—and continue with the Waldorf-Astoria (6.5/6.7), New York's preeminent and beautifully restored skyscraper hotel. We continue with the delightful Goelet Building (6.9), New York's best-kept Deco secret, before plunging into Rockefeller Center (6.10). We close with a Deco artifact of the subway system (6.11) and a visit to the Brill Building (6.12), stump of a planned "world's tallest" tower.

*The walk begins at the southwest corner of First Avenue and East 49th Street. At the northeast corner of the intersection, Mitchell Place runs eastward parallel to East 49th, practically abutting that street.*

## 6.1a ⋆Panhellenic House (now Silver Suites Residences at Beekman Tower), 3 Mitchell Place John Mead Howells, 1927–28

During the same years that he collaborated with Raymond Hood on an apartment building at 3 East 84th Street (10.1), shortly after completion of Hood's American Radiator Building (5.7), John Mead Howells designed the Panhellenic House as a club and residence for "Greek-letter" sorority women—"Panhellenic" meaning "all Greek." The

Brill Building
1619 Broadway
Central IND Substation
126 West 53 Street
Rockefeller Center
Fifth Avenue to Sixth Avenue
West 48 to West 51 Streets
Rockefeller Plaza
Goelet Building (Swiss Center)
608 Fifth Avenue
Former Newsweek Building
444 Madison Avenue
Waldorf-Astoria Hotel
301 Park Avenue
RCA Building (General Electric)
570 Lexington Avenue
Panhellenic House (Silver Suites)
3 Mitchell Place;
2 Beekman Place
Southgate, 433 East 51 Street;
400, 414, 424 and 434 East 52 Street
River House, 435 East 52 Street
Columbus Circle
Times Square
Shubert
Broadway
Bryant Park
Grand Army Plaza
Central Park South
Grand Central
Vanderbilt
Tunnel Exit
Tudor City Pl
United Nations
Mitchell Place
Beekman Pl
Sutton Pl Sth
Sutton Place
Queensboro Bridge
8 Av
7 Av
6 Av (Av of Americas)
5 Av
Madison Av
Park Av
Lexington Av
3 Av
2 Av
1 Av
W
S
N
E
© Tauranac, Ltd., 2016.
All Rights Reserved.

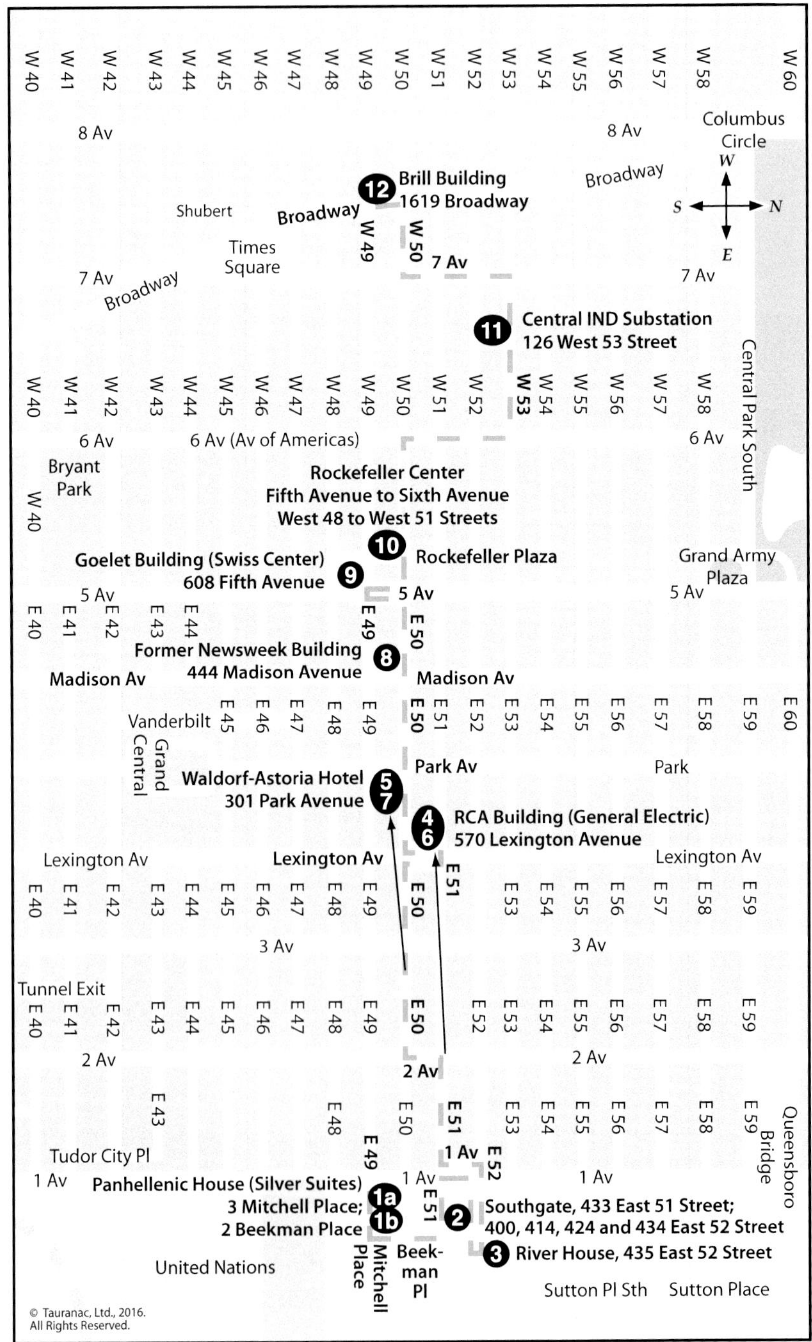

MAP 6

young women in question had graduated college and sought professional positions in New York; the Panhellenic House provided them with affordable—and socially amenable—housing. The Panhellenic's prime mover, Emily Eaton Hepburn (wife of Barton Hepburn, chairman of Chase National Bank), had played a major role in the suffrage movement; she saw the Panhellenic House as the next step: an opportunity to support young college-educated women breaking down professional barriers.

Howells (1868–1959), son of prominent American novelist William Dean Howells (and bearer of the name of his uncle, William R. Mead of McKim, Mead & White), studied at MIT and Harvard and then—like so many of his contemporaries—in Paris, at the École des Beaux-Arts. In an early partnership with I. N. Phelps Stokes, and on his own after 1917, Howells designed in the eclectic styles typical of the times. Then, in 1922, together with Raymond Hood, he won the famed competition for the new headquarters of the *Chicago Tribune*, and as the decade progressed his designs turned modernistic.

The Panhellenic House's design suggests the evolution of an architectural idea—from the Gothic-crowned Tribune Building that, despite its eclectic stylistic overlay, includes such modernist characteristics as vertical windows and chamfered corners; to the American Radiator Building, which straddles the line between neo-Gothic and Art Deco; to the Panhellenic House, largely stripped of its predecessors' eclectic ornament to reveal a solidly geometric form. In a 1928 article in *The American Architect*, tellingly titled "The Verticality of the Skyscraper," Howells promoted "the simple composition of verticals, which some like to call modernistic."

***Cross to the northeast corner of the intersection.***

Though largely free of applied ornament, the Panhellenic includes three enthusiastically sculptural panels by Rene Chambellan, joining his work on such Deco designs as the Chanin Building (5.5), Horn & Hardart (9.10), and Suffolk Title and Guarantee Building (14.10). One sits directly above a narrow entrance in the building's corner—a decorative octagon, topped by a flamboyantly floral fantasy; the other two, more along the lines of a frozen fountain, flank the main Mitchell Place entrance. Look up at the third-story setback to see the tail end of the Gothic in this progression of three Gothic Modern buildings—though what appears to be Gothic is more a series of geometric patterns suggesting that historic style.

The Panhellenic House made a huge impression on the critics. From *The New Yorker*: "John Mead Howells . . . has scored what seems to be another knockout with his Panhellenic House. . . . This is a glorious building on a glorious site and a marvelous example of modernism not gone berserk." And the *New York Times*: "Towering above the East River, the Panhellenic House . . . marks an outstanding example of American skyscraper architecture. . . . In the huge square monolith . . . one feels the vertical steel structure under the sheathing of concrete and brick."

***Walk east along Mitchell Place to the corner of Beekman Place, and cross to the east side of the street, then look back across the street at No. 2 Beekman Place.***

## 6.1b 2 Beekman Place<br>Rosario Candela, 1931

Following her success with the Panhellenic House, Emily Hepburn developed a second apartment house at the other end of Mitchell Place, at the corner of Beekman Place—a posh riverfront residential enclave—and lived there in a penthouse apartment, where she became known as "the Grand Old Lady of Beekman Hill." Instead of Howells, she brought in Rosario Candela, famous for his luxurious apartment layouts. Unlike Candela's earlier and better-known work, No. 2 Beekman is relatively modest, but includes some handsome Art Deco detail, notably the cast-stone floral panels and giant spiral forms above the entrance, as well as some geometric brick and cast stone toward the roof.

As described in a 1931 *New York Times* ad, the building "enjoys all the charm of this exclusive old neighborhood with its quaint houses and gardens, wide views of the River and floods of sunshine . . . an old world charm that emphasizes the truly modern aspect of living at Two Beekman Place where the comforts and convenience of today are built into every apartment."

***Walk north on two-block-long Beekman Place to its end at East 51st Street, where the vista is closed, toward the west, by No. 433 East 51st, a unit of the Southgate complex, most of which faces East 52nd Street.***

## 6.2 Southgate, 433 East 51st Street and 400, 414, 424, and 434 East 52nd Street Emery Roth, 1928–1930

Though enamored of—and best known for—designs based on classical Italian models, Emery Roth occasionally dipped his toes into modernistic waters (for Roth, and his wary relationship with Art Deco, see 9.2). For one of his major clients, Bing & Bing, Roth designed a group of five Deco apartment buildings in the quickly gentrifying far east side of Midtown, one fronting on East 51st street and four directly behind it on East 52nd.

No. 433 East 51st Street, built in 1930, is typical of the five: red brick with white stone trim, suggesting a staid neo-Georgian typical of the East Side, but with bursts of modernistic trim, especially at the entrance (unfortunately somewhat obscured by the now de rigeur awning), where a fruit-and-flowers motif surrounding the doorway combines with more geometric detailing. Still more geometric are the overlapping "Vs" over several ground-floor windows, and geometrically patterned window sills above.

***Walk west along East 51st Street to the corner of First Avenue, turn right, and walk north along First Avenue to East 52nd Street. Cross to the north corner of East 52nd, turn right, and walk east along East 52nd to the middle of the block for a view of the four Southgate buildings on the south side of the block.***

Of the four Southgate apartment buildings on East 52nd Street, those to the west came first, followed by those to the east. As Nos. 400 and 414 neared completion, the *Times* noted: "With the construction of these two houses, the A. M. Bing Corporation will complete a project consisting of five similar buildings, having a total of nearly 500 housekeeping apartments ranging from one to six rooms, all within the block." An ad in *The New Yorker* made the case to prospective renters: "The trend is toward the river. More and more smart New Yorkers are realizing the advantages of living over by the river in SOUTHGATE, that fashionable colony set apart from the rest of the town—and yet five minutes from the center of everything." And another: "Two to five rooms . . . some with river view . . . dropped living rooms . . . log burning fireplaces. Dining galleries or alcoves . . . casement windows . . . tile bath with every chamber . . . full size kitchens. Also Studios . . . Penthouses and Terraces."

A writer in *The New Yorker* described the apartments: "You might like a studio apartment, nicely proportioned, with a deeply sunken livingroom that has a fourteen-foot ceiling. A long window seat runs below the nine-foot high, narrow windows. Alcoves in the living-rooms of the two-room apartments serve very neatly as diminutive libraries or studies."

Despite their overall similarity, each of the buildings features different design motifs. No. 424 East 52nd Street repeats the design of No. 433 East 51st Street, but the others all vary in detail—a walk along the sidewalk looking at door and window trim will turn up many versions of the same basic pattern.

## 6.3 River House, 435 East 52nd Street
## Bottomley, Wagner & White, 1930–31

Opposite Southgate, on the north side of East 52nd Street at the eastern end of the block, the august River House politely ignores its more modest neighbors. Where Southgate's apartments ranged from one to six rooms, River House apartments started at eight-room "simplexes," progressed to eleven-room duplexes and, at the very top, culminated in a seventeen-room triplex—all apartments described by *The New Yorker* in 1931 as "private homes in a skyscraper." Each such home had a river view and luxurious details, but most sumptuous of all was that triplex: "The drawing-room is almost fifty feet long and is two stories high, and its windows command a view of Long Island Sound on the east and of the Bay on the south. There are two terraces, an observation deck on the roof, and a private elevator running between the three floors. In the servants' quarters. . . . a room for a tutor or governess. . . . Price: $275,000."

River House included in its first four stories the River Club, newly organized, noted the *Times*, by "many prominent men and women of New York City," including Mrs. Vincent Astor, Marshall Field, and Harold S. Vanderbilt. Modeled after "certain London clubs," its plan included "two full-size indoor tennis courts, three squash racquets courts, a large gymnasium and a swimming pool. It will have a boat landing for yachts and motor boats and probably will have a mooring pier." The décor would be in the capable hands of Dorothy Draper, interior decorator to New York's high society (see also 7.5 and 10.3).

Such elegance and luxury apparently required a classically sedate exterior, but modernistic impulses occasionally shine forth, notably above the second-floor windows over the 52nd Street entrance: geometric railings on nautical motifs (look closely to see the ropes and anchors at the heart of the design) together with carved stone floral patterns, and also on the huge pylons supporting the gates to the entrance court, and in the molded cast-stone piers flanking the entrance to the building from that entrance court.

***Return to First Avenue, walking west along East 52nd Street, and cross to the west side of First, then turn left and walk south on First Avenue to East 51st Street. Turn right and walk west on East 51st Street to the corner of Second Avenue. Straight ahead, two blocks west, rises the slender, elegant tower of 570 Lexington Avenue.***

## 6.4 *RCA Building (later General Electric/GE Building), 570 Lexington Avenue (introduction, continued in 6.6) (Plate 8) Cross & Cross, 1929–31

The slender tower of 570 Lexington Avenue still rises, isolated, into the skyline—at least from this vantage point—in dramatic contrast to the bulky modern slabs nearby. Tenth-tallest building in the city when it opened, the extraordinary, fifty-story skyscraper initially served as headquarters for the Radio Corporation of America (RCA), a subsidiary of General Electric (GE).

RCA began in 1919 as a creature of government—a federally organized effort to keep the Navy's radio technology, developed during World War I, in American hands. RCA found itself bundled into a collection of related firms under parent company General Electric. RCA's chief mover and soon-to-be president, David Sarnoff, liked to tell the perhaps apocryphal story of sitting by a "wireless" while an office boy at American Marconi Wireless Telegraph and monitoring distress calls radioed from the *Titanic.* In any case, early on Sarnoff saw the commercial potential of the new technology. He imagined a radio in every household, and RCA became the vehicle for his vision.

By the end of the 1920s, the fast-growing RCA had commissioned a fifty-story headquarters from the prominent architectural firm of Cross & Cross. In 1931, however, as the dust settled on the new skyscraper, RCA separated from GE in a complex transaction that left GE the owner of the new tower, while RCA moved across town to become the chief tenant at Rockefeller Center (6.10).

The building's ornamental treatment is better seen close-up, from Lexington Avenue (6.6).

***Turn left on Second Avenue and walk south to East 50th Street. Turn right and walk west on East 50th, staying on the north side of the street; cross Third Avenue and continue west on East 50th, stopping about three-quarters of the way to the end of the block at Lexington Avenue for a view of the Waldorf-Astoria.***

## 6.5 *Waldorf-Astoria Hotel, 301 Park Avenue (introduction, continued in 6.7) Schultze & Weaver—Lloyd Morgan, partner in charge—1929–31

Just one block south of GE, another skyscraper raises not one but two towers into the sky—the Waldorf-Astoria, the world's tallest hotel when it opened. Seen from this angle, it looks every bit as much a jazz-modern skyscraper as its neighbor. Its massing is thoroughly visible in the round (it occupies an entire city block), it has the telltale vertical windows, and it rises 625 feet into the Manhattan skyline with twin towers capped by modernistic copper peaks. And yet, on closer inspection, the building seems rather plain, its walls clad in gray limestone in the lower

stories, with matching gray brick above—no bright colors here. In its detailing, the building seems rather conservative. We'll take a closer look after we visit 570 Lexington.

*Continue west to the corner of Lexington. Turn right and walk north on Lexington to the corner of East 51st Street. Cross to the north side of East 51st, then turn right and walk east a few feet until you can stand behind the subway entrance. Turn around to face west to see 570 Lexington Avenue catty-corner across the intersection. Look up the tower, from the street to the pinnacle.*

## 6.6 ⋆RCA Building (later General Electric/GE Building), 570 Lexington Avenue (continued from 6.4) Cross & Cross, 1929–31

No. 570 Lexington stands in stark contrast to Cross & Cross's earlier eclectic designs—neo-Georgian, neo-Renaissance, neo-Gothic. By 1930 even this conservative firm found itself caught up in the new modern style. The architects designed RCA's new skyscraper as a physical evocation of the modern phenomenon of radio. In the words of John Walter Cross: "Romantic though radio may be, it is at the same time intangible and elusive—a thing which can be captured visually only through symbolism. It is energy in almost the pure state, which challenges us to depict in design the very fundamentals of our universe." Fortunately—given General Electric's long tenure in the building—the architectural symbolism for the elusive radio appears to work equally well for electricity in general.

Like the other great Deco skyscrapers of Midtown, 570 Lexington has a broad base stepping back to a slender tower and the usual vertical window bays. It also has the legally mandated setbacks, on both its main façades, but, unlike other Deco towers, it uses those setbacks to accentuate the tower's verticality—they project out from the building in its center and rise straight up into the tower, coaxing one's eye up toward the crown, a fairy-tale crest of gilded terra-cotta in curving geometrical shapes topped by frozen electric flares in terra-cotta. Outlined against that crest, at the center of each of the tower's four sides, a huge terra-cotta lightning bolt rises into a sculpted figure—the whole sculpture some fifty feet tall—wearing a spiky headdress of "forked lightning" intended, according to the *New York Times*, to

throw out "an aura of colored light at night as a symbol of the speed of radio." Lightning had already become a general symbol of radio transmission, hence a logical choice for ornament on RCA's tower.

*Cross to the west side of Lexington Avenue.*

Electric design pulses across the entire building. It has almost no completely flat surfaces. Here at street level, the storefronts sit within a frame of rippling polished stone at either side, topped by a stone arch that zigzags in and out. A niche in the wall rising above the arch encloses a smaller version of the tower's crowning sculptures—a face atop a lightning bolt. Some have imagined that the lightning bolt suggests sound waves traveling up the stylus of an RCA Victrola, though more likely it represents radio in general. The sculpture as a whole seems oddly suggestive of a boy who's stuck his finger into an electrical outlet. Similar ornament can be found all over the building—zigzags of every kind, brick laid in curving patterns, and odd sculptural suggestions of electric current. The abstract patterns within the terra-cotta spandrels between the windows might suggest an artist's impression of a radio wave.

No. 570 has one of the few curving corners in this otherwise sharply angled city. Above the corner entrance you'll see another sculpture of a hand holding a lightning bolt, surrounded by brick set in curving patterns. Two metal hands project out above the entrance, at the very corner, holding a lightning bolt above a clock face with the letters "GE"—the lightning bolt hiding a light fixture for nighttime illumination.

*Walk south on Lexington to the entrance.*

Similar detail adorns the building's main entrance, above which sits an enormous polished triangular piece of marble; polished stone above the triangle rises to spirals from which hang drop pendants. In the center, another metal sculpture suggests a female figure with a curving vine rising up its middle to a diamond-shaped flower; zigzag marble crowning the figure's head suggests a beehive hairdo.

The building's lobby includes a tiny vestibule leading to a long corridor, both spaces with rippling marble walls, mosaics in a wave pattern, aluminum-coated ceiling, and the original inlaid-wood elevator cabs. A custom-made letter box, which collects mail from the Cutler chutes rising up through the center of the building, repeats motifs from the building's exterior. The hanging chandeliers are a recent addition—originally the lobby was lit only by the sconces still projecting indirect, low-level lighting that bounces off stone segments curving out from the wall just for that purpose. In Cross's words, the sconces reflect light "downward at a thousand angles from the ceiling's bright surface, [and] hint at the broadcast stations which curl their signals into every corner of the land."

Name game: In 1974, GE moved its headquarters to Connecticut, leaving just a few divisions at 570 Lexington Avenue. In 1986, GE reacquired RCA, and in 1988 the RCA Building at Rockefeller Center was renamed . . . the GE Building, even though GE still owned 570 Lexington (it no longer does). So Midtown Manhattan now boasts two Art Deco towers that began life as the "RCA Building" and later became the "GE Building."

*Continue south along Lexington to the corner of East 50th Street, enjoying the view of the Chrysler Building down at 42nd Street (5.4). Turn right, and walk west along 50th Street to Park Avenue. Cross to the northwest corner of Park Avenue and 50th Street, then turn around for a view of the Waldorf-Astoria.*

## 6.7 ★Waldorf-Astoria Hotel, 301 Park (continued from 6.5) Schultze & Weaver—Lloyd Morgan, partner in charge—1929–31

From this vantage point, the Waldorf's modernistic twin skyscraper towers . . . disappear. Instead, the hotel presents a solid mass of stone and gray brick. That brick—called "Waldorf Gray"—was invented specifically to match the stone, suggesting an attempt to make the building's façades, well, dull.

*Cross back to the northeast corner of Park Avenue, then turn south, cross 50th Street, and continue south on Park to the hotel's main entrance.*

Above the entrance canopy, an appropriately modernistic Art Deco geometric metal grille covers the windows. But above that, the gilded reliefs flanking the hotel's name, "Waldorf-Astoria," look like something out of classical antiquity. A metal strip with handsome geometric patterns runs across the top of the doorways, but the seemingly abstract geometric ornament of its supporting columns turns out to be the flowing drapery of sculpted maidens.

Inside, the foyer, lined with square columns mimicking a Greek temple, sports murals of mythological figures—an old-fashioned look, at odds with the modern towers this hotel puts into the skyline. No question that this is also Art Deco—those pastoral murals are the work of French artist Louis Pierre Rigal, who had exhibited at the 1925 Paris exposition—but the softer, flowery version rather than the more geometric Machine Age skyscraper style of its neighbor. (The mosaic in the floor is a 1939 replica of Rigal's 1938 enormous round rug, "The Wheel of Life.")

Is there a reason for these stylistic contrasts? Yes indeed, and it's bound up with the hotel's unusual history. Simply put, this isn't New York's first Waldorf-Astoria—it's the second. The modern skyscraper hotel of 1931 has roots deep in the nineteenth century, where it connects with the social aspirations and real-estate dealings of the Astor clan.

The Astors came to New York from the town of Walldorf in Germany some two centuries ago. They prospered in the fur trade, but also dabbled in real estate, in 1827 acquiring a farm that today we call "Midtown Manhattan." In 1859, two Astor brothers—John Jacob Astor III and William Astor—built adjoining houses on Fifth Avenue between West 33rd and 34th Streets. In the mid–nineteenth century, much of society partying took place in private ballrooms, none more notable than Mrs. William Astor's—said to hold four hundred people, which number gave birth to the expression "the New York Four Hundred" signifying the city's high society.

Following John Jacob Astor's death in 1890, his heirs replaced his mansion with the Hotel Waldorf, a thirteen-story Victorian colossus. In 1897, a seventeen-story annex—the Astoria—opened on the site of his late brother's house. Before long, the two hotels had been joined together as the "Waldorf-Astoria." What Mrs. Astor's ballroom had been—the legendary home of New York society and its grand parties—the public rooms at the Waldorf-Astoria became: "New York's unofficial palace" according to the *New York Times*. The maitre d' who choreographed the parties—Swiss immigrant Oscar Tschirky—became known simply as "Oscar of the Waldorf." A corridor connecting two public rooms—the Palm and the Empire—became known as Peacock Alley, so named for all the finery worn by guests parading back and forth.

A generation later, just before New Year's Day of 1929, a changing neighborhood and changing fashions led to the sale of the Waldorf-Astoria site to the Empire State Building's developers, and the hotel's move to now-fashionable Park Avenue. The new Waldorf-Astoria rose higher into the sky than all but a handful of the city's skyscrapers. Yet at the same time, its builders saw it as a reincarnation of the old Waldorf—an established, conservative institution with a high-society clientele. Lucius Boomer, manager of the old Waldorf, led the new hotel. Oscar of the Waldorf postponed his retirement. A new Peacock Alley was born—three times larger than the original.

Boomer's architects—Schultze & Weaver—specialized in high-end hotels, having designed such conservative stalwarts in New York as the Sherry-Netherland and the Pierre. For this, their last hotel commission, they pledged, according to the *New York Times*, "to incorporate in the future Waldorf-Astoria all of the outstanding features of the old which helped to make it famous."

Hence the Waldorf's split personality—an up-to-the-minute, jazzy Art Deco skyscraper in the skyline, with a genteel interior almost Victorian in flavor. The *New York Times* approved of the stylistic split, describing the hotel as a combination of "smart contemporary effects and beautiful period interpretations." (In *The New Yorker*, Lewis Mumford less kindly described the overall effect as "Modernism, revivalism, eclecticism and plain gimcrackery.")

The main area looks rather like an imported Greek temple—one in which a couple of interior decorators have been allowed to run riot. Mythological figures mingling with baskets of flowers adorn the ceiling and the wall areas just below it. It's hard to believe that this building is an exact contemporary of the electrically designed GE Building—and that, apparently, was the idea.

***From the main entrance, turn right, walk north on Park Avenue to the corner of East 50th Street, cross to the north side of 50th, then cross to the west side of Park Avenue and continue walking west, fifty feet in toward Madison Avenue.***

Once you are safely across Park Avenue, turn around, and once again the Waldorf will appear as a 1930 twin-towered skyscraper. Look down at the street bed for a moment—either Park Avenue or 50th Street—and you will notice steel bands crossing the pavement. These serve as expansion joints for what is effectively an enormous steel bridge over Grand Central Terminal's sunken rail yard—trains rumble in and out beneath your feet. Buildings along Park Avenue—including the Waldorf—don't have normal foundations, being supported instead on enormous steel pillars. As a result, the Waldorf accommodates a rail spur (no longer in regular use) connecting the main train line to a siding beneath the hotel—once planned to allow wealthy residents with their own private rail cars to arrive at the hotel underground. Ah, the Waldorf.

*Continue west on 50th Street one block to the corner of 50th and Madison Avenue, and look catty-corner across the intersection at the southwest corner.*

### 6.8 444 Madison Avenue
### Robert D. Kohn, 1930–31

Madison Avenue has long been synonymous with the advertising industry, and, since advertising has long been intertwined with publishing, that industry has also located here. No. 444 Madison Avenue, built as a generic office building, became the Newsweek Building in 1959 when that weekly news magazine leased five of its floors. When *New York Magazine* leased three floors in 1996, the Newsweek Building became the New York Magazine Building. Two blocks to the north, the white brick building with the curving corner at 488 Madison Avenue (Emery Roth & Sons, 1949–50) similarly took the name of one of its publishing tenants, *Look Magazine*—prompting an indignant fellow tenant, *Esquire Magazine*, to sue, unsuccessfully, to stop the deal.

No. 444 is a modest example of Art Deco. Nevertheless, it has all the markings of the skyscraper style—a narrow tower rising above setbacks, vertical columns of windows, and abstract patterns. The first two stories, once faced with polished black limestone and gilded geometric details, have, sadly, been redesigned, as has the lobby.

*Continue west one more block to the corner of Fifth Avenue; turn left and walk south one block on Fifth Avenue to East 49th Street. Cross to the south side of East 49th Street and look west across Fifth Avenue at the Goelet Building.*

### 6.9 **Goelet Building (now Swiss Center Building), 608 Fifth Avenue (Plate 9)
### Victor L.S. Hafner and Edward Hall Faile, 1930–32

The old Goelet Building may seem relatively modest on the outside, but inside you will find one of New York's best-kept Deco secrets. Robert Goelet, scion of an old New York banking and real-estate dynasty, inherited the family mansion at 608 Fifth Avenue in 1929, added the site to the two-story art gallery he'd commissioned next door a decade earlier, and replaced them both with a ten-story office building. Goelet's building stood catty-corner from Saks Fifth Avenue, the grand department store, but across the street from the construction site of Rockefeller Center, the new office-building complex. Goelet wanted his building to be flexible enough to function either way—department store or office building. Hence the double-story glass storefronts along Fifth Avenue, above which rise eight stories of office space. The light-court on the 49th Street façade provided light to those offices—but the architect designed the building's floors to handle the extra weight should Goelet decide to fill in the light-court to convert the entire structure to department store use.

*Cross to the west side of Fifth Avenue to reach the entrance.*

The offices are reached via a narrow elevator lobby squeezed in next to the wide shops. Inside, a small entrance vestibule leads into a slightly larger vestibule, leading in turn into the small but amazingly ornamental elevator lobby. Every inch of this space gets the full Deco treatment. In the small entrance vestibule, strips of black marble rise from a red marble baseboard to a plaster coved ceiling covered with geometric patterns in aluminum leaf. Each corner is quite overwhelmed by a floor-to-ceiling aluminum grille filtering light into the room. Even the doors to the next room—including their remarkable handles—are all about geometric patterns. In the larger vestibule, narrow aluminum strips separate dark- and light-brown marble bands on the walls, while up at the edge of the ceiling light is hidden behind an embossed metal band. Geometric patterns on the ceiling surround a swan—an image taken from the Goelet family crest. But it's the elevator lobby around the corner that explodes in ornament—marble bands, aluminum ceiling, and cast-metal elevator doors. Even the original elevator cabs survive, with vertical strips of baked enamel and corner aluminum light fixtures adorned with a mix of geometric forms and stylized floral patterns. It's just the luck of the draw that this lobby survived over the decades almost entirely unchanged until its designation as an official interior landmark.

*Cross back to the east side of Fifth Avenue, turn left, and walk to the corner of Fifth and East 49th Street. Stand on the southeast*

***corner of Fifth Avenue and 49th Street and look across and north along the avenue.***

## 6.10 **Rockefeller Center, Fifth Avenue to Sixth Avenue, West 48th to West 51st Streets The Associated Architects, 1932 ff.

Rockefeller Center—which has been the subject of half-a-dozen full-length books—deserves (and usually gets) its own tour, focusing on more than just its Art Deco connections. Please consider this entry a small introduction to a much larger topic.

The Center began life as "Metropolitan Square"—a project to build a new home for the Metropolitan Opera and surround it with a commercial development whose rents would underwrite the usual opera deficits. John D. Rockefeller, Jr., the philanthropist son of the founder of Standard Oil, stepped in to help finance and organize the project—acquiring the property, hiring the architects, proposing an initial plan—but then the Opera decided to stay put, leaving Rockefeller with a project but no centerpiece. The result: instead of building Metropolitan Square, he built Radio City, today called Rockefeller Center.

Rockefeller's people hired a team of three firms who styled themselves the Associated Architects—a group including, among others, modernists Raymond Hood, Harvey Wiley Corbett, and Wallace K. Harrison (for Hood, see 5.1; for Corbett, see 2.9). Faced with an enormous three-block site, stretching from Fifth to Sixth Avenues, the architects brought order and coherence to the project by organizing the plan around three visual axes: (1) from 49th to 51st Streets along Fifth Avenue, (2) from Fifth Avenue west along the Channel Gardens to the RCA tower, and (3) along the newly created north-south street of Rockefeller Plaza. Around these axes they organized a dozen buildings of various shapes and sizes, ranging in height from six to seventy stories, all centered on a sunken plaza that today serves as a skating rink (or a café in warm weather). Though the various buildings differ in shape and size, they nevertheless form a coherent whole, in part because of the axial planning and in part because of their generally uniform design: faced in buff-colored limestone, with windows organized in vertical columns, window spandrels designed in abstract geometric patterns, and entrances marked by lively, colorful art designed by a dozen artists, including such prominent figures as Rene Chambellan, Lee Lawrie, Paul Jennewein, Gaston Lachaise, and Paul Manship.

Standing at the corner of East 49th Street, look north up Fifth Avenue: what appear to be four identical six-story buildings, draped in flags, form the grand entrance to Rockefeller Center. That effect is somewhat illusory—the first two buildings are indeed separate structures, but the third and fourth in the distance are actually wings of the taller skyscraper rising behind them.

***Cross 49th Street and continue walking north up Fifth Avenue till you're half way up the block and can see down the gardens that separate the first two six-story buildings.***

Now look west, between the first two six-story buildings, along the line of the gardens—and you will find yourself admiring a dramatic view of the seventy-story RCA (later renamed General Electric, and now called Comcast) Building, in its day the third-tallest skyscraper in the city. That's the second axis, and it leads your eye from the Center's grand entrance directly into its heart.

The four buildings or wings of the grand entrance have names. From south to north: La Maison Francaise, the British Empire Building, the Palazzo d'Italia, and . . . the International Building North. With the loss of the Opera as a philanthropic identity for the complex, Rockefeller turned to another passion: promoting international understanding. The plan was to lease the four low Fifth Avenue structures to foreign governments—but this was in 1933, and Germany, potentially the fourth tenant, declined to participate. The skyscraper attached to the third and fourth structures became the International Building, hence the name of the fourth element of the plan (originally to be called Deutches Haus).

***Walk up to the crosswalk in the middle of the block, and cross Fifth Avenue to the British Empire Building.***

The governments leasing these buildings chose the ornament. For the British Building, Paul Jennewein designed a sculpture of the British coat of arms and bronze figures representing the industry and commerce of the British Empire.

*Turn left and walk down the sidewalk to the Maison Francaise, and look at the entrance.*

For the Maison Francaise, Alfred Janniot designed the figure of "Marianne"—a generic symbol of France—bearing the torch of Liberty, with beneath her the motto of the French Revolution (a natural counterpart to the royal coat of arms on the British building). In the large relief below, two women, representing Paris and New York, cordially greet each other—Rockefeller's hopes for world peace—while below, three figures are called *Poesie* (poetry), *Beauté* (Beauty), and *Elegance* (elegance). So interesting, the different images these two world powers sought to project.

*Turn right and walk back up the sidewalk till you reach the gardens that separate the Maison Francaise from the British Empire Building.*

The gardens separating the French and British Buildings are called the "Channel Gardens" after the English Channel separating France and Britain. The six bronze figures adorning them are the work of Rene Chambellan.

*Walk down the left side of the path, halfway toward RCA, and stop right by the side entrance to the Maison Francaise.*

The national symbolism continues here in the reliefs by Lee Lawrie above the side entrances of each building. On the Maison Francaise: "Scattering the Seeds of Good Citizenship" (the seeds in the shape of the fleur-de-lis); on the British Empire Building: Mercury, the god of commerce. The figures in each relief stand on geometric patterns running along the top of their respective entrances.

*Walk down to the central plaza.*

At the far end of the plaza, Paul Manship's enormous gilded bronze statue (for Manship, see 12.12) shows Prometheus bringing fire to humanity—an appropriate symbol to guard the headquarters of the Radio Corporation of America.

*Turn right, walk along the edge of the rink and continue up the stairs to West 50th Street.*

Across the street you can see the flank of the International Building, with more of Lee Lawrie's foreign fantasies. To the west (on your left), a polychromatic limestone screen with symbolic figures, representing "The Races of Mankind," "Regions of the Earth," "Religions of the World," and more. To the east (on your right) above a secondary entrance is Lawrie's representation of Isaiah's famous prophecy: "And they shall beat their swords into ploughshares."

*Continue walking east, towards Fifth Avenue.*

The next entrance leads to the Palazzo d'Italia—and here it suddenly becomes apparent that the Palazzo is merely a wing of the International Building. Above the entrance, Lee Lawrie has done another nationally representative relief—an image of St. Francis, patron saint of Italy, preaching to the birds (who carefully form a halo around his head).

*Walk back, west, to the sunken plaza, and continue to Rockefeller Plaza, the three-block-long private street Rockefeller Center added to the Midtown street grid.*

Here is the Center's third axis, running parallel to Fifth and Sixth Avenues and breaking up the very long blocks between them. Look north, to your right, and you'll see the vista closed by another Rockefeller Center building that actually sits outside the three-block area—it's across the street, on the north side of West 51st Street. To your left, on the west side of Rockefeller Plaza, between West 50th and 51st Streets, an enormous stainless steel image of "News" by Isamu Noguchi overwhelms the entrance to the Associated Press Building.

*Turn back and walk south on Rockefeller Plaza, crossing West 50th Street, and continue halfway down the block, then turn right to face the entrance to the RCA Building.*

While world peace and international symbolism dominate the artwork on the eastern half of the complex, the western half is, so to speak, the business end, lined with corporate headquarters. Rockefeller's people hired a group of advisors, including a philosophy professor, to propose appropriate themes for these buildings, and they do show up on many of them. Above the entrance to the RCA (now Comcast) Building is Lee Lawrie's multicolored stone and glass representation of Wisdom—whose compass crosses the inscription and sets off waves in the 240 Pyrex glass blocks below.

***Walk through the doors and into the lobby of 30 Rockefeller Plaza.***

For the lobby of the RCA Building, Rockefeller's people famously hired the Mexican muralist Diego Rivera to paint a grand mural—only to stop him halfway when his mural proved too politically socialist for comfort. That mural is gone—replaced by the work of Spanish artist Jose Maria Sert, *American Progress, the Triumph of Man's Accomplishments through Physical and Mental Labor*. Like many murals inside skyscrapers of the period, it includes a representation of the very building in which you're standing.

***Continue walking west through the RCA Building; follow the long, narrow hallway all the way to the end, and exit into the porch next to the sidewalk along Sixth Avenue. Turn around to see the large mosaic over the entrance.***

The mosaic, by Barry Faulkner, represents "Intelligence Awakening Mankind," a somewhat convoluted allegory, hard to interpret despite the names helpfully inscribed beneath many of the figures.

***Turn right on Sixth Avenue and walk north to the corner of West 51st Street, where you'll be able to see the great neon signs and entrance for Radio City Music Hall—Rockefeller's replacement, in a sense, for the Metropolitan Opera.***

High up on the West 50th Street façade of the Music Hall, three enormous roundels represent Dance, Drama, and Song. They were designed by Hildreth Meière (who did the mosaics at One Wall Street, 1.3, and the ceiling at the Long Lines Building, 2.10), and cast by metallurgist Oscar Bach (who did the duralumin roundels in the Empire State Building lobby, 3.6, and the symbols of public health on the Health, Hospitals, and Sanitation Building in the Civic Center, 2.8).

Though there's so much more to see and say about this extraordinary complex in the heart of Midtown Manhattan, we have to move on.

***Cross to the west side of Sixth Avenue, turn right, and walk north along Sixth Avenue to West 53rd Street. Turn left on West 53rd and walk west halfway down the block to the IND Substation.***

## 6.11 Central IND Substation, 126 West 53rd Street Squire J. Vickers, 1932

New York City has three major subway lines—the IRT, the BMT, and the IND. The IRT (Interborough Rapid Transit) opened in 1904, and the BMT (Brooklyn and Manhattan Transit) in the following decade—both as private companies. But in 1932 the City of New York opened the first section of a City-owned "Independent" line—the IND, whose trains today are identified by the first letters of the alphabet— A, B, C, D, E, F, and G. Their stations, designed beginning in the late 1920s by Squire J. Vickers (for Vickers, see 11.1), show the influence of Art Deco, as does this IND substation. The largest such substation in the system at the time of its completion in 1932, it originally provided electricity for the B, D, and E trains.

The new IND substations made use of new technology—notably, a mercury arc rectifier—that eliminated the need for certain manually operated equipment. It is only fitting, then, that the new substations should take their architectural cue from Machine Age design. Though just five stories tall, the brick and limestone façade includes such skyscraper-style details as vertical window bays set between projecting brick piers, and geometrically patterned ornament—those zigzag lightning bolts at the top of the building wouldn't be out of place on the fifty-story GE building (6.4/6.6).

***Continue walking west on West 53rd Street to Seventh Avenue, turn left, and walk south on Seventh Avenue to West 50th Street, then turn right on West 50th and walk west to Broadway; look across Broadway at the Brill Building.***

## 6.12 *The Brill Building, 1619 Broadway Victor A. Bark, Jr., 1930–31

This short building had a rough start in life. Initially planned to be the world's tallest building, it became instead a small office building named in memory of the developer's son, only to be renamed for the original owner of the property—and then went on to have an entirely unplanned history as the home of American popular music.

The Brill Building takes its name from the Brill Brothers—owners of a chain of men's clothing stores, one of which stood on this site. Toward the end of the 1920s, the location caught the attention of garment-manufacturer-turned-real-estate-developer A. E. Lefcourt, active in the nearby Garment Center as well as around town generally, and here he proposed erecting the world's tallest building—at 1,050 feet just barely taller than the proposed Chrysler Building (5.4). Unfortunately for Lefcourt, the stock market crashed three weeks later and brought the project down to earth, just ten stories tall.

Architect Victor Bark, who often worked on Lefcourt projects, had produced typically eclectic historicist designs for the developer, but by 1929, like most other architects of the day, he had turned modernistic. His simple design for Lefcourt's building includes the usual vertical windows, in this case set in pairs, with a nod to earlier classical styling in the first three stories that suggest pairs of columns at either end. Deco ornament shows up in the strip running between the second- and third-story windows—handsome and colorful terra-cotta reliefs combining Vs and floral patterns—and again in abstractly styled floral patterns atop pairs of windows in the building's center, above the third story. The lobby has wonderful floral Deco designs on the elevator doors, radiator grilles, and even the mailbox.

Most unusual, however, is the extraordinary zigzag brass arch above the central entrance, which rises to a niche cradling a portrait bust—with a matching bust at the roofline in more traditional materials. Lefcourt's obituary identified the brass bust as a portrait of Lefcourt's son, Alan, who died young in 1930 as the building went up. Lefcourt initially named the building for his son, but after his own death in 1932 the name changed to Brill.

And then came the unexpected history. As the Brill Building, 1619 Broadway developed a reputation as the center of the popular music publishing business, from the days of Tin Pan Alley right through rock-and-roll. Over many decades, it sheltered dozens of music publishers, who published hundreds of songs, as well as musicians including the likes of Tommy Dorsey, Duke Ellington, Cab Calloway, and Nat King Cole. Various nightclubs once operated here, as did, until recently, Colony Records, the emporium of rare recordings, which regularly lived up to its motto, "I found it at the Colony!" Though the songwriters have moved on, the Brill Building still keeps alive the memory of half a century of the American music industry.

# ITINERARY NO. 7
# FROM BLOOMINGDALE'S TO THE SOFIA APARTMENTS

This itinerary skirts the northern edge of Midtown, from east to west, for the most part along 57th and 59th Streets. It begins with a look at three commercial buildings just below the border with the Upper East Side: Starrett & Van Vleck's extension of Bloomingdale's (7.1), Walker & Gillette's Fuller Building (7.2), and Ely Jacques Kahn's Squibb Building (7.3). It continues along Central Park South (the grand name adopted by West 59th Street between Fifth and Eighth Avenues) with a look at three of Midtown's more exclusive apartment hotels: the Barbizon Plaza (7.4), Hampshire House (7.5), and Essex House (7.6). And it concludes with Viennese architect Joseph Urban's whimsical base for what would have been William Randolph Hearst's skyscraper citadel (7.7); a modest loft building that originally serviced Twentieth Century Fox (7.8), and an unlikely apartment house that began life as an automated parking garage (7.9).

***The walk begins at the southwest corner of Lexington Avenue and East 59th Street, looking across the intersection at Bloomingdale's on the northeast corner.***

## 7.1 Bloomingdale's, 743–765 Lexington Avenue (officially 1000 Third Avenue) Lexington Avenue extension Starrett & Van Vleck, 1930–32

Following the general trend northward of Manhattan's development, most of Midtown's fabled department stores moved to their current locations from further south on the island—but not Bloomingdale's. Located at the edge of the Upper East Side since its founding in 1872, the store moved to Third Avenue and East 59th Street in 1886, and gradually expanded westward towards Lexington Avenue as it

10 Av
Twentieth Century Fox Building
(High School for
Environmental Sciences)
444 West 56 Street
8
10 Av
Amsterdam Av
9 Av
Columbus Av
Kent Automatic
Parking Garage
45 Columbus Avenue
9
Broadway
Hearst Magazine Building
300 West 57 Street
7
Columbus
Circle
Central Park West
8 Av
Broadway
Times
Sq
7 Av
Central
Park
Central Park
South
Essex House
160 Central Park South
6
Hampshire House
150 Central Park South
5
Barbizon Plaza
106 Central Park South
4
6 Av (Av of Americas)
Rockefeller
Plaza
Grand Army Plaza
5 Av
Squibb Building
745 Fifth Avenue
3
Madison Av
Vanderbilt Av
Fuller Building
41 East 57 Street
2
Park Av
Lexington Av
Bloomingdale's
Lexington Avenue Extension
743–765 Lexington Avenue
1
3 Av
W
S
N
E
© Tauranac, Ltd., 2016.
All Rights Reserved.

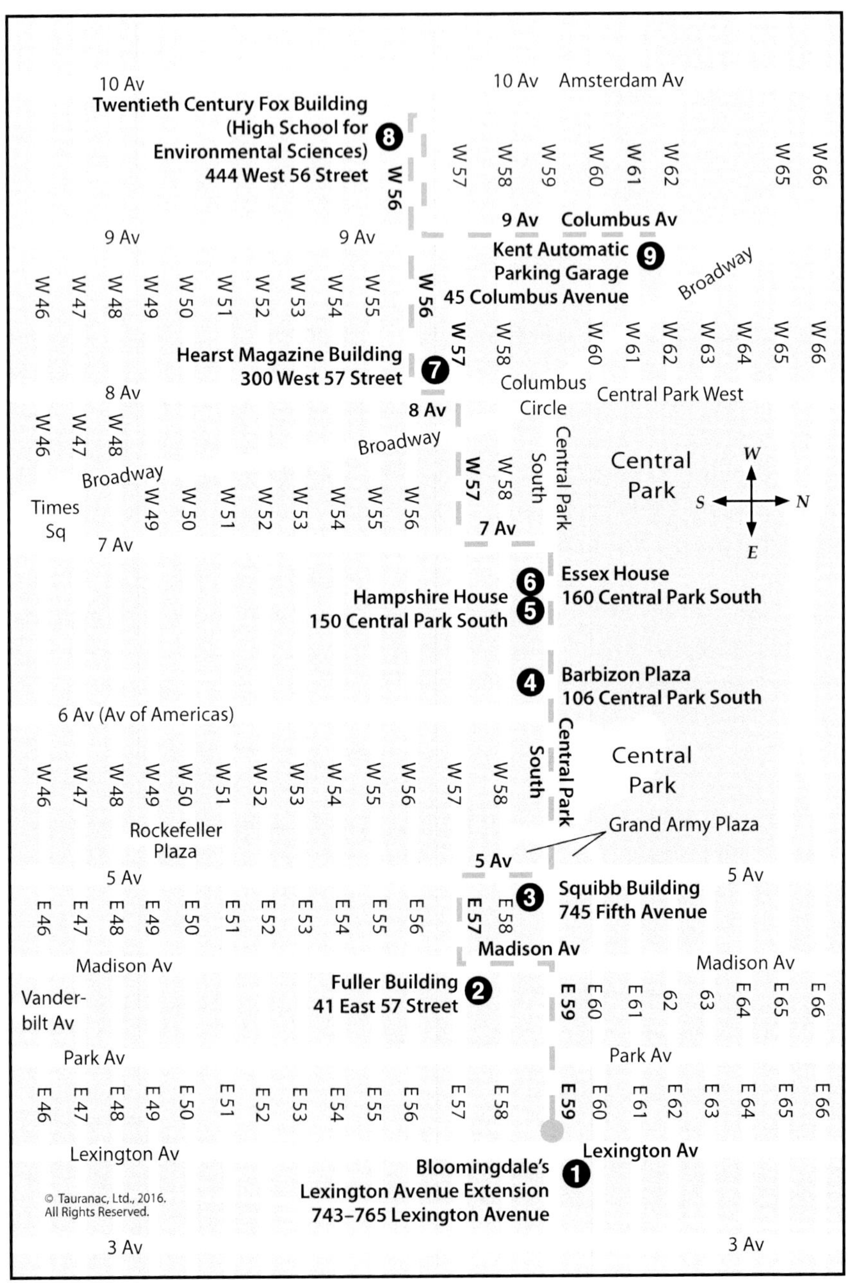

MAP 7

grew into one of the city's pre-eminent shopping destinations. As early as 1904, Bloomingdale's had taken over almost the entire block, with a Parisian-style shopping arcade extending to Lexington. As described that year by the *New-York Tribune*, "No store is more conveniently located for the majority of shoppers. . . . Every car line either runs directly or by transfer to its very doors, and all the ferries connect with car lines which in many cases run directly by it. . . . And so from the accessibility of this great shopping headquarters sprang the appropriate phrase 'All cars transfer to Bloomingdale's.'"

In 1930, the store completed its takeover of the block—bounded by Third and Lexington Avenues and East 59th and 60th Streets—by commissioning a major addition on Lexington from the firm of Starrett & Van Vleck (for Starrett & Van Vleck, see 1.1). The ceremonial cornerstone-laying in April of that year included a second, larger cornerstone meant to be opened in the future—two centuries in the future. Wrote the *Times*: "Specialists in art, literature, politics, sports and other fields have written predictions of conditions which will prevail two hundred years from now. . . . Three savings bank books, each recording a $25 deposit, also will be placed in the stone, these accounts to run for 200 years with compound interest, the total sum at the end of that time, about $614,400, to be distributed among three charitable institutions. A radio set, cocktail shaker, a current phonograph record and other articles of modern times will be included."

If Bloomingdale's survives to 2130, our descendants may learn something about the city of 1930—and the vagaries of predictions—from the contents of that cornerstone. But even today, we can learn something about 1930s New York from the details of Starrett & Van Vleck's stylish addition: tall, uninterrupted piers stretching up the façade; abstract geometric metal grilles above the entrance doors; and small but stylish modernistic vestibules just inside those entrances.

*Walk west along East 59th Street to Park Avenue; cross Park Avenue, and continue walking west to Madison Avenue. Cross to the west side of the avenue, then turn left and walk south on Madison two blocks to East 57th Street. Cross to the southwest corner of East 57th Street and Madison Avenue, then turn around to look catty-corner across the intersection at the northeast corner.*

## 7.2 **Fuller Building, 41 East 57th Street (Plate 10) Walker & Gillette, 1928–29

The construction company founded by nineteenth-century skyscraper pioneer George A. Fuller became one of the most prolific in the nation. In New York City, Fuller's legacy includes such legendary historic structures as the original Penn Station and the Plaza Hotel, and such seminal modern skyscrapers as Lever House and the Seagram Building. In the early twentieth century, the company built two Manhattan skyscraper headquarters for its own operations: the famed Flatiron Building (originally also called the Fuller Building) at East 23rd Street and Fifth Avenue, in 1902; and the new Fuller Building (which managed to hang on to its name, with the help of prominent inscriptions over the entrances) on East 57th Street and Madison Avenue, designed in 1928 by Walker & Gillette (for Walker & Gillette, see 2.2).

Fuller chose a location in an up-and-coming retail section at the north edge of Midtown. The *Times* quoted a company rep as explaining: "It is in the belief that the street presents the most exclusive retail area in the world that [we have] undertaken the construction of the new Fuller Building." In particular, New York's art galleries had begun relocating to the area. Capitalizing on the retail potential, Fuller commissioned a hybrid skyscraper: a modern office building, to be sure, but with its first six stories devoted to retail space, its intermediate stories given over to art dealers, and standard commercial office space above. In a *Times* article of December 1928, Fuller described the six stories of retail space as "vertical shops," which "make it possible for tenants to rent space fronting on either Madison Avenue or Fifty-seventh Street, and duplicate the space for five stories above." The shops included their own private elevators servicing just those six stories. The architects called the Fuller Building "the first high-class multiple-purpose skyscraper" in New York.

Walker & Gillette's design neatly expresses the building's three distinct uses—enormous retail shop windows on the first six stories, framed by black granite piers; then a bulky midsection for the art dealers; and finally a slender tower for business offices. The design relies on the contrast between white and black brick and black granite, and the tower's generally blocky geometry. Ornamental geometry shows up in the bronze spandrels under the shop windows—wavy lines running across upside-down ziggurats—but especially over the East 57th Street double-height entrance, with its black and white patterned piers and its extraordinary statuary above the inscription "FULLER BUILDING." Said statuary—two muscular male figures flanking an octagonal clock, with a backdrop of geometrical patterns that might represent skyscrapers (or, if not, then rather large sheaves of wheat)—was produced by Elie Nadelman, a European sculptor who came to the United States in 1914 and became friendly with Walker while doing a portrait of the architect's young son.

*Cross to the north side of East 57th Street and then the east side of Madison Avenue to see the entrance up close.*

The building's ornamental treatment continues inside the lobby, with stylized classical details in marble and bronze, a double "F" for "Fuller" on the floor, and ornamental wings and waves. The elevator doors sport images of construction work. But most impressive are the three major mosaics on the lobby floor—they illustrate three of the company's buildings, including the Flatiron Building and this new Fuller Building, thereby continuing a trend in Art Deco towers of incorporating images of the building in its ornamental treatment.

*Cross back to the west side of Madison Avenue and walk west on East 57th Street one block to Fifth Avenue. Cross to the west side of Fifth Avenue, then turn right on Fifth Avenue and walk north halfway up the block toward West 58th Street. Then turn to look back across the avenue at the Squibb Building.*

## 7.3 Squibb Building, 745 Fifth Avenue Ely Jacques Kahn, 1929–1930

At East 59th Street, the ritzy eastern half of commercial Midtown merges into the residential

Upper East Side. Abe Adelson (for Adelson, see 1.2) commissioned Ely Jacques Kahn (for Kahn, see 3.4) to design a speculative showroom and office building at this very posh location, just across from the Bergdorf-Goodman department store (also a Kahn design), the Plaza Hotel, and Central Park—and on the site of one of Fifth Avenue's grandest residential blocks, the so-called Marble Row, a group of white-marble-faced row houses of 1871 at one time considered among the finest on the avenue. Adelson later noted that the location enjoyed "the advantages of freedom from noise and outstanding accessibility for the executives and personnel of large organizations" and "an exclusive neighborhood." Originally named simply with its address—745 Fifth Avenue—the building soon took on the name of its principal tenant, pharmaceutical giant E. R. Squibb & Sons.

Though it might seem surprising—given, say, the polychromatic wonders of Two Park Avenue (3.4)—Kahn considered this building his masterpiece. On instructions from Adelson, he deliberately chose to face his tower in white marble in memory of the Marble Row. Even as the Marble Row disappeared, the influence of its white marble fronts lived on in the (now demolished) Savoy Plaza Hotel and the façades of Bergdorf-Goodman.

Because of alterations to the first six stories, it's hard to picture Squibb in its original condition, but the upper stories in glazed white brick, with matching white marble window spandrels, still rise majestically in receding setback blocks.

***Cross to the east side of Fifth Avenue and approach the main entrance.***

Kahn's idiosyncratic, finely detailed ornamental treatment shows up in the elaborate abstract grille above the Fifth Avenue entrance, and again in grilles in the lobby.

The crowning glory of the lobby, however, is its enormous ceiling mural. Painted on canvas by Arthur Covey, it superimposes abstract multicolored zigzags and streamlined airplane profiles, along with the names and symbols of various intellectual disciplines, over a map of Manhattan's rigidly geometric street grid.

*Walk north along Fifth Avenue to the corner of East 58th Street, cross to the west side of the avenue, then turn right and walk north along Fifth Avenue (which at this point means along the side of Grand Army Plaza) to Central Park South, the westward extension of East 59th Street. Turn left on Central Park South, walking through Grand Army Plaza to the corner, then turn right and cross Central Park South to the park side. Then turn left and walk west along Central Park South (the park will be on your right) to the corner of Sixth Avenue (Avenue of the Americas) and look across the intersection at the southwest corner of Sixth and Central Park South.*

## 7.4 Barbizon Plaza, 106 Central Park South
Murgatroyd & Ogden, 1928–1930

The Barbizon Plaza—with more than fourteen hundred rooms spread over forty stories—takes its name from the Barbizon school of French painters, a choice reflecting its original marketing as "New York's first residential hotel catering to artists." Well, artists "whether engaged in the ART of BUSINESS or the BUSINESS of ART."

According to one boosterish publication, "The Barbizon has proximity to art galleries, music halls, libraries, clubs, cafes and recreation. Among its appeals are: Atmosphere . . . Intimacy . . . Sun-tan Glass enclosed Roof . . . Deck tennis courts . . . Library . . . Art gallery . . . Salon de Musique . . . Sound-proof studios . . . Studio for sculpture and painting . . . Business Men's Art Club . . . And many other features appealing to artists, musicians, singers, writers, reporters, students and to business people interested in any form of art, even though it be commercial."

In a somewhat more sober account, the *New York Times* on opening day declared that the Barbizon provided the city with "the first fully equipped music-art residence centre in the United States."

The Barbizon Plaza's developer, William Silk, had earlier helped found the Allerton hotels, which one writer described as "a semi-philanthropic hotel chain for young men or women at moderate rates" providing, according to an Allerton brochure, the "wholesomeness of a home, the service of a hotel and the sociability of a club of modest rates." In 1928, Silk built two grander residential complexes as an upscale version of the Allerton originals. One, the Barbizon on East 57th Street, housed young women finding their way in artistic careers. The other, the Barbizon Plaza here on Central Park South, targeted art-loving businessmen. Silk brought in Murgatroyd & Ogden, architects of the original Allerton group, to design both new buildings.

While their earlier buildings hewed to the romantic eclecticism so typical of the earlier 1920s—the Lombard Romanesque, the North Italian Renaissance, the Moorish Revival—with the Barbizon Plaza, Everett Murgatroyd and Palmer Ogden turned to the modernistic. The plain gray stone façade is somewhat reminiscent of the lower stories of the Waldorf-Astoria (6.5/6.7), and like the Waldorf it sports progressively more geometrically elaborate ornament as it rises into the Midtown skyline, from stylized floral panels to heavy ribbed piers forming a skyline crown.

***Walk south on Sixth Avenue to West 58th Street, then turn right and walk west partway down the block toward Seventh Avenue.***

The bulk of the hotel sits not on Central Park South but on the corner of Sixth Avenue and West 58th Street, and its entrance was originally on West 58th, moving to Central Park South only in 1952. That former entrance has been altered, but surviving above it at the third story are three sculpted roundels suggesting the hotel's original artistic ambitions: to the left a writer with a book, in the center a lyre, and at the right a painter with an easel.

***Return to the north side of Central Park South, turn left, and continue walking west along Central Park South halfway to Seventh Avenue.***

## 7.5 Hampshire House, 150 Central Park South Caughey & Evans, 1931 and 1937

Architects Caughey & Evans, like Murgatroyd & Ogden down the block, enjoyed a modest practice designing apartment buildings and apartment

hotels in a variety of historic styles, notably Tudor and Renaissance, but by the end of the 1920s they too had turned in more modern directions. Their first plan for this building—to be called "Medici Tower" and imagined as home to suites for doctors and dentists (*medici* being Italian for "doctors")—included a jazzy tower and dome. In the end, they designed a cross between the two stylistic approaches of the 1920s, what the *Times* described as "an adaptation to the modern tall building of the Georgian style such as is found in many old homes in the County of Hampshire, England." The owners chiseled that ambition into the building's cornerstone, which still bears the inscription, "Dedicated to Yesterday's Charm and Tomorrow's Convenience."

Within a few months of the *Times* encomium, however, the project fell victim to the Depression: foreclosed, in receivership, and "boarded up and left to the mercy of the elements." For six long years, Hampshire House stood empty and forlorn. Only in 1937 did the project come back to life—a fortuitous year, in that with some imaginative use of a chisel, the date "1931" on the cornerstone could be modified to read "1937."

Caughey and Evan came back to complete the construction, and new management brought in Dorothy Draper, grand doyenne of interior design (for Draper see also 6.3 and 10.3). Draper decided to use English Georgian styling to camouflage the interior of a modern tower as, in the words of the *Times*, "a traditional London town home."

Caughey & Evans's exterior does much the same, rising thirty-four stories into the sky, with a series of modernist setbacks, leading to—of all things—a steeply sloping roof topped with chimneys, modeled on old Georgian stately homes. Traces of modernism persist, however—certainly in the vertical arrangement of windows, but also in a series of cast-stone panels at the third floor in which a grand capital H has been ensconced within typically Deco stylized floral patterns.

## 7.6 Essex House, 160 Central Park South Frank Grad, 1929

How did a New Jersey–based architect like Frank Grad snag the commission to design one of New York City's largest apartment hotels? By pleasing New York developer A. E. Lefcourt, for whom Grad had just designed two new towers in downtown Newark (for Lefcourt see 6.12.) Lefcourt initially called his forty-three-story project on Central Park South the "Seville Towers Hotel," because it replaced a large chunk of the old "Spanish Flats"—an early luxury apartment complex occupying much of the block—as did also, for that matter, neighboring Hampshire House. Like Hampshire House, unfortunately, Seville Towers fell to foreclosure in 1931, and its new owner preferred a name suggesting old England rather than Spain.

Grad, the son of an Austrian painter, studied architecture and engineering in Vienna before immigrating to the United States in 1902 and becoming a major Newark architect. Despite his great success in that city, he remains best known for Essex House.

Unlike its neighbor, Essex House is unabashedly modernistic in its styling—vertically arranged windows, of course, and blocky geometric setbacks, but also lots of abstract geometric patterned brickwork and cast-stone ornament. Particularly notable—especially because they've been gilded—are the sculpted "frozen fountains" at the second and third stories, and the explosion of (also gilded) abstract stylized floral patterns rising for four stories above the main entrance. Unlike Hampshire House, but like the Barbizon Plaza, Essex House extends through the block to West 58th Street, where its façade—especially at the entrance—sports similarly floral ornament.

***Continue walking west to Seventh Avenue. Cross to the west side of the avenue, turn left, and walk south two blocks to West 57th Street. Turn right, and walk west to Eighth Avenue. Look across the street at the southwest corner of Eighth and West 57th.***

## 7.7 ⋆Hearst Magazine Building, 300 West 57th Street Joseph Urban and George B. Post & Sons, 1927–28; sculpture, Henry Kreis

It takes a certain amount of willful suspension of disbelief, but try to picture this building without the huge glass-and-steel tower that now rises above it—and imagine, instead, an old sled named Rosebud . . . because you're standing in front of the truncated dream of urban glory of William Randolph Hearst, inspiration for the publishing mogul in Orson Welles's classic film, *Citizen Kane*. The San Francisco–born son of a U.S. senator, Hearst turned the failing San Francisco *Examiner* into a publishing empire including the *Journal American* and the *Daily Mirror* in New York, as well as newspapers in almost every major American city—not to mention such magazines as *Cosmopolitan*, *Good Housekeeping*, and *Harper's Bazaar*.

A major player in Roaring-Twenties New York, Hearst met his future mistress, actress Marion Davies, while she worked as a chorus girl in the Ziegfeld Follies. Hearst went on to back Florenz Ziegfeld in a number of 1920s theatrical ventures—notably the modernistic Ziegfeld Theater, which once stood just two blocks to the east (56th Street at Sixth Avenue). Through Ziegfeld, Hearst met architect Joseph Urban, the Vienna-born and -trained architect who brought a Viennese Sezession sensibility with him to America—first to St. Louis, where he designed the Austrian pavilion in the 1904 World's Fair, then to Boston as art director of the Boston Opera, and eventually to New York, where Ziegfeld hired him in 1914 to design the stage sets for his Follies. By the 1920s, Urban was designing stage sets for the Metropolitan Opera and remodeling or building theaters for Hearst, including the Ziegfeld.

Hearst and Urban found themselves in the late '20s planning the transformation of Columbus Circle into a major theatrical and cultural center, to be centered on a new Hearst tower. The *New York Times*, in the Times Tower on Times Square, heart of the Broadway theater district, would be supplanted by the Hearst organization in the Hearst Tower on or near Hearst Plaza (Columbus Circle), heart of a new theater district. Hearst at one time had designs on each of the three blocks facing onto Columbus Circle, but in the end settled on 57th Street, two blocks to the south.

Carnegie Hall had long since occupied the corner of West 57th Street and Seventh Avenue. In 1926, the Metropolitan Opera announced plans to build a new home on the same street, just west of Hearst's building, as part of a new skyscraper to be designed in part by Urban. Hearst intended his own new Urban-designed headquarters also to rise, eventually, to skyscraper height (hence the architectural collaboration with George B. Post & Sons, experienced high-rise designers). In the end, the Opera backed out, the theater district stayed put, and Hearst's building never rose more than six stories—until the beginning of the twenty-first century when the Hearst corporation brought in British superstar architect Norman Foster to design the incongruous addition now hovering above Urban's original.

Urban's design for the Hearst Building is perhaps more theatrical than specifically Art Deco, and combines classical leanings—underpinned by the architect's Sezession roots—with World's Fair pomp, but it does share with, for instance, the General Electric Building (6.4/6.6) such details as vertical window bays and chamfered corners. Most unusual are the pairs of enormous stone fluted pylons that rise into the sky carrying urns adorned with typically Deco zigzag patterns. Urban illustrated Hearst's grand intentions for his building's role in the cultural life of the city by flanking each of these pylons with a pair of allegorical statues, by German-born and -trained Henry Kreis (for Kreis, see also 12.1).

The statues represent—counterclockwise from south to north—*Sport and Industry* at the corner of 56th Street, *Comedy and Tragedy* to the left and *Music and Art* to the right above the Eighth Avenue entrance, *Printing and the Sciences* at the corner of 57th Street, and *Comedy and Tragedy* and *Music and Art* repeated in the middle of the 57th Street façade.

***Cross to the west side of Eighth Avenue for a closer look at the Hearst Building. Then turn left and walk south along Eighth Avenue to West 56th Street. Turn right on West 56th and walk to Ninth Avenue, cross Ninth Avenue, and continue halfway down 56th Street toward Tenth Avenue.***

## 7.8 Twentieth Century Fox Building (now High School for Environmental Studies), 444 West 56th Street (Plate 11) Joseph J. Furman, 1929–30

The great American film studio, Twentieth Century Fox, had its headquarters in Los Angeles, but also maintained a presence in New York City. The company built the Fox Exchange, at 345 West 44th Street, for sales and distribution, while Fox Movietone News had quarters on West 54th Street—here, according to the 1939 *WPA Guide to New York City*, "newsreels are edited for release. Shots taken in the afternoon can be made ready for a Broadway showing on the same evening." Fox also maintained a suite of rooms for its executives in Hampshire House (7.5).

The company built No. 444 West 56th Street as offices and a film storage facility, bringing in Joseph J. Furman, architect of the West 44th Street facility. Furman (1890–1975), born in Kingston, New York, learned his trade as an apprentice and opened his firm in 1923. Much of his work was commercial, but also included the early-Modern Forest Hills Jewish Center (1949).

For West 56th Street, Furman designed a simple five-story loft building on a street otherwise occupied by modest tenements. But he dolled up the building's façade with abstract brick patterns and fanciful cast-stone panels—the kind of inexpensive ornament that could make even a simple loft building seem stylish, up-to-date, and fashionable. The patterned brick work is most notable in the zigzag roofline, but also shows up as rectangular layering in the simple columns separating the windows.

The cast-stone geometry can also be found at the roofline, but positively explodes at the main entrance in shapes suggesting orange slices, sine curves, boomerangs, panpipes, and more.

***Walk back to Ninth Avenue, turn left, and walk north along Ninth Avenue five blocks to West 61st Street. Across the street, on the northeast corner of West 61st Street and Columbus Avenue, stands the Sofia Apartments.***

## 7.9 *Kent Automatic Parking Garage or Kent Columbus Garage (now Sofia Apartments), 45 Columbus Avenue Jardine, Hill & Murdock, 1929–30

The last building on our walk is a relic of a time when the west side of Midtown, stretching north along Broadway and beyond, housed New York's automobile industry. Descended from the horse-and-carriage district of the Victorian city, centered around Long Acre Square before its renaming for the *New York Times*, the automobile industry moved west to Eleventh Avenue—even today lined with car dealerships—and north along Broadway as far as 72nd Street. General Motors once stood at 57th Street, and the U.S. Rubber Company at Columbus Circle, with buildings for Ford, B. F. Goodrich, and the Automobile Club of America nearby. The Kent Columbus Garage, today the sole survivor of automobile row on this stretch of Columbus Avenue, once counted among its neighbors on the block a Packard Motor Car Company showroom.

As cars entered early-twentieth-century Midtown in ever greater numbers, the need for adequate parking emerged as a major urban puzzle. In

1927, the Kent Automatic Parking Garage company announced the construction of a twenty-eight-story "motor hotel" on East 43rd Street, to open in 1928, and in 1929 built a second facility here on Columbus Avenue. By 1930, Kent had built half-a-dozen "skyscraper" or "vertical" garages, including outlets in Newark, Philadelphia, and Chicago. As the Kent company described its automated system: "The customer drives into the garage, shuts off his motor, accepts his check and leaves. From that time until he himself starts his motor to drive the car away, his automobile is never moved by its own power. All handling and parking of the automobile while in the building is done entirely by electric service"—that service provided by "the new Kent electric parkers" designed to grab hold of a car's rear axle and drag it from "high speed, self leveling elevators" to its designated parking spot. The company failed in 1931—perhaps due to a combination of crashed stock market and broken axles—but the Columbus Avenue building, with a capacity of a thousand cars, continued in use as a garage. In 1944 the building—even then one of the largest garages in the country—fell into the hands of Sofia Brothers, who pulled out the parking equipment and operated the former garage as a warehouse until its conversion to condominium apartments in 1984.

Such a modern building type might seem to call for a "modernistic design." Nevertheless, the architects, Jardine, Hill & Murdock—a firm dating back to Victorian days as D. & J. Jardine—used a Renaissance-inspired style for the East Side Kent garage. Only here on Columbus Avenue did they opt for Deco. As this is a parking garage, rather than a corporate headquarters, it has a modest design, relying on geometrically patterned brick in several colors, and glazed terra-cotta ornament mildly suggestive of Aztec influence.

*Cross to the east side of Columbus Avenue and walk to the entrance.*

The combination of geometric patterns, vivid colors, and vertical window bays clearly links the building to the newly modern metropolis. The terracotta is particularly pronounced at the roofline and setbacks, but especially around the wide ground-floor openings—originally the garage's entrance, here on Columbus, and exit, around the corner on West 61st (leaving the open space at the corner for use as a gas station). Take a close look at the angular stonework and contrasting colors of the terra-cotta.

The 1984 condo conversion punched dozens of windows into the formerly blank 61st Street façade, and the widening of the windows on the Columbus Avenue façade, but otherwise did little damage to the original design.

Plate 1
Cities Service Building, 70 Pine Street (originally "60 Wall Tower") (1.6)

PLATE 2
New York Telephone Company (Barclay-Vesey) Building,
140 West Street (2.4)

PLATE 3

Health, Hospitals and Sanitation Building, 125 Worth Street (2.8)

Plate 4
Two Park Avenue Building (3.4)

Plate 5
Chrysler Building (5.4)

Plate 6
Chanin Building (5.5)

PLATE 7
Film Center Building, 630 Ninth Avenue (5.11)

Plate 8
RCA (later GE) Building, 570 Lexington Avenue (6.4/6.6)

Plate 9
Goelet Building, 608 Fifth Avenue (6.9)

PLATE 10
Fuller Building (7.2)

Plate 11
Twentieth Century Fox Building, 444 West 56th Street (7.8)

Plate 12
Eldorado Apartments (8.9)

PLATE 13
888 Grand Concourse Apartments (12.3)

Plate 14
Park Plaza Apartments, 1005 Jerome Avenue (12.4)

Plate 15
1150 Grand Concourse (12.7)

Plate 16
Paul J. Rainey Memorial Gates (12.12)

# ITINERARY NO. 8
# UPPER WEST SIDE: CENTRAL PARK WEST

We take a pleasant stroll along Central Park West for a closer look at the buildings that form Manhattan's major residential skyline, including the great twin-towered skyscraper-apartment houses—the Century (8.1), the Majestic (8.3), and the Eldorado (8.9)—that tower over Central Park, and other multicolored Jazz Age fantasies of high living.

*The walk begins at Central Park West and West 62nd Street, on the Central Park side.*

You are standing at the southern tip of the Upper West Side's most prestigious avenue, and near the southwest corner of the grand park whose proximity created the neighborhood. Once well to north of the center of town, the Upper West Side began to attract land speculators in the 1860s, thanks to the hatching of plans for Central Park. Compared to the east side of the park, development here came late, not really getting underway until the mid-1870s. Once the Ninth Avenue elevated began service in 1880, development picked up enormously, and by 1900—just twenty years later—tightly packed rows of houses lined formerly empty side streets, while flats and tenements proliferated along Columbus and Amsterdam Avenues. Central Park West, on the other hand, attracted speculators who simply bought and resold property at a profit—as late as 1893, city maps showed most of its blocks as vacant, with a few exceptions like the American Museum of Natural History (1874–77) at West 79th Street and the Dakota Apartments (1880–84) at West 72nd Street.

In 1890, a prescient real estate broker wrote, "Central Park West seems to have only one future—it is destined to become an avenue of grand apartment houses and hotels. Everything tends that way. It is too public a thoroughfare to become a private residential avenue." And indeed, over the next thirty-five years, Central Park West sprouted Beaux-Arts apartment houses, including the Prasada at 65th Street, the Langham at 73rd, and the Kenilworth at 75th, with small religious and cultural institutions scattered in between, like Ethical Culture at 63rd Street, the Second Church of Christ,

336 Central Park West
Ardsley Apartments
320 Central Park West
El Dorado Apartments
300 Central Park West
Society for the Advancement of Judaism
15 West 86 Street
5 West 86 Street
40 West 86 Street
241 Central Park West
10 West 74 Street
Majestic Apartments
115 Central Park West
55 Central Park West
Century Apartments
25 Central Park West
86 St Transverse
79 St Transverse
Manhattan Square
Central Park
Lincoln Towers
Lincoln Center
Columbus Circle
Central Park South
Central Park West
West End
Broadway
Amsterdam
Columbus
© Tauranac, Ltd., 2016. All Rights Reserved.

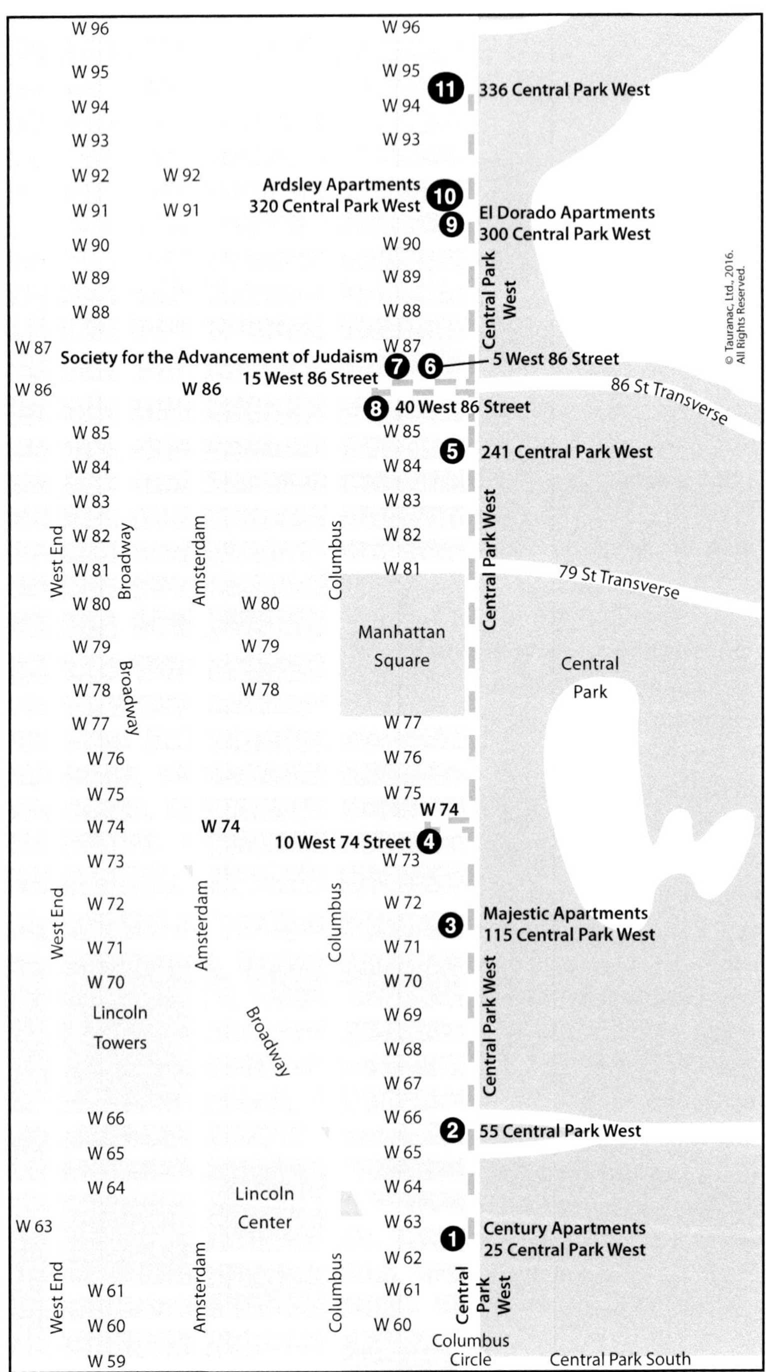

MAP 8

Scientist at 68th, and the Shearith Israel synagogue at 70th. Development continued into the 1920s with more apartment houses in typically eclectic styles. By the late 1920s, Central Park West seemed largely complete—but one last burst of construction awaited. From 1928 to 1932, half a dozen major buildings brought color and jazz to the formerly sedate boulevard, while four twin-towered buildings—three of them Art Deco—transformed Central Park West's skyline almost overnight.

Part of that transformation can be attributed to the 1929 Multiple Dwelling Act of New York State. As the *Times* noted in July of 1930:

> The benefits of the multiple-dwelling act in respect to fine residential dwellings are being clearly demonstrated this year, both in architectural style and the addition of many terraced or set-back apartments, giving the latter many of the conveniences of the penthouse apartment. This new type of apartment building is especially noticeable this season on Central Park West, where every one of the five new multi-family home structures reveals very distinctly the marked difference in apartment architecture from that which prevailed in the older houses. . . . Central Park West seems . . . assured of becoming an avenue of which New Yorkers may justly be proud.

***Look across the street at Central Park West, between West 62nd and 63rd Streets.***

## 8.1 ★(HD) Century Apartments, 25 Central Park West Irwin S. Chanin, with Jacques Delamarre, 1931

With the construction of just two buildings, the Century Apartments and the Majestic Apartments (8.3), built in barely one year, Irwin Chanin made a bigger splash on the skyline of Central Park West than any other architect or developer. He also brought a French connection, having spent a month in Paris in 1925 visiting the famed Exposition. On his return to New York, he became one of the country's first architects to adopt Art Deco ornament for large building projects, including his company headquarters, the Chanin Building (5.5) on East 42nd Street.

Chanin developed plans for his two Central Park West towers more or less simultaneously, acquiring the Majestic plot in April 1929 and the Century plot in May. Each took its name from a building formerly on the site—the Majestic from the old Majestic Hotel, and the Century from the former Century Theater. The Century Theater dated back to 1909, built as the New Theatre when it looked like Columbus Circle might overtake Times Square as New York's theater district. Chanin became interested in theaters in the 1920s, building six Broadway houses, including a complex of three theaters and a hotel on 44th and 45th Streets between 7th and 8th Avenues. The Shubert family controlled most of the other Broadway theaters. They'd also acquired the Century Theater in 1920, but in 1929 Chanin set his sights on it. In a major property swap, the Shuberts took over Chanin's theaters in Times Square—in what is now called "Shubert Alley"—and gave Chanin the Century Theatre. But Chanin didn't want the theater for dramatic purposes—he coveted its site for a dramatic new building.

That building was not the Century Apartments. Chanin initially concocted plans for a sixty-five-story tower, intended as a French-American collaboration, to be called the "Palais de France." With joint French and American financing, the Palais would have included three stories of exhibition space for French products, twenty-seven stories for a hotel, and thirty stories on top of that for various French offices—not to mention, according to the *Times* in September 1929, an "Academie des Beaux-Arts" to teach French language and history, art and literature, music, drama, and ballet. Add to that the French Consulate, Commercial Attaché, and National Tourist Bureau, and the Palais would have become the "center of French activities in America." Naturally, Chanin wanted to design it in a French-inspired style—in other words, Art Deco.

But Chanin didn't plan a mock-French tower. The *Times* quoted him on the subject: "While Europe is the motherland in the development of the so-called modernistic tendencies in design, it is my own opinion that America is rationalizing these ideas and is making them fit into the scheme of things more successfully than Europe. I did not see abroad any modernistic interiors or furniture that approaches either in beauty or usefulness that which is becoming fairly common in New York." Chanin characterized his design as "modern French style adapted to the exigencies of American skyscraper construction." Instead of a Palais de France—a French Palace—he designed an American skyscraper.

Unfortunately for Chanin, his plans for the Palais de France collapsed in 1930, along with the stock market. Chanin replaced the scrapped project with a twin-towered apartment house, at thirty stories tall just half the height of the Palais, and remarkably similar to the Majestic, which he had just designed. No question that Chanin's French connection shows up in both designs—but by the time the Century opened, in January 1932, the *Times* could describe it as "modern American"—so much for French style. France, of course, didn't build skyscrapers. Chanin adapted the modernistic American skyscraper to residential use. The Century Apartments' details owe more, perhaps, to Raymond Hood's contemporary Daily News Building (5.1) than to anything Chanin might have seen in France.

***Stand at the corner of West 62nd Street and look up at the towers.***

The Century's twin-tower silhouette reflects the requirements for light and air of the new 1929 Multiple Dwelling Act. Four such twin-towered buildings mark the Central Park West skyline. Emery Roth designed the first, the San Remo at 75th Street, using a style based on Italian Renaissance forms. But the next three—the Eldorado (8.9), the Majestic (8.3), and the Century, all built within a year of each other—adopted the new modernistic approach. (A fifth twin-tower project on Central Park West, at 102nd Street, was announced in the press in October 1930, but nothing came of it.)

Century Apartments

Standing at the corner of West 62nd Street, you can see both the Central Park West and the West 62nd Street façades of the Century, and take in its impressive bulk. Even at thirty stories instead of sixty-five, the Century takes up its entire block front and a good chunk of the entire block back toward Broadway, and has a massive, three-dimensional presence, very much like an enormous piece of sculpture. Its towers rise three hundred feet—about the same height as the towers of St. Patrick's Cathedral. The red and white color cuts both horizontally and vertically, but the main thrust comes from the six broad lines of wide bays with slightly rounded windows across the Central Park West façade, with red brick spandrels reminiscent of those at the Daily News Building. Look carefully: the lines of the casement windows run into lines of

Daily News Building

brick set in ornamental crisscross patterns, carrying the vertical thrust up and down the façade.

Corner windows before long became standard for 1930s apartment buildings, but Chanin's were among the first. He called the corner window a "solarium" and outfitted each one with imported English glass said to allow ultraviolet rays into the apartments—just one of the building's many interior luxuries, along with sunken living rooms, fireplaces, and "creak-proof" hardwood floors.

*Cross to the west side of Central Park West.*

Take a close look at the building's details: abstract stone patterns surrounding the main entrance; horizontal lines at the base, just above the sidewalk, and especially the corner-store entrance at West 62nd Street, directly below the corner windows. The windows above, with no corner columns, suggest a sensation of floating above the street, but at street-level the recessed entrance of the storefront makes that sensation palpable.

*Walk west along West 62nd Street to see the building from the rear.*

According to the Century's original sales brochure: "Towers, roofs and terraces make the building as interesting from the air as from the street." Its wonderful geometries show up better when seen from Broadway—especially the geometric fantasy of the tower caps, and the building's cascading levels.

Though Chanin completed the Majestic and Century almost simultaneously, he designed the Century second, and later said that he preferred it to the Majestic, especially the more complex crown of the towers, and the details of the bay windows and balconies. Chanin chose the Century for his own use, and lived here well into his nineties.

*Return to the east side of Central Park West, turn left, and walk north along Central Park West to the southeast corner of West 65th Street. Look north on Central Park West toward the southwest corner of West 66th Street.*

## 8.2 (HD) 55 Central Park West
## Schwartz & Gross, 1930

How peculiar—the higher up this building you look, the more its color seems to lighten. That's not an illusion. Like several skyscrapers built the same year—Raymond Hood's McGraw-Hill (5.8/5.12) and Ralph Walker's Western Union (2.6)—No. 55 has that color change built into the materials.

It's not just that the color gets lighter as the building rises. The building has two principal colors at the bottom. Most of the façade is a dark red, forming a contrasting background for a lighter orange cast-stone ornament. There's something fiery about those bright orange cast-stone forms—they suggest flames licking their way up the façade, and casting bright light onto the brick spandrels in the three center bays directly above them. As the building rises, the red and orange gradually merge into a single, lighter shade in the upper stories. Those cast-stone flame forms return at the building's top stories at each of the building's setbacks.

*Cross to the north side of West 65th Street.*

Look carefully, and you can spot the lines where one color shades into the next. The first change happens just above the fourth story—try to follow the changing brick all the way up.

Architects Simon Schwartz (1877?–1956) and Arthur Gross (1877–1950), both graduates of New York's Hebrew Technical Institute, formed their partnership in 1902, and churned out dozens of apartment houses and hotels. Their early work took inspiration from the usual classical and eclectic sources, but by the late 1920s they had turned modernistic. Their building at No. 55—seventeen stories tall—replaced not a row house, but a nine-story apartment building, suggesting just how dramatically population density was pushing up building heights on Central Park West.

*Cross to the west side of Central Park West.*

Take a closer look at the details. The flaming orange projections at the base are especially wide at the entrance. The window spandrels—whether orange or red—have simple, slightly projecting brick lines that alternate in length, suggesting an up-and-down motion. (Note the damage that through-the-wall air conditioners can do to historic buildings—many here are rammed straight through those spandrels. Through-the-window air conditioners might seem unsightly, but they don't hurt the building fabric.) As you look up, notice that even in what seem to be separate sections of brick, the colors vary from one brick to the next.

Don't miss the metal marquee shading the entrance, or the wonderful candy-cane spiral and floral ornament built into the door frames.

*Cross to the northwest corner of West 66th Street.*

Most of the casement windows on Central Park West have been replaced with picture windows—no doubt for the enjoyment of unobstructed park views. On the West 66th Street façade, however, the casements survive more or less intact, so you can see the important part they play in the building's geometric design.

***Cross back to the east side of Central Park West, turn left, and walk north to the southeast corner of Central Park West and West 71st Street to look at the Majestic Apartments, occupying the block between West 71st and 72nd Streets.***

## 8.3 ★(HD) Majestic Apartments, 115 Central Park West Irwin S. Chanin, 1930–31

The Majestic looks remarkably like its slightly younger sibling ten blocks to the south (8.1)—though some details do differ. Late in life, Chanin told historian Andrew Dolkart that he considered the Majestic "experimental"—wondering if the market would accept such a modernistic approach in a residential building (though in fact Blum and Blum had already designed No. 210 East 68th Street [10.7] two years earlier).

Chanin's original plan in 1929 called for a forty-five-story "full-service apartment hotel" described by the *Times* in April as having "large dining rooms, a grand ball room and smaller quarters for social activities." In June of 1930, the Crash cut the project down to size, just as it had the Century—leading to another thirty-story twin-towered apartment house.

Noticeable differences from the Century include the colors (more red and white at the Century), the arrangement of the windows across the façade, and the Century's somewhat more sculptural windows—the Majestic has no bowed curving window bays. On the other hand, the Majestic façade in general seems more three-dimensional than the Century's, with projecting brick horizontal courses and vertical brick piers. Other details are identical—notably the metal balustrades in the upper levels, and the corner windows (his "solariums").

Chanin considered those windows a major innovation, "made possible by the omission of the usual supporting vertical steel columns at the corners of the building" and the cantilevering of the floors on "heavy central columns"—an arrangement he credited to German examples. He suggested that in the summer, "the glass in the solariums may be removed to provide an open terrace." According to the *Times* in July 1930, he also planned "a large solarium on the roof."

***Cross to the northwest corner of Central Park West and West 71st Street.***

Take a closer look at the details, especially the various brick patterns and the window arrangements. Look carefully at the top of the three-story stone base on West 71st Street, just below the tall vertical window bays set between projecting brick piers. Where the brick piers meet the stone base, a series of notches marks their transformation into stone—a small detail, but a careful one.

***Cross back to the park side, and walk north to the northeast corner of Central Park West and West 72nd Street.***

From this corner, you can see both the Central Park West and the West 72nd Street façades. You can also compare the Majestic with its nineteenth-century opposite number on the north side of West 72nd Street—the Dakota Apartments. In the mid-1880s, the Dakota's architect, Henry Hardenbergh, seems to have asked himself what would be the appropriate model for a building housing hundreds of people, and answered—typically for his day—with an established European prototype, modeling the Dakota on German Renaissance palaces. In the late 1920s, Irwin Chanin answered the same question by modeling the Majestic not on an ancient European palace but on a modern New York skyscraper.

***Walk north along Central Park West to West 74th Street; the San Remo occupies the block front between West 74th and 75th.***

The comparison of Chanin's Century and Majestic with Emery Roth's San Remo is stunning. The San Remo is the same twin-towered building, but clothed in traditional garb. Chanin took the new twin-towered residential skyscraper and brought it up to date with 1930 zigzag modernism.

***Cross to the west side of Central Park West and walk west a short distance on West 74th Street to No. 10.***

## 8.4 (HD) 10 West 74th Street H. Herbert Lilien, 1940

From thirty-story, multicolored, Roaring-Twenties, twin-towered giants on Central Park West to a ten-story, all-white, modest side-street late-Depression-era building might seem like quite a leap—but these buildings do have some things in common. No. 10 might look more comfortable in Washington Heights or the West Bronx—not surprisingly, since that's where Herbert Lilien did much of his work. Compared to the Central Park West towers, the strong vertical lines are gone, and the wild brick patterns subdued, but something of the modernistic approach survives here, even if it's better called Moderne than Art Deco. Chanin's solarium corner windows, a brick façade rising above a stone base with horizontal speed lines, geometrically patterned brickwork at the roof line—though much simpler than anything on Central Park

West—and even a certain amount of blocky geometry thanks to the inset entrance, all link this building to its grander neighbors.

***Return to Central Park West, cross to the park side, turn left, and enjoy a pleasant stroll north along Central Park West to the southeast corner of West 84th Street. Look across the intersection at the northwest corner.***

## 8.5 (HD) 241 Central Park West
## Schwartz & Gross, 1930–31

Loud, brightly colored cast-stone sculptural ornament against a brick background—yes, No. 241 Central Park West is another design by Schwartz & Gross, begun shortly after they'd completed No. 55 (8.2). No color growing lighter here as the building rises, but the architects brought the same sense of brightly contrasting colors of brick and cast stone. Instead of flame-like forms at the base and setbacks, they designed what look like modernistic versions of calla lilies.

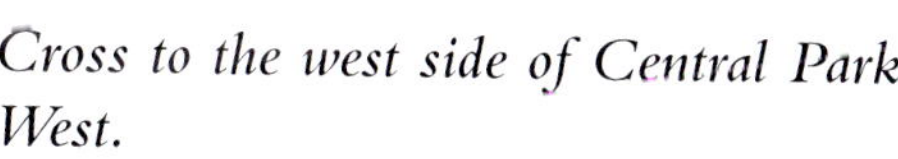

***Cross to the west side of Central Park West.***

Up close, those calla lilies are huge—two stories tall, projecting dramatically from the brick façade. The first-story cast-stone façade from which they spring is thoroughly ribbed—nothing flat here. The brick spandrels are, as usual, slightly recessed, but instead of a geometric pattern—as at No. 55—they simply sport a startling purple color in the center of each façade.

This nineteen-story building replaced eight row houses, not unlike the rare surviving group that fills out the block at the corner of West 85th Street. Though lacking the corner windows of Chanin's buildings, the apartments also enjoy sunken living rooms, considered a great attraction at the time. As described in an April 1931 *Times* ad: "Much of the charm of the Living Room is achieved in the Dropped Floor. That's what is so unusual about 241 Central Park West. Every apartment has a dropped-living room which lends itself so much better to interior arrangement. The railed gallery gives the final artistic touch. Bathrooms color tiled, kitchens white tiled throughout with metal kitchen cabinets. Suites of 3 to 7 Rooms. Bath to every chamber. Occupancy August 1st."

The building briefly became less famous for its sunken living rooms than for its notoriety in 1932 as the residence of former bouncer "Salvy Spitale," one of two men authorized as go-betweens for the Lindberghs in potential negotiations with their baby's kidnappers.

***Continue north along Central Park West to West 86th Street. Turn left onto West 86th Street and walk west a short distance until you're across the street from Nos. 5 and 15.***

## 8.6 (HD) 5 West 86th Street
## Boak & Paris, 1937

The tall apartment house at No. 5 and the adjoining low synagogue at No. 15 (8.7) might look like one project, but in fact they are two separate buildings, built a year apart, to designs by two different architectural firms.

Boak & Paris (for Boak & Paris, see 11.6) always bring their own particular flavor to Art Deco buildings. A much simpler building than its fancier cousins around the corner on Central Park West, No. 5 uses modest materials—brick, cast stone, and terra-cotta—in modest ways, but with corner windows, casements, and a set-back tower, making it unmistakably part of the Deco family. Particularly inventive ornament: the two-story cast-stone base with ribbed piers between the second-story windows; a cast-stone band course in the form of waves running across the seventh story; more cast-stone bands at the setbacks, with odd wheels over a long fasces (bundle of sticks tied together); and patterned brickwork. Note the interesting break in symmetry at the building's center: two columns of wide windows, separated by a projecting brick course, seem to mark the building's midpoint, but at the base, where you'd expect to find two entranceways, one under each set of windows, you'll find only one.

No. 5 replaced five row-houses, one of which had earlier been the home of the infamous "Diamond Jim" Brady.

## 8.7 (HD) Society for the Advancement of Judaism, 15 West 86th Street Albert Goldhammer, 1938–39

The Society for the Advancement of Judaism bought a house on this site in 1925 and converted it into "a modern house of study" with a school, auditorium, gymnasium, and library. Thirteen years later, the growing institution commissioned a new façade from Albert Goldhammer. Whether or not intentionally, Goldhammer designed a cast-stone first story and brick and cast-stone façade above that roughly matches its neighbor at No. 5. Goldhammer certainly designed his share of Art Deco buildings. On closer inspection, however, the details of his synagogue turn out to be based on more traditional forms, and on Jewish motifs, rather than on zigzags. Some have called the building's style "Modern Semitic."

*Continue west on West 86th Street to No. 40.*

## 8.8 (HD) 40 West 86th Street Jacob M. Felson, 1930–31

This is a much earlier work than Felson's buildings (for Felson, see 11.2) in Washington Heights (11.2, 11.4b, 11.13, 11.15) and the Bronx (12.8, 12.9), and quite different in its details—an unusual design unlike most other Art Deco buildings in New York. It's a collection of typically Deco ornament, in terra cotta and cast stone, but set against a background of brick in varied patterns and glazes. The glazed terra-cotta spandrels below the third-story windows at either end sprout multicolored vegetation, while the spandrels above are set in wavy brick. The entryway is framed by ribbed columns with fanciful capitals, and the windows to either side by yet another geometric pattern. The more you look at the details of this relatively simple façade, the more you'll see.

*Walk west to the corner of Columbus Avenue, cross to the north side of West 86th Street, then walk back east along West 86th until you're across the street from No. 40.*

From here you can see the brightly colored terra-cotta panels at the top of No. 40. The only comparable example would be the flash of colored terra-cotta at the top of the Towne House apartments on West 38th Street (3.1).

*Continue walking east on West 86th Street to Central Park West, cross to the east side, turn left, and walk north on Central Park West to West 89th Street. Look north to the Eldorado Apartments, occupying the block front from West 90th to 91st Streets.*

## 8.9 ⋆(HD) Eldorado Apartments, 300 Central Park West (Plate 12) Margon & Holder and Emery Roth, 1929–31

Central Park West's first Art Deco twin-towered apartment building came not from Chanin's office, but from the lesser-known firm of Margon & Holder, in association with, of all people, Emery Roth, who generally resisted the modernistic (for Roth, see 9.2). According to his biographer, Steve Ruttenbaum, Roth—master of the apartment-house type—handled the apartment layouts and general massing of the building, neither much different from his recently completed San Remo. Roth's few drawings for the project show either classical or Romanesque-inspired detailing. Margon & Holder sprinkled modernistic details across the façade.

*Walk to the middle of the block on Central Park West between West 89th and 90th Streets.*

Like the Century (8.1) and the Majestic (8.3), the Eldorado takes its name from the buildings it replaced—two eight-story buildings called the "Eldorado" flats. The new project went through several stages, beginning as a sixteen-story building, but eventually its towers rose to three hundred feet.

Little is known about the partnership of Irving Margon (c.1888–1958) and Adolph M. Holder. Margon designed tenements and apartment houses from as early as 1916, working alone until 1921, then in partnership with Charles Glaser, and finally joining forces with Holder in 1928. Back on his own in 1932, Margon continued designing apartment buildings into the 1950s. Margon and Glaser designed apartment buildings in the Bronx as well as Manhattan, so Margon might have had connections with the Eldorado's Bronx-based developer, Louis Klosk. In any case, none of Margon & Holder's known works in Manhattan comes close to the exuberance and inventiveness of the Eldorado.

The building's overall arrangement is not the most sophisticated. Lacking the contrasting horizontal lines of Chanin's towers, the Eldorado relies almost entirely on verticals—with columns alternating between light and dark brick, and shallow projections or projecting piers, to divide the façade into eleven sections, two, three, or six windows wide. Where the Eldorado shines, rather, is in its color and ornament.

Unlike, say, the red and white of the Century, the Eldorado—appropriately enough for a building named for the mythical golden kingdom of South America—glows with yellow cast stone and yellow terra-cotta, contrasting with tamer tan and brown brick.

***Cross to the west side of Central Park West to see the ground-floor details.***

Unlike either the Century or the Majestic, which seem to follow Raymond Hood's example of simple, even stark, geometries, Margon & Holder's design is more in line with Cross & Cross's G. E. Building (6.4)—slathered with decorative forms, particularly the cornucopia of abstract geometrical flourishes surrounding the grand double-story triple entrance on Central Park West. Far more elaborate than any other Deco entrance on the avenue, the three entryways, set in angled bronze frames, sport elegant filigreed grilles crisscrossing their glass, while polished bronze birds flock at the upper corners, looking up at ornamental plaques stamped with lush Deco ornament. To the left and right, similar glass doors have filigreed grilles and simple curving handrails.

*Cross back to the east side of Central Park West.*

Across the Eldorado's middle stories, the architects have scattered stone and terra-cotta balconies with patterned brickwork and Art Deco railings. Terra-cotta panels and balconies continue up into the towers. But by far the most dramatic features are the darker, elaborate cast-stone pinnacles that crown each tower and make the Eldorado instantly recognizable from afar.

*Continue north along Central Park West to the corner of West 92nd Street to see the Ardsley Apartments on the southwest corner.*

## 8.10 (HD) Ardsley Apartments, 320 Central Park West Emery Roth, 1930–31

Emery Roth's design for the Ardsley—unlike most of his work—falls squarely into the Art Deco camp (for Roth, see 9.2), but in its own quite distinct version. Its façades offer a cascade of geometrically patterned cast stone and brickwork. Look carefully—the black brick lines project slightly beyond the buff brick background. A lot of low-relief work crosses still more low-relief work.

When asked about his use of the Moderne style, Roth explained, in the *New York Sun* in May 1931: "Architecture at all periods and at all times was 'moderne'. . . . Each building can be equally good and each would equally represent the spirit of these times. . . . I have a suspicion that these 'modern movements' have been going on ever since there was architecture." Roth went on to compare changing styles in architecture to changing tastes regarding beauty in women: "Art Nouveau . . . went in for curves, while the 'modernistic' is going in for long straight lines. . . . This I can only explain [by] the fact that our ideal of beauty in 1900 was Anna Held and Lillian Russell of large curves, and the architects went for curved lines. Our ideals now are for the long and slim, and our architecture follows our taste in ladies."

*Cross to the west side of Central Park West.*

Wildly stylized zigzag cast-stone patterns show up everywhere—around the smaller entrances, in a narrow band above the first story, and especially at the main entrance, set within a triple-height surround. Perhaps the most interesting ornament is the multicolored band of cast stone that runs across the second story but dips to the first story at either corner.

Note the casement windows. Unlike other Central Park West buildings, where casement windows leave no room for an uninterrupted park view, at the Ardsley Roth made use of "view windows" surrounded by multipane sections. Roth made that decision as a part owner of the Ardsley.

*Walk north along Central Park West to West 92nd Street and cross to the north side of the street.*

The West 92nd Street façade is much longer than the façade on Central Park West. Follow it down the street to find yet more remarkable Deco ornament.

*Cross back to the east side of Central Park West, then turn left and walk north to the southeast corner of West 94th Street. Look across the street at 336 Central Park West on the southwest corner.*

## 8.11 (HD) 336 Central Park West
## Schwartz & Gross, 1928–29

Earliest of the Schwartz & Gross buildings on this walk (for Schwartz & Gross, see 8.2), No. 336 shows no sign of the color explosions to come over the next two years, but its modernistic detail, designed in 1928, puts it right

up front with the city's earliest Deco apartment buildings. And it shares with the firm's other Central Park West buildings an inventive approach to brick and cast stone. Details to watch for: the two-story-tall cast-stone entranceway, which bows out over the doors, and the inventively patterned brick, which varies in color and shape, and projects out or is recessed in—note the patterns, for instance, directly below the first-story windows. Most unusual is the handling of the brick at the roofline—laid out in a wavy pattern with something of the flavor of ancient Egypt.

# ITINERARY NO. 9
# UPPER WEST SIDE: BROADWAY AND RIVERSIDE DRIVE

The Upper West Side has so much Art Deco that it requires a second, separate walk along its western edge. This walk takes us from West 84th Street to West 104th Street, principally along Broadway and Riverside Drive. We see work by such stalwart Manhattan Deco icons as Sugarman & Berger, Boak & Paris, and Harvey Wiley Corbett, as well as architects less well known for their Deco productions, including Emery Roth and Rosario Candela. Highlights include Roth's Normandy Apartments (9.2) and Corbett's Master Apartments (9.12); the Broadway Fashion Building (9.1)—four stories of commercial space in a Moderne glass box; Joan of Arc Junior High School (9.6); Boak & Paris's Midtown (now Metro) Theater (9.9); and one of Manhattan's last surviving Horn & Hardart automat buildings (9.10), with splendid Art Deco terra-cotta.

***The walk begins at the northeast corner of Broadway and West 84th Street. Look across the intersection at the southwest corner.***

## 9.1 (HD) Broadway Fashion Building, 2315 Broadway Sugarman & Berger, 1930–31

That remarkable four-story building across the intersection, with the curving corner, has a façade almost 90 percent glass. According to the *Times* in November 1930, the building would include "a system of exterior and interior illumination [that] will give the structure an unusual appearance at night." Twenty years later, the all-glass look became the hallmark of International Style office buildings, but Sugarman & Berger beat them to it (for Sugarman & Berger, see 4.4).

The reason for the all-glass façade had to do with the building's rental strategy: while more typical commercial buildings

Riverside Park
W 106
West End
Broadway
W 105
W 104
315 Riverside Drive
Master Institute
310 Riverside Drive
Former Horn & Hardart
2710 Broadway
W 103
W 102
W 101
W 100
Riverside Dr
Broadway
Amsterdam
Columbus
Manhattan
Henry Hudson Parkway
Midtown Theater (Metro)
2624 Broadway
W 99
W 98
Park West
W 97
W 96
W 95
W 94
Riverside Dr
West End Av
Westwind Apartments
175 West 93 Street
Joan of Arc
154 West 93 Street
W 93
W 92
180 West 93 Street;
175 West 92 Street
Central Park West
Riverside Park
W 91
W 90
W 89
W 88
W 87
57 West 86 Street
Normandy Apartments
140 Riverside Drive
W 86
565 West End Avenue
New Amsterdam Apartments
200 West 86 Street
W 85
W 84
Broadway Fashion Building
2315 Broadway
W 83
W 82
W 81
W 80
W 79
W 78
Manhattan Square
© Tauranac, Ltd., 2016.
All Rights Reserved.

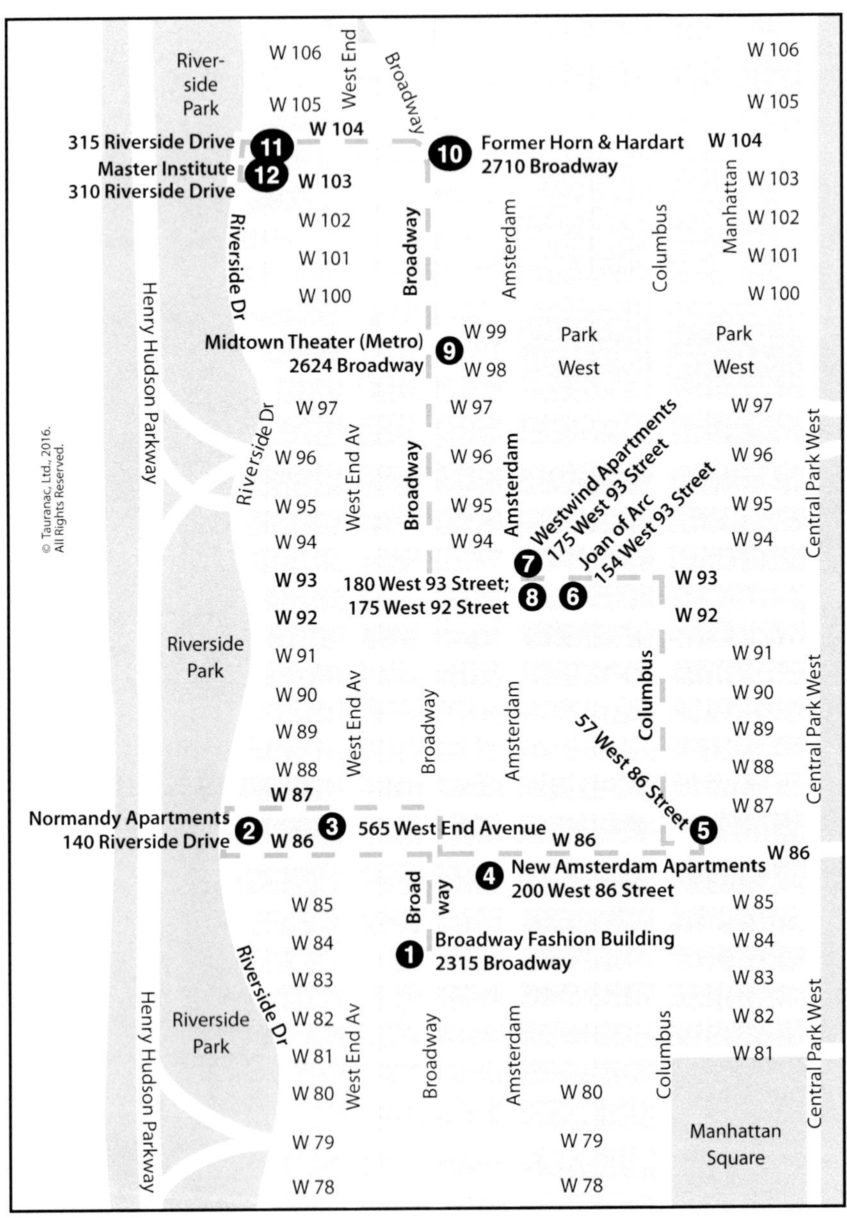

MAP 9

had storefronts on the ground floor with offices above, the Broadway Fashion Building offered four stories of storefronts, all brilliantly lit by daytime sunlight. Tenants in the upper stories included such light-sensitive enterprises as the Marlborough Galleries, which held art auctions on the third floor, while down on the ground floor Geffner's Restaurant and Bakery advertised its new home as a "Modern Uptown Eating Place."

*Cross to the west side of Broadway for a closer look.*

The building's nonglass 10 percent includes white stainless metal spandrels with flashy geometric patterning set between black glazed terra-cotta columns, and a roofline of stylized floral patterns that seem positively alive.

*Walk north along Broadway to West 86th Street; turn left on West 86th and walk west to West End Avenue; cross West End Avenue and continue west along West 86th Street to Riverside Drive. Cross to the Riverside Park side of the Drive, and stand at the southwest corner of West 86th Street and Riverside Drive looking back across the intersection to the Normandy Apartments, occupying the block of Riverside Drive from West 86th to 87th Streets.*

## 9.2 *(HD)Normandy Apartments, 140 Riverside Drive Emery Roth & Sons, 1938–39

Towering eighteen stories above Riverside Park, overlooking the mighty Hudson River, the Normandy was the last of the grand pre–World War II apartment houses built on the Upper West Side, and the only one that brought the twin-towered skyline profile of Central Park West over to Riverside Drive. Not surprisingly, it is among the last designs of Emery Roth, one of New York's preeminent twentieth-century designers of apartment houses and hotels, who designed two of the four twin-towered buildings on Central Park West—the San Remo and, as a consultant, the Eldorado (8.9)—at the beginning of the decade.

Emery Roth came to the United States alone, at age thirteen; got himself a draftsman's job at the 1893 World's Columbian Exposition in Chicago, where he met architect Richard

Morris Hunt; moved to New York to work in Hunt's office—and developed a great love of classical and Italian Renaissance architecture that he never gave up, even in the 1930s. Roth designed the San Remo, the first, but also the only non-Deco, twin-towered apartment house on Central Park West. Ten years later, he turned to the modernistic for the Normandy. Yet even here, Roth kept something of the Italian Renaissance he so loved, mixing classical details with modernistic design.

At the Normandy, Roth acted both as architect and, with three partners, as developer. The partners announced their intention to build "one of the largest multi-family edifices ever erected on Manhattan Island." True to Roth's inclinations, they announced its design as "in the Italian Renaissance style of the same character as the San Remo Towers." In the *New York Sun* in September 1938, Roth explained his conception of the building's style: "Every building is ultra modern when erected, whether it is inspired by any one of the historic periods of architecture or whether it was planned with a conscious search for originality. . . . I am fond of so-called old Italian architecture. If today I designed a building of old Italian architecture it would emerge nevertheless as a modern structure, always to be recognized as of 1939."

Many have wondered if the Normandy took its name from the great Art Deco French ocean liner, the *Normandie*. The ship did attract much attention when it embarked on its much-ballyhooed hundredth trans-Atlantic crossing on July 13, 1938, just six weeks before Roth filed plans for his new building. Press coverage included a large photo and a page-three story in the *Times*. But if any connection existed, Roth apparently never mentioned it.

From across the street, the Normandy's blocky massing, its curving corners, and the horizontally striated lines incised in the stone base at the first and second stories, all have a distinctly Moderne flavor. Only up at the twin towers do specifically Italian details emerge—classical capitals on corner pilasters, and broken pediments over windows.

***Cross back to the east side of Riverside Drive, and walk east along the north side of West 86th Street to the West 86th Street entrance.***

The remarkable curving entrance on West 86th Street (and its twin on West 87th) looks strictly modernistic, especially the abstract geometric mosaic patterns—though Roth might have imagined them as up-to-date versions of Roman mosaics. They bear a striking resemblance to the entrance at No. 888 Grand Concourse (12.3), a Bronx apartment house designed by Roth in 1937.

*Walk west back to Riverside Drive, turn right, and walk north along Riverside Drive to the middle of the block.*

Normandy

Unlike the Central Park West twin-towered buildings, the Normandy has a garden court in a set-back area, where a balustraded fence with giant urns brings an Italian flavor. Perhaps the Normandy is best thought of as neither Renaissance nor Moderne—but, simply, as Emery Roth.

888 Grand Concourse

*Continue north on Riverside Drive to West 87th Street, turn right, and walk east on West 87th Street to the middle of the block.*

## 9.3 (HD) 565 West End Avenue Hyman I. Feldman, 1937

From the middle of the block on West 87th Street, you can see the top stories of a multicolored Art Deco apartment house, at the northwest corner of West 87th and West End Avenue, completed just a year before construction began at the Normandy.

*Continue east on West 87th Street to West End Avenue and cross to the east side of West End Avenue, then turn around to look back at the west side of West End.*

Unlike Emery Roth, Hyman Feldman apparently had no qualms about modernistic design. Corner windows—check. Sharp, geometric corners—check. Red and black patterned brick reminiscent of the Century Apartments or the Daily News Building—check again. And apartments featuring the usual sunken living rooms.

According to the *Times* in October 1937, "Much of the success in renting suites in the building is due to the fact that each apartment is different in layout and design, points out Mose Goodman, builder. The plan of individual suites, he explains, follows closely current trends in exclusive suburban home construction."

***Continue walking east on West 87th Street to the corner of Broadway and West 87th Street. Look across the street.***

The twin-towered look made a comeback in the 1980s, as in the rather bland example at the northeast corner of Broadway and West 87th Street (No. 2380 Broadway)—which even has curving corner windows in the towers—designed in 1983 by the Gruzen Partnership. Called the Montana—because, according to reporting in the *Times* in January 1983, "it's north of the Dakota"—it deliberately evoked an older Upper West Side style. The local community board, which weighed in on the plan, considered the proposal "something of a modern El Dorado or Majestic." The *Times* continued: "It is no accident that this building, rosy gray in color with a wide base built to the street line to a height of 13 stories and with narrower towers above, will have an old New York look in harmony with West Side buildings generally. The new special zoning district for land on the Upper West Side encourages construction in that manner."

***Walk south on Broadway to West 86th Street; turn left, cross to the east side of Broadway, and walk east on West 86th Street to Amsterdam Avenue. Look across the street at the long West 86th Street façade of 200 West 86th Street.***

### 9.4 (HD) New Amsterdam Apartments, 200 West 86th Street Schwartz & Gross, 1930

Though nothing like as eye-catching as Schwartz & Gross's three Central Park West buildings (8.2, 8.5, 8.11), the New Amsterdam shares with them some details—endless projecting brick piers, abstract geometric spandrels, and geometrically adorned balconies. Slender, ribbed cast-stone piers rise along the second and third stories and reappear at the setbacks, not unlike the orange flames at

55 Central Park West (8.2) or the calla lilies at 241 Central Park West (8.5), but flatter, and without the bright colors that make those two buildings so memorable.

*Continue east on West 86th Street to the northwest corner of West 86th Street and Columbus Avenue, and cross to the northeast corner of the intersection.*

## 9.5 (HD) 57 West 86th Street Fellheimer & Wagner, 1929

This small building has been through a lot. Built as two five-story houses in 1888 (architect John G. Prague), they were later joined and converted to apartments. Then the Corn Exchange Bank bought the property and hired Fellheimer & Wagner to create a new façade, with a new home for the bank on the first floor and apartments above. As the *Times* noted in reporting the conversion: "West Eighty-sixth Street has undergone a rapid transition from a block of high-class private houses into a street lined with fifteen-story apartment houses and hotels, and the rapid development and the rebuilding of Central Park West will greatly enhance this location from the standpoint of business and banking."

Alfred Fellheimer (1875–1959) and Steward Wagner (1886–1958) specialized in, among other things, banks. Their new façade for the Corn Exchange Bank makes use of all the typical modernistic wiles available for such a small project—an odd ribbing pattern at the top of the second-story windows; a geometrically patterned metal grill over the service door on the east; a stylized floral pattern, suggesting cornstalks (as in "Corn Exchange Bank") with flowers and vines, over the main door at the west; and ribbed columns stretching from the third to the fifth stories, standing on what look like modernistic tiptoes.

***Cross back to the west side of Columbus Avenue, turn right, and walk north on Columbus Avenue to West 93rd Street; turn left, and walk west on West 93rd Street, continuing halfway toward Amsterdam Avenue.***

## 9.6 Joan of Arc Junior High School, 154 West 93rd Street Eric Kebbon, 1939–40

Still a school, though no longer called "Joan of Arc," Eric Kebbon's building is one of the city's few Art Deco public schools, the other notable example being the Herman Ridder Junior High School (12.13) on Boston Road in the Bronx.

In 1938, Mayor Fiorello La Guardia appointed Kebbon (1891–1964) superintendent of school buildings for the New York Board of Education—effectively making him architect for all the city's schools—succeeding Walter C. Martin, architect of the Herman Ridder School (12.13). Kebbon, trained at MIT, had earlier designed new buildings at his alma mater, become a partner with William Welles Bosworth, and then designed post offices and courthouses for the U.S. Department of the Treasury. Eventually he designed more than a hundred New York public school buildings, but Joan of Arc—built to accommodate two thousand students—was among the first.

In 1939, the mayor presided over the school's groundbreaking ceremony—by one account, he intended to "touch off the first dynamite explosion at the site." Kebbon's design struck many as looking less like a school and more like a miniature tall office building. As described in the *Times* in November of 1940, "Known as the 'skyscraper' school, this is the only junior high school in New York City built in 'vertical' design." Apparently Martin's equally vertical Bronx junior high school of a decade earlier had been forgotten.

Kebbon's design earns the "vertical" label with its pairs of windows set between unbroken brick piers. Ornamentally, it is fairly severe—not unusual for 1940—but does include a wonderfully fanciful triple-height entrance inscribed at the top with the school's name, flanked by the French fleur-de-lis. Running up the middle of the entranceway, an extraordinary vine appears to grow out of a flowerpot and wrap around clusters of grapes, a crown, and a flaming brazier, as well as spears and swords—all no doubt symbolic of the story of Joan of Arc.

***Continue walking west on West 93rd Street to Amsterdam Avenue. At the intersection of Amsterdam Avenue, West 93rd Street is flanked by two period buildings: the "Westwind" on the northeast corner, and No. 565 West End Avenue on the southeast corner.***

## 9.7 Westwind Apartments, 175 West 93rd Street Rosario Candela, 1928

Rosario Candela made his mark with opulent 1920s apartment buildings on the Upper East and Upper West Sides—ten- to twenty room apartments wrapped in restrained versions of historical styles, especially neo-Georgian. His Westwind shows the influence of modernistic trends on its otherwise classical detailing, including the ribbed piers with stylized capitals at the entranceway and the cast-stone framing around selected windows at the second and third stories and again just below the roofline.

## 9.8 180 West 93rd Street and 175 West 92nd Street Horace Ginsbern, 1940

Horace Ginsbern (for Ginsbern, see 12.4) combines modernistic details—such as the rounded corners and porthole windows at the entrance to No. 180 and the geometrically patterned brick joining neighboring windows—with a horizontal emphasis and simplicity more suggestive of the budding International Style.

*Walk south to the middle of the block.*

These two buildings, designed as one project on the site of the Methodist Episcopal Home, represented, according to the *Times*, "the largest individual operation of the season" in "the West Side residential area." They opened the same year as the junior high school directly behind them.

*Continue south on Amsterdam Avenue to West 92nd Street, then turn right, cross Amsterdam Avenue, and walk west on West 92nd Street one more block to Broadway, then turn right and walk north on Broadway to West 99th Street. Cross to the west side of Broadway for a view of the midblock Midtown Theater.*

## 9.9 ★Midtown Theater (now Metro Theater), 2624 Broadway Boak & Paris, 1932–33

Though not one of their usual apartment houses, the Midtown Theater may be Boak & Paris's best-known Art Deco design (for Boak & Paris see 11.6). The great period of two-, three-, four-, and five-thousand-seat movie palaces ended with the Roaring Twenties. Several large Deco palaces did get built in California, but in New York, with the sole exception of Radio City Music Hall, Art Deco movie theaters were conceived as small-scale neighborhood houses. Not too many survive, and none can compete with the old Midtown Theater for its façade of beige and black glazed terra-cotta. Note that the vertical Deco features are joined by horizontal banding—a nod to the emerging Art Moderne—notably in the four chrome bands encircling the marquee and also the stripes flanking a side door at the theater's northern edge.

Despite the theater's original name, Broadway at 99th Street is not, by any stretch, Midtown Manhattan. Curiously, however, the façade's most striking element—the central circular panel with two dancers flanked by the masks of comedy and tragedy—looks remarkably similar to one of the much larger panels, designed by Hildreth Meière, adorning the flank of

Midtown Theater

Radio City Music Hall

Radio City Music Hall (6.10) built just one year earlier—perhaps a deliberate reference to the most famous "Midtown" theater of them all.

***Walk north along Broadway to the southeast corner of West 104th Street.***

## 9.10 *Former Horn & Hardart, 2710 Broadway F. P. Platt & Brother, 1930.

Horn & Hardart automats once not only dotted the city, but defined an urban way of life. They began in 1890s Philadelphia as an attempt to create a modern, automated dining service. They morphed in New York City, in the 1910s and 1920s, into a fast-food operation, and declined during the Depression years into sad hangouts where down-and-out New Yorkers famously put free ketchup into free hot water to make tomato soup and free lemons into free hot water to make lemonade. They survived into the 1950s and 1960s as a budget alternative and a great favorite with kids, who adored watching the change lady dole out hundreds of nickels with a sweep of her hand, and then choosing sandwiches or slices of pie released from stainless-steel compartments by a deposit of the appropriate number of nickels.

Despite their former ubiquity in the city, very few former Horn & Hardart buildings survive, in part because some decades ago Burger King acquired the company and revamped most of the automats in the image of that fast-food hamburger chain.

The original New York automat, built on Times Square in the first decade of the twentieth century, was an elaborate essay in Art Nouveau, but many of the automats built in the 1920s took on the modernistic coloration of their surroundings. Louis Allen Abramson, who designed a number of them, recalled, in an interview with the author, being instructed by the company's representative, "we like Modern, not Moderne." Abramson later said he had no idea what the man meant, but his own essays in automated dining indulged in Deco.

F. P. Platt & Brother (that would be Frederick Putnam and Charles Carsten Platt) designed by far the bulk of the New York automats. Though this one had seen its ground floor altered, enough of the original survived to have earned New York City Landmark designation—and as of late 2014 the original ground floor has been uncovered once again. The façade is especially notable for its glazed polychromatic terra-cotta—blue, green, tan, and gold. Details abound, but by far the most interesting are the panels along the top row of windows. Stylized floral patterns are standard Deco items, but this batch is particularly wild and inventive, suggesting to the Landmarks Commission staff that it might have been designed by Rene Chambellan, author, for instance, of the extraordinary ornamental bands at the Chanin Building (5.5) on East 42nd Street, or the Suffolk Title and Guarantee Building (14.10) in Queens.

***Walk west along West 104th Street to the southeast corner of Riverside Drive.***

## 9.11 315 Riverside Drive
## Boak & Paris, 1930–31

Yet another Boak & Paris design—once you know what they look like, they're hard to miss. The color is often a major clue, dark red brick with contrasting light cast-stone ornament. The color scheme here suggests a modern version of the Georgian. Patterned brick arrangements at the first and second stories suggest Georgian columns, but with cast-stone stylized floral patterns at the base;

at the top, they blossom into thoroughly modernistic projecting forms framing metal balcony railings. The windows directly above are then framed in a purely geometric cast-stone fantasy.

The double-story entranceway on West 104th combines generically wavy lines with a floral explosion to either side. Early ads for the building touted the usual "dropped living rooms," but no corner windows.

*Cross Riverside Drive, then walk half a block south for a view of the Master Building at the northeast corner of Riverside Drive and West 103rd Street.*

## 9.12 ★Master Building (formerly Master Institute of United Arts), 310 Riverside Drive Harvey Wiley Corbett of Helmle, Corbett & Harrison, with Sugarman & Berger, associated architects, 1928–29

What an unlikely team for a residential tower: Harvey Wiley Corbett (for Corbett, see 2.9), one of New York's most prominent modernists, better known for commercial blockbusters like Rockefeller Center (6.10), combining talents with apartment-house-and-hotel experts Sugarman & Berger (for Sugarman & Berger, see 4.4). But Corbett's involvement here was not accidental—nor was this just a residential building.

Tall, angular and severe, the Master Building rises twenty-nine stories above Riverside Drive, towering over the Hudson River; on this western shore of the Upper West Side, only the tower of Riverside Church is taller. One of the first Art Deco residential buildings in New York City, it was commissioned by Louis and Nettie Horch, devoted followers and patrons of Russian artist and mystic Nicholas Roerich. They created the building—named for Roerich's Master Institute of United Arts—to combine small apartments with an art school, library, conference hall, and even what *The New Yorker* described as a "copy of a Tibetan monastery library," and a museum containing more than a thousand of Roerich's paintings. *The New Yorker,* noting that Corbett himself belonged to the Roerich Society, recounted that "like every other zealous member he's devoted to Unity and to various other 'ideals of brotherhood and culture through art and science' as expressed in the paintings and teachings of Nicholas Roerich." Corbett described the building's purpose as inaugurating a "new era in art as the first living home of art . . . where art and human beings will grow and develop side by side."

Unlike later West Side Art Deco twin-towered apartment buildings, Corbett's Master Building rises to a single, tapering pinnacle, more like a Midtown skyscraper—suggesting how Central Park West might have turned out without the 1929 law encouraging twin-towered residential buildings. His design relies on geometric patterns, angles, and colors. The corner windows are said to be the first in a tall New York building (yet another claimant to this particular title), with splendid views of the park and river.

The color of the building's patterned brickwork gradually shades from dark at the base to light at the tower. As Corbett explained to the *New York Times* in September 1929, "For the first time in the history of steel and brick construction, colored brick has been used to give to a building the effect of a growing thing. At the base the building is of a deep purple hue, and gradually the color changes to lighter shades until at the very summit the tower gleams in pure white against the background of the sky." The building's angled setbacks and sheer walls suggest the austere purity of a glass and brick prism—a striking modernistic contrast to the opulent Beaux-Arts classicism of its neighbors.

*Cross to the east side of Riverside Drive.*

Though the museum closed in 1938, the cornerstone at the corner of West 103rd Street still bears an inscription of a capital "M" ("Master") enclosing a smaller "R" ("Roerich") set within a circle, above the date 1929. The side-street entrance is still marked "RIVERSIDE MUSEUM," referring to a later institution that the Horches brought in to replace Roerich. And the Master Apartments still dominates the skyline on this stretch of the Hudson River.

# ITINERARY NO. 10
# UPPER EAST SIDE

The Upper East Side—Manhattan's Gold Coast—maintains an aura of conservative respectability, and perhaps as a result never attracted as much Art Deco flash as its counterpart on the west side of Central Park. Nevertheless, tucked among the Beaux-Arts town houses and sedate neo-Georgian apartment buildings, the neighborhood has some remarkable examples by some of the best architects, including an apartment house (10.1) by Raymond Hood (built for the owner of the *Daily News,* 5.1); one of Manhattan's very few Art Deco town houses (10.2), by Harry Allen Jacobs; the elegant Carlyle Hotel (10.3); and apartment houses by Sloan & Robertson (10.4), architects of the Chanin Building (5.5); Horace Ginsbern (10.6), architect of the Park Plaza (12.4) and other West Bronx wonders; Henry S. Churchill (10.8); and George and Edward Blum (10.7)– the Blums having designed some of the very first Art Deco apartment buildings anywhere in the city.

*The walk begins on the southeast corner of Fifth Avenue and East 84th Street.*

The creation of Central Park and the introduction of mass transit (horsecar lines at first, then elevated trains, and finally the subway) spurred the development of the Upper East Side in major leaps, starting in the 1870s and continuing to the 1930s. Fifth Avenue to Park Avenue became the city's Gold Coast. Fifth Avenue once boasted a fabulous collection of mansions; most gave way to luxury apartment buildings in the 1910s and 1920s, about the same time that similar buildings rose along Park Avenue; grand town houses still survive on the side streets. Further east, an immigrant working-class population dwelled in tenements, while middle-class residents occupied brownstone row houses. Post-World-War-II development—mostly of plain white (and occasionally blue) brick-faced apartment buildings—took over Second and Third Avenues once the elevated trains above them came down. As a result, architectural styles range from the Italianate late-nineteenth-century brownstones and tenements, to Beaux-Arts turn-of-the-century town houses, to neo-Georgian 1920s apartment houses, to nondescript

1 3 East 84 Street
2 49 East 80 Street
3 Hotel Carlyle
35 East 76 Street
4 895 Park Avenue
5 240 East 79 Street
6 225 East 74 Street
7 210 East 68 Street
8 The Lowell
28 East 63 Street
Central Park
Grand Army Plaza
Queensboro Bridge
5 Av
Madison
Park Av
Lexington
3 Av
2 Av
1 Av
E 87
E 86
E 85
E 84
E 83
E 82
E 81
E 80
E 79
E 78
E 77
E 76
E 75
E 74
E 73
E 72
E 71
E 70
E 69
E 68
E 67
E 66
E 65
E 64
E 63
E 62
E 61
E 60
E 59
© Tauranac, Ltd., 2016.
All Rights Reserved.

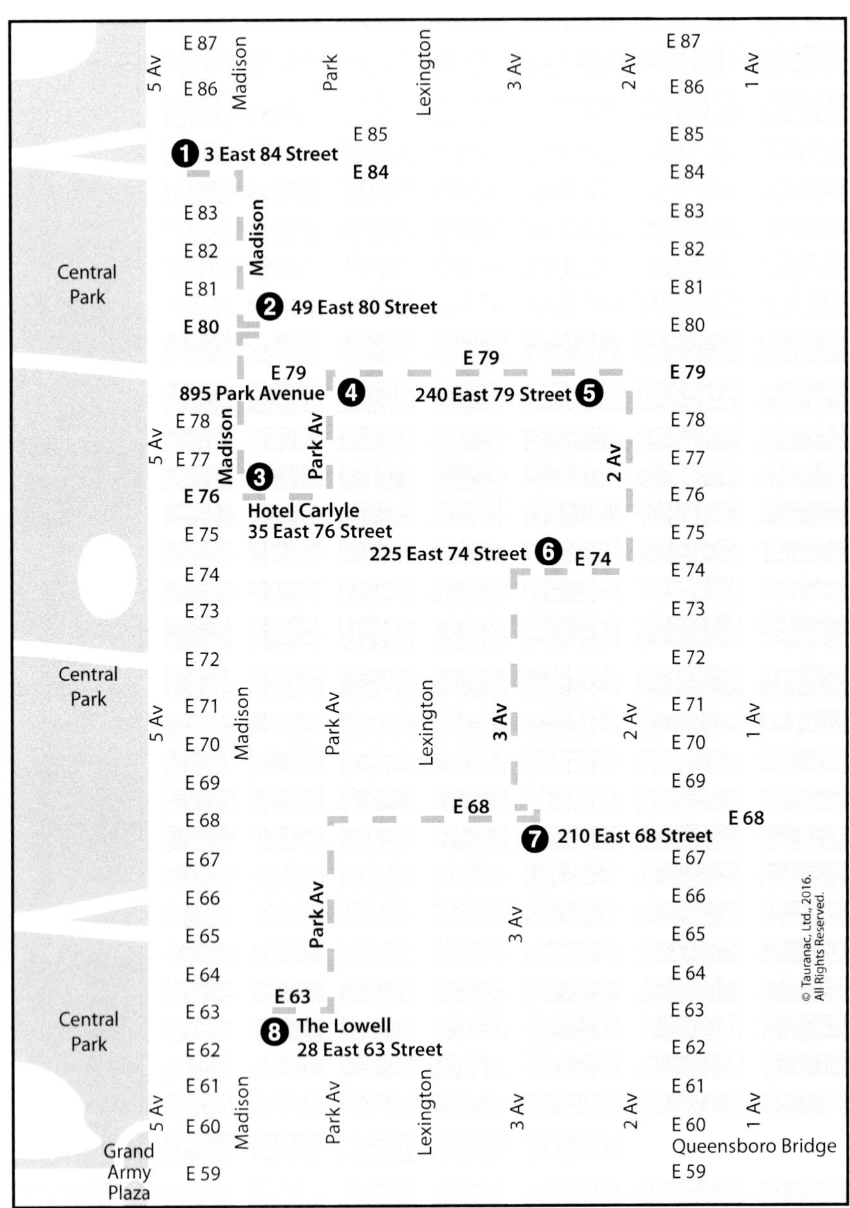

MAP 10

towers from the 1960s and later. Art Deco has no particular spot in this landscape—individual examples just pop up unexpectedly, sometimes in the unlikeliest places.

## 10.1 (HD) 3 East 84th Street
## Raymond Hood and John Mead Howells, 1927–28

Two years before he commissioned the Daily News Building (5.1), the newspaper's owner, Capt. Joseph Medill Patterson, hired Howells and Hood (for Howells, see 6.1a; for Hood, see 5.1) to design this small apartment building. Patterson had been living in a smaller apartment house on the site, then bought it, demolished it, and built this larger one. Taking the penthouse suite for his own use, he rented each of the remaining nine floors as single apartments, each one said to have ten rooms and four baths.

Hood's New York skyscrapers (5.1, 5.7, 5.8/5.12, 6.10) generally avoid the typical Art Deco ornament of abstract geometric patterns and stylized floral patterns—for which reason some prefer to call them "early Modern" rather than "Art Deco"—but not this apartment house. Geometry rules the window spandrels, where large and small chevrons mingle with diamonds and overlapping circles. An elaborate geometric frieze zigzags above the entrance. Directly over the door, partially hidden by the awning, stylized floral patterns and quatrefoils surround the cursive inscription "No 3." And the ornamental zing continues up to and including the building's parapet.

In 1928, the New York Chapter of the American Institute of Architects awarded Hood's building a medal. The award's language sums up Hood's design approach as understood in that year: "The building at 3–5 East 84th street is in the modified form of the so-called modern style. By this I mean that it has no cornice, a setback and the treatment of the spandrels between the windows is simple, with such decoration as there is, of a non-historical sort. In other words, Messrs. Hood and Howells, the architects, have designed the building of modern materials and ornamented it with design invented by themselves, and not gotten out of a book."

*Continue east on East 84th Street to Madison Avenue. Turn right on Madison and walk south to East 80th Street. Cross to the south side of East 80th, then cross to the east side of Madison Avenue and continue east along East 80th a short distance.*

## 10.2 (NR) Lionello and Carolyn Perera Residence, 49 East 80th Street Harry Allen Jacobs, 1929–30

As Harry Allen Jacobs told a reporter from the *New York Times*: "The house is designed in a modernistic spirit in decoration as well as in materials as representative of this materialistic, artificial and practical age. I believe it is the first single-family home of this type to be built entirely in this mode in Manhattan." Since 1930 saw the construction of exactly four town houses in Manhattan, and the Depression put an end to such houses generally, it might also be Manhattan's only example.

Venice-born Lionello Perera founded a private bank, which later merged with the Bank of America. His wife, Carolyn Allen, became a major philanthropist devoted to Italian cultural causes, founding the Toscanini Memorial Archives, avidly collecting Verdi-related material, and holding musical evenings as fundraisers in this house. (Music and fundraising of a different sort came in 1970, when Barbra Streisand bought the house and hosted a fundraiser for first-time Congressional candidate Bella Abzug. Streisand collected Art Deco objects—which would make this house her largest such collectible.)

During the 1910s and 1920s, Jacobs churned out neo-Renaissance or neo-Classical town houses for well-to-do New Yorkers, as well as a Tudor-Revival headquarters for the Friars Club. He also indulged in far-fetched planning schemes—like filling in the East River to connect Brooklyn and Manhattan. Only during the last two years of his life, 1930 and 1931, did he turn to modernism in architecture, writing a series on the subject in the *Times* in which he condemned cornices as "ridiculous overhanging projections" and cheered the elimination of "expensive detail and carving." As he memorably put it, "This is a materialistic, scientific and practical age that Jules Verne could not picture with his wildest imagination. Radio, the spanning of the continent with the telephone, the talkies, television, the airplane and dirigible, mass production, newest machinery and what not, cannot be expressed in an Italian Renaissance or other styles of the past."

The Perera house gave Jacobs the chance to put his new principles into practice. As befits an Upper East Side town house, its severe brick façade displays a very restrained version of the "modernistic spirit." Bands of geometrically patterned brick separate the upper stories from each other, but most ornamental detail keeps to the first story. A stone band separating the first and second stories combines overlapping zigzag lines with abstract shields. A cast-stone ornamental band above the entrance includes an inscription with the numerals "49."

The remarkable decorative metal entrance is made of Monel, one of the new alloys that became popular in the period, rather like the Chrysler Building's Nirosta (5.4). The contrast with the adjoining traditional brownstone and limestone houses—with their "ridiculous overhanging projections"—must have pleased Jacobs.

***Return to Madison Avenue, cross to the west side of Madison, then turn left and walk south on Madison to the northwest corner of East 77th Street. Look across the intersection at the Hotel Carlyle, which occupies the block of Madison between East 77th and 76th Streets.***

## 10.3 (HD) Hotel Carlyle, 35 East 76th Street Bien & Prince, 1930

The Carlyle opened in 1930 as a residential hotel—a popular institution at the time, described by the *Times* as offering "freedom from drudgery, the servant problem, plus the many responsibilities that go with maintaining large private homes." Such hotels replaced the single-family town house whose construction in Manhattan petered out in the early 1930s.

Who stayed at the Carlyle? Debutantes and bridal parties; visiting royalty and American presidents. Bobby Short sang at the Carlyle for decades—in a bar decorated with murals by Ludwig Bemelmans.

The Carlyle actually includes two separate buildings designed to look like one, standing side by side in what the *Times* called "the English residential plan known as London chambers."The shorter building, entered on East 77th Street, is an apartment house; the hotel occupies the tower, entered on East 76th Street. The Carlyle tower still dominates this generally low-rise section of the Upper East Side.

Austrian-born architect Sylvan Bien (d. 1959) worked with the august firm of Warren & Wetmore (designers of Grand Central Terminal) before going out on his own, and eventually designed more than a hundred New York buildings. He became known in the 1930s and '40s for his many Upper East Side apartment buildings on Fifth, Park, and Madison Avenues, but the Carlyle stands out because it is, well, the Carlyle.

Named after English writer Thomas Carlyle, a favorite of the developer's daughter, the "London chambers" building has been compared to London's Byzantine-inspired Westminster Cathedral, with which it shares a slender tower with horizontal stripes. Closer inspection, however, reveals modernistic ornament—those stripes, in beige terra-cotta, are incised with endless V patterns, some right side up, others turned on their sides, as well as stylized floral patterns and ribbed panels. Spandrels in one column of windows use vertically geometric brick patterns. Bear in mind, though, that this is Madison Avenue, and the modernism is, accordingly, sedate.

The black-and-white-tile aesthetic in the hotel's public spaces, incidentally, doesn't fit into the Deco rubric, but is notable nevertheless as the breakout moment of famed interior designer Dorothy Draper (see also 6.3 and 7.5).

*Cross to the east side of Madison Avenue. Turn right and walk south along Madison to East 76th Street; turn left and walk east on East 76th Street to see the Carlyle's south façade. Continue walking east on East 76th Street to Park Avenue. Turn left on Park and walk north to East 79th Street. Cross to the northwest corner of East 79th and Park and look across the intersection at the southeast corner.*

## 10.4 (HD) 895 Park Avenue Sloan & Robertson, 1929–30

Park Avenue is lined with prestigious, expensive, and rather dull apartment buildings, almost all in one eclectic style or another. And then there's No. 895, which cautiously flirts with styling advertised as "a modern adaptation of classical motifs"—still sedate, but with a certain modernistic flare.

John Sloan and T. Markoe Robertson, who formed their partnership in 1924, designed a number of Art Deco office buildings, notably the Chanin Building (5.5) and 29 Broadway (1.2), as well as the late lamented House of Detention for Women that once stood on Sixth Avenue in Greenwich Village. At No. 895, one of their rare apartment buildings, John Sloan acted not just as architect but also as developer. Planned as a cooperative, the nineteen-story building had just thirty-five apartments, including two "duplex penthouse suites," one with twelve rooms and five baths, the other with fourteen rooms and six baths. Residents could enjoy the building's many special amenities, notably a squash court, a gym, and locker rooms in the basement. To maintain an appropriately hushed atmosphere, the architects included two layers of special sound-proofing materials separated by an "air space" in all the floors and ceilings. Ah, Park Avenue.

The design's "classical motifs" include the three-story rusticated limestone base, and the enormous pilasters stretching from the fourth to the twelfth story. The "modern adaptation" shows up in the details—those pilasters rest on rectangular bases with typically Deco stylized floral patterns, and they're capped by similarly modernistic ornamental panels. At the top—with the penthouse duplexes—the building gets quite blocky, almost cubistic, with more modernistic details.

*Cross back to the south side of East 79th Street, and then to the east side of Park Avenue, and walk up to the entrance on East 79th.*

Around the corner, at the building's main entrance on East 79th Street—safely out of view from Park Avenue—the modernism overtakes the classicism. The entrance doors, set beneath a deep light-court, are flanked by two wide, flat, ribbed piers rising to jazz-modern jungle-pattern capitals (well, from a Park Avenue perspective), with a similarly exotic window directly above the entrance. Look under the canopy at the doorway: it's set within a rounded, geometrically patterned surround, and topped by an octagonal panel with more jungle vegetation. Scandalous!

***Walk east on East 79th Street to Lexington and then to Third Avenue; cross Third and continue east on East 79th three-quarters of the way toward Second Avenue.***

## 10.5 240 East 79th Street
## Godwin, Thompson & Patterson, 1929

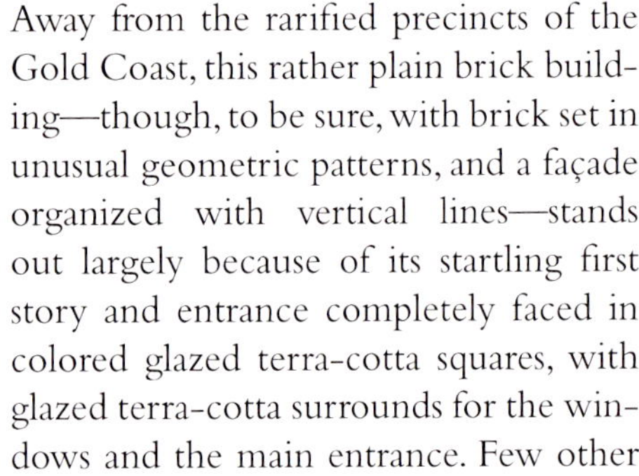

Away from the rarified precincts of the Gold Coast, this rather plain brick building—though, to be sure, with brick set in unusual geometric patterns, and a façade organized with vertical lines—stands out largely because of its startling first story and entrance completely faced in colored glazed terra-cotta squares, with glazed terra-cotta surrounds for the windows and the main entrance. Few other New York buildings have anything like this, but you will see two more on this walk: No. 210 East 68th Street (10.7), and the surprisingly similar Lowell at East 63rd Street (10.8). The entrance design includes ribbed piers and, at the top, an inscription (hard to see, just above the awning) with the building's address.

Above the inscription sits an octagonal piece of stone, set within a terra-cotta frame and capped by a flowering form that curves out from the façade to hover protectively over it. Frederick Godwin, the architect, was a great-grandson of American poet William Cullen Bryant—and his ornamental treatment here is quite poetic.

*Continue east on East 79th Street to Second Avenue. Turn right on Second Avenue and walk south to East 74th Street. Turn right and walk west on East 74th to the middle of the block.*

## 10.6 225 East 74th Street Horace Ginsbern, 1937

Horace Ginsbern's firm designed any number of six-story apartment buildings in the West Bronx (for Ginsbern, see 12.4) and Washington Heights (11.4a, 11.8), but also worked in Manhattan. His 1930s buildings generally featured white brick with contrasting red and black brick geometric patterns. For this long, low apartment block, however, he turned to darker, patterned brick with cast-stone ornament—at the bottom and top—in the form of long, slender, molded brick piers, suggestive of a modernistic take on the neo-Georgian style once popular for Upper East Side apartment buildings. In style, No. 225, so unlike Ginsbern's other buildings, bears an uncanny resemblance instead to the mid-1930s work of Boak & Paris (10.6). One block further east, at No. 310 East 74th Street, Ginsbern designed in the same year a smaller but similar apartment house for the same developer (Bricken Brothers). Architects have always borrowed from each other—but these buildings' similarity to Boak & Paris's work is striking.

*Continue walking west to Third Avenue; turn left, and walk south on Third Avenue to East 68th Street. Walk a short distance east on East 68th, then look across the street at 210 East 68th Street, at the southeast corner of Third Avenue.*

## 10.7 (NR) 210 East 68th Street George & Edward Blum, 1928

Glazed terra-cotta in bright colors—green, black, orange—along with abstract geometric patterns, mark No. 210 as a Deco design. But George and Edward Blum (for the Blums, see 3.11) design patterns unlike anybody else's. At the eastern edge of the building, the first story is covered in orange terra-cotta squares similar to those at 240 East 79th Street (10.5). The ornamental band above it, however, is pure Blum brothers, based on angled diamond forms that alternate in both color and shape—the light diamonds point upward, the dark ones point downward. Alternating light and dark circles mark each diamond in a band directly below. This first-story band stretches right up to the main entrance—and then jumps up to the second story. Why? Because East 68th Street slopes uphill toward the west, and at the western, Third Avenue, end the terra-cotta band appears, once again, at the first floor level. But that jog up one story affects the building's entire design.

*Stand across the street from the entrance.*

Just as the terra-cotta band above the first story jumps up a story at the entrance, so do a series of brick bands above the third, fifth, seventh, ninth, and eleventh stories—it's as though the whole façade jumps up a notch.

*Continue walking west on East 68th Street to the corner of Third Avenue and cross to the northwest corner of Third and East 68th.*

Working that same pattern, the Blums jump those brick bands (but not the terra-cotta band) up one more story at the corner of Third Avenue, and bring them back down again around on the avenue side—and down again one more story at the far end of that side. What began as an awkward site condition becomes the source for an unusual design—lemonade from lemons. Take a closer look at those brick bands—each one is composed of four lines of tiny brick, in two different patterns, and each one projects slightly beyond the next. Such attention to detail!

Up toward the building's top, two stories below the roofline, a terra-cotta band in a completely different pattern zigzags its way around the building, as though on a geometric roller coaster or racetrack. Amazing how a building standing stock still can seem to be in motion!

One block to the east, at 315 East 68th Street at the corner of Second Avenue, the Blums' third apartment building from this period offers a more understated modernism, its design resting entirely on contrasting shades of brick—buff, brown, and black—set in various patterns.

***Walk west on East 68th Street, past Lexington Avenue to Park Avenue. Turn left and walk south on Park Avenue to East 63rd Street. Turn right, cross Park Avenue, and continue walking west on East 63rd Street to the middle of the block.***

## 10.8 (HD) The Lowell, 28 East 63rd Street Henry S. Churchill, with associate Herbert Lippman, 1926; mosaic by C. Bertram Hartman

The earliest building on this itinerary is also one of the most colorful, thanks to the involvement of two men devoted to architectural color: architect Henry S. Churchill, and artist Bertram Hartman. They designed it as an apartment hotel, with a first-floor restaurant, for Leo H. Wise, a long-time resident of a row house on the site. (The name "Lowell" dates to the building's acquisition in 1928 by the Lowell Leasing Corporation.)

Churchill, a talented early modernist much involved in housing projects, during the 1920s expressed strong feelings about the use of color in architecture: "People are tired of the monotonously colorless façades that line our business streets. Personally I am strongly in favor of the use of *color* in office buildings." Churchill noted that building design used to rely in part on shadows cast by variations in a building's façade, either "projections or depressions." New regulations, however, eliminated overhanging projections, leaving only the possibility of "depressions"—but such depressions sacrificed valuable space. Walls consequently became flat and shadowless. His solution: the application of color to flat walls, giving "the architect the opportunity to bring out whatever lines he wishes without difficulty. . . . Attractive colors in pleasing patterns and designs present a field of their own for the architect desiring beauty."

Churchill's façade for the Lowell makes use of tapestry brick, as well as blocky geometric setbacks at the uppermost stories outlined in white terra-cotta, but the most startling color effects define the first story, with its rippling pink piers set against a white, glazed-terra-cotta background.

Churchill also brought in other artists to add color. Edgar Brandt's New York shop (for Brandt, see 3.5) provided iron gates—sadly missing—for the first-story restaurant. And Churchill commissioned a brightly colored octagonal mosaic, manufactured in Germany from Bertram Hartman's design, directly above the entrance—still there, though now partially hidden from view by a canopy.

A modernist painter who had studied in Germany, where he discovered the Jugendstil movement, Hartman also worked in batik, did magazine illustrations, and designed mosaics and glass for new buildings. The same year he designed the Lowell's mosaic, he also provided illustrations for Ely Jacques Kahn's *Times* article, "Our Skyscrapers Take Simple Forms," and he designed a ceiling mosaic for one of Kahn's buildings in the Garment Center (the Millinery Center Building at 39th Street and 6th Avenue). As he wrote to a friend, also in 1926, "Gradually our architects are able to convince these clients to use artists to decorate their buildings." Many of his paintings focused on skyscrapers, including his 1929 work, *Razing Number One Wall Street*, depicting the demolition making way for Ralph Walker's new Irving Trust building (1.3).

Though Hartman filled his paintings with architecture, at the Lowell he softened the architecture with a mosaic depicting a rustic scene—triangular evergreens surrounding a tree, with skyscrapers in the background—perhaps meant to represent Central Park, just one block to the west.

# ITINERARY NO. 11
# WASHINGTON HEIGHTS

High up on a hill, its streets lined with modest but attractive six-story Art Deco apartment houses, Washington Heights has more in common with West Bronx neighborhoods just across the Harlem River than with the rest of Manhattan. Many of the same architects who worked on the Grand Concourse also designed apartment buildings on or near Fort Washington Avenue—we will see work by Horace Ginsbern (11.4a, 11.8), Jacob Felson (11.2, 11.4b, 11.13, 11.15), Israel Crausman (11.7), Miller & Goldhammer (11.11), Charles Kreymborg (11.12), and H. Herbert Lilien (11.14). Modest buildings, on a modest scale, with modest budgets, they are quite unlike the twin-towered luxury buildings on Central Park West, but definitely related. Two taller apartment buildings, by Boak & Paris (11.6, 11.10), offer a more idiosyncratic take on the modernism of the 1930s. Besides the apartment buildings, our walk includes a one-story taxpayer (11.5), and one of the city's few frankly Deco subway entrances (11.1). But the star attraction is the Fourth Church of Christ, Scientist (11.3, now the Hebrew Tabernacle of Washington Heights), one of perhaps a dozen or so Art Deco houses of worship anywhere in the city.

***The walk begins at the Fort Washington Avenue exit of the 181st Street stop of the Independent subway (the A train). Exit at the north (uptown) end of the station and take the elevator up to Fort Washington Avenue, at West 184th Street (according to the street sign, even though there is no street here). Cross Fort Washington and enter Bennett Park.***

Washington Heights stretches from the Harlem River on the east to the Hudson on the west, and from West 155th Street on the south to Dyckman Street on the north. Our walk takes in a more condensed area between West 181st Street and Fort Tryon Park, from Fort Washington Avenue to Cabrini Boulevard. Art Deco can be found elsewhere in Washington Heights—notably at Columbia-Presbyterian Hospital (now New York–Presbyterian

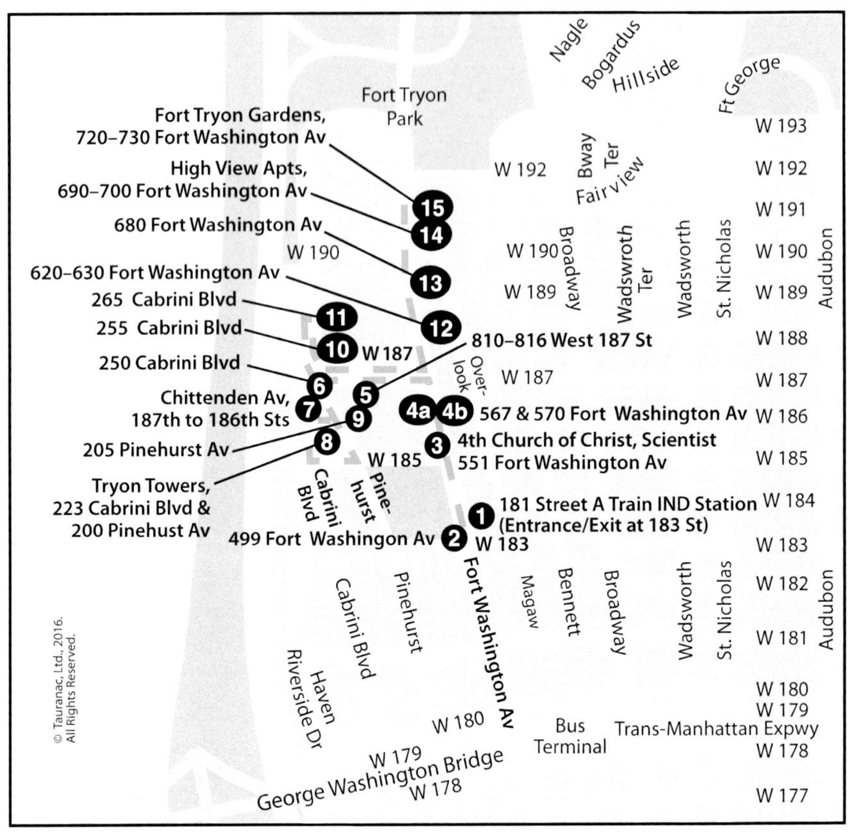


MAP 11

Hospital) at West 168th Street west of Broadway—as well as in Inwood, the neighborhood to the north, but this section includes a particularly large and interesting cluster.

The area's history revolves around two famous names: George Washington and John D. Rockefeller, Jr. The neighborhood takes its name from Fort Washington, which the Continental Congress erected during the American Revolutionary War roughly on the site of Bennett Park, near appropriately named Fort Washington Avenue. Following the Revolution, the Heights became known for country estates with generous river views, and remained largely rural until the beginning of the twentieth century. As always, the coming of the subways brought denser development. The IRT reached 157th Street at Broadway in 1904, bringing residential buildings to the valley to the east. When the IND opened in 1932, offering very fast express service to midtown and downtown, its stations at 181st Street and 190th Street included elevators to lift passengers up the hill to Fort Washington Avenue—and brought with them a wave of new Art Deco apartment buildings.

Rockefeller made his contribution between 1936 and 1941, gifting large amounts of property to the City of New York while selling other property nearby to developers. The city-owned property became Fort Tryon Park, home to the Cloisters, housing the medieval art collection of the Metropolitan Museum. The speedy, direct subway service, the spectacular views, and the splendid new park combined to make this section of Washington Heights a very desirable location indeed.

## 11.1 IND (Independent line) subway exit, 181st Street station on the A train; Fort Washington Avenue at West 184th Street Squire J. Vickers, 1932

It's only appropriate to begin a walk through a neighborhood made possible by the subway system with a look at the Art Deco subway entrance at West 184th Street. The Independent line—so called because, unlike the earlier, privately operated (though city-financed) IRT and BMT lines, it was operated independently by the City of New York—was planned during the late 1920s and opened on Saturday, September 10, 1932 (carrying 171,267 passengers during its first twenty-four hours, according to the *New York Times).*

Squire (his name, not his title) J. Vickers studied architecture and painting at Cornell University before joining the subway's staff in 1906 for what turned out to be a thirty-six-year career, during which he oversaw the design of the system's stations. His early work for the IRT and BMT reflected an Arts and Crafts aesthetic, but by the late 1920s Vickers had discovered the Machine Age, using long strips of black, blue, yellow, or red tiles along the platform walls—even the original maps of the IND system used brightly colored angular lines with a Deco flare. The subway entrance on Fort Washington Avenue is a deceptively modest one-story vestibule, leading to elevators that connect to a vast interior deep underground. Its cast-stone façade offers the station's most recognizable Art Deco ornament, from the overlapping zigzag lines with diamond patterns framing the pointed-arched entranceway—more elaborately on the underside of the arch—to the blocky cut-out letters spelling "SUBWAY" in the vertical light fixture above it, and the wavy zigzag lines running across the top.

***Walk south one block along Fort Washington Avenue to the northwest corner of West 183rd Street.***

## 11.2 499 Fort Washington Avenue Jacob M. Felson, 1936

Jacob Felson designed No. 499 as a classic mid-1930s six-story apartment building. Like so many of his contemporaries designing Art Deco apartment houses, Felson (1886–1962) came of immigrant Eastern European Jewish stock, arriving in New York, barely two years old, with his family in 1888. Like other poor young men interested in architecture, he studied at tuition-free Cooper Union. From 1910 until his death in 1962 (his obituary described him as "semi-retired"), Felson designed hundreds of buildings, including movie theaters, private homes, and garages, but especially apartment houses—in many cases acting as both architect and developer.

Felson designed No. 499, for Samuel Barkin of Fort Tryon Properties, on a prominent corner site opposite Bennett Park. An ad in the *New York Times* described it as "A Barkin Apartment—The Apartment Pride of Washington Heights," and boasted of its sunken living rooms, colored tile, casement windows, Otis elevators, Venetian blinds, "General Electric refrigeration," and especially its location: "1/2 Block from 8th Ave. Subway Station. 2 Blocks from John D. Rockefeller Jr. $7,000,000 Fort Tryon Park." Felson's Deco detailing includes blocky massing, corner windows (their casements, sadly, replaced), and just enough red and black brick geometry to liven up a mostly white brick façade—especially in the vertically oriented window spandrels but also as horizontal bands at the corners, and a strong vertical red and black line rising from the recessed West 183rd Street entrance to the roofline.

*From 183rd Street, walk back along the edge of (or through) Bennett Park to West 185th Street, across from the Hebrew Tabernacle at the northwest corner of Fort Washington Avenue and West 185th Street.*

## 11.3 (NR) Fourth Church of Christ, Scientist (now Hebrew Tabernacle of Washington Heights), 551 Fort Washington Avenue Cherry & Matz, 1932

By far the most unusual Deco structure in the neighborhood, the Fourth Church is a rare example of an Art Deco church in New York, and an even rarer example of an Art Deco Christian Science church anywhere in the country.

Begun in 1896 by Elizabeth Skinner and Caroline Frame, students of the religion's founder, Mary Baker Eddy, the Fourth Church initially rented space on West 82nd Street. Following the loss of its lease, the congregation relocated to Washington Heights and built a new home.

As a new American religion, Christian Science initially had no architectural tradition other than standard Western revival styles—neo-Gothic, neo-Romanesque. The church never formally adopted any architectural style, but before long a clear preference emerged for the neo-Classicism of the 1893 World's Columbian Exposition in Chicago. Under the influence of architect Solon Beman—himself a Christian Scientist—who designed several Exposition buildings, the churches became grand, columned structures with centrally planned interiors under dramatic domes with skylights. The Fourth Church commissioned Beman to design its new home on Fort Washington Avenue, in what became the architect's last design, and his only Christian Science church in New York City—not this building, but its immediate predecessor, fifteen blocks to the south on West 178th Street. Completed in 1918, that grand structure stood barely two decades, falling victim to condemnation to make way for the George Washington Bridge.

Given Beman's prime position in Christian Science architecture, and the Fourth Church's status as his sole New York City church design, it seems remarkable that the congregation willingly gave up neo-Classicism and embraced the new modernism. Christian Science churches rarely used the style, and "modernistic" churches in New York were exceedingly rare in general—a phenomenon generally ascribed to a conservative sensibility among traditional institutions. The same architectural journals that in 1931 highlighted such inventive Art Deco structures in New York as the Empire State Building, the Waldorf-Astoria, the Brooklyn Telephone headquarters, and Bloomingdale's, had to make do with churches in neo-Gothic, neo-Georgian, or neo-Romanesque styles. Only the Catholic Church experimented to any extent with modernistic styles, mostly in the work of Henry J. McGill (14.2, 14.4). Cherry & Matz, architects of the Fourth Church, invariably worked in more traditional styles. The choice, clearly, was the congregation's. "The Fourth Church took great pride in its up-to-date new home, describing it as . . . a very modernistic building, beautifully lighted and well equipped. . . . Standing on one of the highest points of Manhattan Island, opposite a small park which marks the site of Fort Washington, the church edifice built of pearl grey Waldorf brick and limestone, is of unique beauty and interest."

Note the reference to the "pearl grey Waldorf brick"—that's the new color of brick that had just been created for the Waldorf-Astoria (6.5). The press noticed the "modernistic design," and the *Times* reported that the building was "believed to be the first such church of its denomination in America."

The new design suggests a modernistic interpretation of Solon Beman's original. The blocky massing repeats the original's generally square shape, as well as the contrast in height between the taller central sections and the shorter corners. The triple entrance on West 185th Street, framed by four modernistic piers, repeats the triple entrance of the original framed by four Ionic columns. But instead of elaborate classical detailing, the ornament is abstract and geometric. The 185th Street façade includes metal doors adorned with superimposed ornamental squares piled up like a flat pyramid, and topped by a metal grille whose details suggest mechanical gears. Above the doors, the limestone wall blossoms with stylized leaves, flowers, and clusters of grapes. Around the corner on the Fort Washington side, tall, elaborate aluminum grilles sporting spirals and miscellaneous floral patterns protect the ground-floor windows.

***Walk north along Fort Washington Avenue halfway toward West 187th Street. No. 567 Fort Washington Avenue will be on your left, and No. 570 across the avenue on your right.***

## 11.4a 567 Fort Washington Avenue
## Horace Ginsbern, 1935

## 11.4b 570 Fort Washington Avenue
## Jacob M. Felson, 1939

567 Fort Washington Avenue

Entrance to
570 Fort Washington Avenue

From West 185th Street, Fort Washington Avenue—lined with six-story apartment buildings—forms a grand boulevard leading to Fort Tryon Park. Horace Ginsbern—one of the most innovative firms active in the Bronx (for Ginsbern, see 12.4)—designed No. 567 with the usual corner windows and vertical lines, but set in a remarkably three-dimensional façade that steps in by degrees to a recessed central entrance, faced in rippling stone with a central stylized vase sprouting stone vegetation. Even though it is just six stories tall, this building has a skyline effect—stone ornament capping the projecting brick columns bend up and over the building's roofline, whose angular corners are matched by a set of curving metal rods. Felson's design (for Felson, see 11.2) across the avenue is simpler, but also includes a recessed entrance flanked by rippling stone.

***Continue north along Fort Washington Avenue to West 187th Street; turn left and walk west on West 187th to the middle of the block.***

## 11.5 810–816 W 187th Street
## George Meisner, 1929

The block of West 187th Street between Fort Washington Avenue and Pinehurst Avenue functions as a major shopping street for the neighborhood. On the south side of the street, a one-story taxpayer (for taxpayers, see 2.2)

includes half a dozen storefronts topped with quirky geometric terra-cotta rooflines—each storefront slightly taller than the next because 187th Street slopes upward toward the west. On the north side, what appears to be another one-story taxpayer is in fact a wing of No. 255 Cabrini Boulevard (11.10).

***Continue west on 187th Street to Cabrini Boulevard and look across Cabrini at No. 250, on the southwest corner of West 187th.***

## 11.6 250 Cabrini Boulevard
## Boak & Paris, 1936

At nine stories one of the tallest Art Deco apartment buildings in the neighborhood, 250 Cabrini Boulevard was built for developer Sam Minskoff, a plumber with a sideline in construction who went on to found a major Manhattan real-estate empire. During the 1920s, Minskoff worked with architect Emery Roth, but eventually the two had a falling out. In the 1930s, Minskoff commissioned buildings from Russell Boak and Hyman Paris, two younger architects who had met while working in Roth's office (Boak started with Roth as a draftsman after finishing eighth grade) and then gone out on their own in 1927. Boak & Paris's buildings have a very particular take on Art Deco. Their Midtown Theater (now the Metro, 9.9) on Broadway at West 99th Street has one of the most unusual Art Deco façades of any New York movie theater, black and maroon terra-cotta with banded aluminum bars and a huge circular terra-cotta medallion. Their design for 250 Cabrini differs from the typical Washington Heights Deco most notably in the color—red brick with cast-stone trim, instead of white brick with red and black brick geometry. They use patterned brick, but more as an accent of existing lines than as additional ornament. And their cast-stone forms are like nobody else's work.

***Cross Cabrini Boulevard and continue west halfway down West 187th Street.***

The main entrance on West 187th Street, surrounded by startling red marble, sports metal window and door grilles with unusual asymmetric geometric patterns, as well as a rippling stone areaway wall.

***Continue west on West 187th Street to Chittenden Avenue; turn left and walk south on Chittenden Avenue.***

## 11.7 Chittenden Avenue, from West 187th to 186th Street

25 Chittenden Avenue

Here at the western extremity of the neighborhood, pause to look out at the spectacular view of the Hudson River, with the George Washington Bridge to the left and the Palisades across the river in New Jersey. No. 250 Cabrini Boulevard anchors this block at the north end, with two more Art Deco apartment buildings to the south. The modest façade of 25 Chittenden Avenue (Samson V. Becker, 1937) includes attractive geometric brickwork above the entrance, which is flanked by brick piers with typically geometric stone caps. No. 17 Chittenden is a late work by Israel Crausman (1939)—the red and black brick of his earlier Art Deco designs banished in favor of the curving corner windows of the later Moderne. The southern end of the block opens onto the vista of Castle Village, a complex of eleven-story apartment towers (George F. Pelham II, 1938–39) marching south along Cabrini Boulevard.

17 Chittenden Avenue

*Continue south on Chittenden Avenue to West 186th Street (Alex Rose Place); turn left on West 186th and walk east to the corner of Cabrini Boulevard; turn left on Cabrini Boulevard and walk north back toward West 187th Street.*

## 11.8 Tryon Towers, 223 Cabrini Boulevard and 200 Pinehurst Avenue Horace Ginsbern, 1935–36

Ginsbern's Tryon Towers has equally interesting front and rear façades thanks to the narrow angle at which Cabrini and Pinehurst meet at 187th Street (for Ginsbern, see 12.4). On Cabrini, Ginsbern includes the usual corner windows and vertical strips of windows with geometric spandrels. To these he has added a dotted-line effect, with small squares surrounding and outlining the corner windows.

*Walk around to the Pinehurst Avenue façade.*

Pinehurst, however, clearly has the major façade, with its central recessed entrance, and a skyline effect similar to what Ginsbern designed, the same year, at 567 Fort Washington Avenue (11.4a).

## 11.9 205 Pinehurst Avenue Charles E. Greenberg, 1947

Directly across the street from Tryon Towers, No. 205 Pinehurst Avenue must be one of the last Art Deco apartment buildings constructed in the neighborhood. The immediate post-war years saw the morphing of the 1930s modernistic into 1950s modernism—but not everybody made the transition so quickly. Greenberg's design has left behind the use of bright colors, and his ornamental brick patterns tend horizontal rather than vertical, but it still has a sense of continuity with neighboring 1930s designs.

***Walk north to the corner of West 187th Street and Cabrini Boulevard; look north across the intersection at 255 Cabrini Boulevard on the northeast corner of West 187th.***

## 11.10 255 Cabrini Boulevard Boak & Paris, 1936–37

One year after 250 Cabrini, catty-corner across the intersection, Boak & Paris designed a combination taller apartment house (eight stories) and one-story taxpayer. Though later than No. 250, this building seems less obviously modernistic—there's something of a neo-Georgian flavor, sort of a "modern Georgian" approach analogous to the Modern Classic of the same decade. The entranceway suggests a modernistic interpretation of a typical neo-Georgian version, with a classical urn set within a broken pediment—but given a geometric or streamlined flare no neo-Georgian would display.

The one-story portion of the building along West 187th Street extends a cast-stone parapet with geometric patterns across its ten storefronts.

***Cross West 187th Street and continue walking north along Cabrini Boulevard to the adjoining building at 265.***

## 11.11 265 Cabrini Boulevard Miller & Goldhammer, 1936

Things happened quickly at this corner—233 Cabrini in 1935–36, 250 and 265 Cabrini in 1936, and 255 Cabrini in 1936–37. Miller & Goldhammer's design for No. 265, adjoining No. 255 on the north, makes clear the difference between the more typical white brick Washington Heights Deco with geometric red patterns, on the one hand, and the more idiosyncratic red brick versions of Boak & Paris, on the other.

*Walk south back to West 187th Street and turn left, walking east along West 187th to Fort Washington Avenue, then turn left and walk north a short distance on Fort Washington.*

## 11.12 620–630 Fort Washington Avenue Charles O. Kreymborg, 1936

Another architect with buildings on both Fort Washington Avenue and the Grand Concourse, Kreymborg was the New York–born son of a cigar manufacturer from Bavaria, and brother of American poet Alfred Kreymborg. One of his apartment buildings—No. 1 Jane Street, in Greenwich Village—attracted the admiration of *New Yorker* architecture critic Lewis Mumford. Though Mumford decried such Deco extravaganzas as the Chrysler Building ("inane romanticism, meaningless voluptuousness, void symbolism") and disliked Rockefeller Center ("mediocrity—seen through a magnifying glass"), in 1939 he wrote about recent new apartment buildings that "present to the eye the simple vernacular of our period: wide steel casement windows; a plain, unadorned façade of clean, soberly designed entrances; and shops that have been treated as an integral part of the building." He particularly liked No. 1 Jane Street, because "the architect, Charles Kreymborg, has given an extra grace to the wall with horizontal bands of brick—a pleasant variation within the pattern. But the point is that these new buildings exemplify a decent, honest, and often quite handsome formula, as good as Bloomsbury was in the eighteenth century or parts of Beacon Hill in the early nineteenth." No. 620–630 Fort Washington neatly fits Mumford's description.

*Continue walking north to the corner of West 190th Street.*

## 11.13 680 Fort Washington Avenue Jacob M. Felson, 1941

The final two blocks of Fort Washington Avenue, on the east side, are lined with large apartment complexes designed during the waning years of the Depression. Like Charles Greenberg's 1947 design for

205 Pinehurst, these buildings have given up the use of bright colors and strong vertical lines. Compare Felson's design for No. 680, of 1941, to his work at 499 Fort Washington Avenue (11.2) five years earlier: flat and white, though still using patterned brick ornament. These are the kinds of buildings that Mumford admired as unadorned, clean, and soberly designed.

*Continue north on Fort Washington Avenue, crossing to the north side of West 190th Street.*

## 11.14a High View Apartments, 690 Fort Washington Avenue H. Herbert Lilien, 1940

## 11.14b High View Apartments, 700 Fort Washington Avenue H. Herbert Lilien, 1944

These two apartment complexes designed by H. Herbert Lilien, four years apart, sit on the former site of the original "Cloisters," or, as described in the *Times* in 1943, "George Grey Barnard's old Cloisters, museum, home and studio where many of the late sculptor's works were executed and where he painstakingly assembled his outstanding collections of Romanesque and early Gothic art treasures." Barnard (1863–1938) had lived in France before the First World War, and supported himself in part by buying and selling medieval sculpture, keeping much of it for his own collection. He later moved with his collection into what was described as a "churchlike brick structure" on Fort Washington Avenue—the original Cloisters, which the Metropolitan Museum later called "the first installation of medieval art of its kind in America." John D. Rockefeller, Jr., bought the collection in 1925, added works from his own collection (notably the Unicorn tapestries), and donated it all to the Metropolitan Museum. In 1937, having converted sixty-six acres to the

north into Fort Tryon Park, Rockefeller built the new Cloisters in the new park and, while he was at it, donated seven hundred acres on the opposite shore of the Hudson to the state of New Jersey, to protect the view from the new park and museum.

Doorway,
700 Fort Washington Avenue

Rockefeller then sold Barnard's property for development. No 690 Fort Washington Avenue curves around and down along West 190th Street; it sports the usual plain white brick and corner windows of the period, but includes an intact surviving doorway—tangential metal circles and long slender metal lines—deeply recessed beneath a cantilevered corner. (Across the street, at the corner of West 190th Street and Overlook Terrace, 802 West 190th is yet another late building, 1941, designed by Jacob M. Felson.) No. 700 (originally proposed the same year, but delayed until 1944) sports the same doorway, minus the cantilever.

## 11.15 Fort Tryon Gardens, 720–730 Fort Washington Avenue Jacob M. Felson, 1938–39

As reported in the *Times* in 1938: "While Fort Tryon Park was under construction after John D. Rockefeller Jr. had donated the land to the city, there were reports that the Rockefeller interests might develop some of their holdings in the vicinity with multi-family dwellings." And so they did. At Nos. 720–730—similar to No. 680 (11.13), designed the following year—Jacob Felson gave up the bright colors of his earlier work, and de-emphasized vertical lines. He gave these two buildings recessed and sunken central entrances flanked by concave curves and wide ribbed piers.

***Fort Washington Avenue ends at the entrance to Fort Tryon Park. A walk north through the park leads to the Cloisters.***

# ITINERARY NO. 12
# THE BRONX

Of all the boroughs beyond Manhattan, none can match the Bronx's reputation as an Art Deco stronghold—hundreds of six-story Deco apartment buildings, especially in the West Bronx on or near the Grand Concourse. The image of a glittering Art Deco boulevard doesn't quite match the reality—most of the Concourse and its side streets had already been developed earlier in the century—but the Deco buildings sparkle as highlights of color and geometry among the staid earlier designs.

The following group of Art Deco buildings, selected from the hundreds scattered across the borough, includes some of the most interesting or unusual examples of the style—many apartment houses, among them what may be the borough's very first in the new style, Park Plaza (12.4), but also a number of public buildings including a bank (12.11), a rare Deco junior high school (12.13), the central Bronx Post Office (12.1), a park recreation center (12.15), an office building with a rare intact Deco lobby (12.10), the Bronx County Courthouse (12.2), a grand entrance to the Bronx Zoo (12.12), and the Orchard Beach Bathhouse (12.15).

Though most of the sites can be reached by public transportation, because of the distances involved they do not lend themselves to a walking tour. They are organized here in geographical clusters.

### *Grand Concourse and vicinity*

The only one of New York's five boroughs on the mainland, the Bronx also offered the city its first opportunity to expand beyond Manhattan Island—New York annexed the West Bronx (everything west of the Bronx River) from Westchester County in 1874, adding the rest of the borough in 1895, before incorporating the other three boroughs in 1898. Once a rural outpost of small villages and large estates, the West Bronx quickly evolved into a set of dense urban districts—its population had soared past the million mark by 1930—and huge numbers of six-story apartment houses sprang up, well, almost everywhere.

Laid out originally (conceived in 1891, begun in 1902, opened in 1909) as a recreational thoroughfare, often compared to the Champs Élysée in Paris, the Grand Boulevard and Concourse redeveloped after World War I as a major residential urban artery. Most of its buildings present quietly respectable versions of European styles to the street, but several dozen Deco additions bring zigzag pizzazz and color to this formerly sedate bastion of middle-class respectability. The West Bronx suffered from economic decline and urban decay in the 1970s and '80s, and many Grand Concourse buildings, sadly, lost their original casement windows and idiosyncratic doorways, but they still form one of the country's great Deco collections—especially when added to the many Deco examples scattered on other streets throughout the West Bronx. And the Concourse also boasts several major public buildings in the style. Of the many Art Deco apartment buildings on the Concourse, just a few of the most interesting or representative are included here.

## 12.1 **Bronx Post Office, 560 Grand Concourse (at East 149th Street) Thomas Harlan Ellett, 1935–37

The Bronx Post Office—largest of New York City's twenty-nine Depression-era post offices (see 2.3)—might not seem like much of an Art Deco design. Nevertheless, the *Architectural Forum* of June 1938 considered it an "excellent example" of the cross between "the continuing tradition of 'government classic'" and "a distinct modern influence," seeing it as a modern interpretation of more traditional Georgian design, perhaps most obviously in its large plain windows set within round marble arches. Architect Ellett attended the University of Pennsylvania and fell under the influence of Paul Cret, an advocate of the Modern Classic—as did Marvin Fine, of Horace Ginsbern's office, who a few years before the Bronx Post Office commission designed perhaps the earliest Art Deco apartment building in the Bronx (12.4).

Like so many others from the period, this post office includes specially commissioned, publicly funded works of art. Outside, two statues—chosen in a national competition judged by Ellett and several sculptors, including Paul Manship (for Manship, see 12.12)—flank the entrance. On the left, Charles Rudy's *Noah* carries a gazelle under his arm, while gazing intently at a dove bearing a message (hence the connection to the postal service) that the great Flood has abated. Offering a more contemporary connection,

Henry Kreis's *The Letter*, on the right, shows a mother and child with the eponymous communication.

But the building's best-known artwork, by far, sits just inside the doors—a set of thirteen murals, in egg tempera on plaster, painted by Ben Shahn and his wife Bernarda Bryson, in 1938 and '39.

The long, narrow main hall housing the murals presents a typical Modern Classic layout—a series of plain Ionic columns supporting a beamed ceiling, but all stripped down to essential forms. The murals, by contrast, show iconic, oversized figures that look like they might burst through the surrounding columns at any moment.

Shahn and Bryson met while working for Diego Rivera on his doomed mural at the RCA Building in Rockefeller Center (6.10). Their Bronx murals, *Resources of America*, represent men and women at work throughout the country—everywhere from cotton and wheat fields in rural states to textile factories and steel mills in big cities. "My idea," said Shahn in a 1944 interview, "was to show the people of the Bronx something about America outside New York." The murals owe something of their sense of realism to photos of Americans at work that Shahn had taken during his travels around the country.

Shahn took inspiration from Walt Whitman's poem, "I Hear America Singing"; the murals include verses from the poem, and an image of Whitman speaking about democracy to a crowd of workers. Shahn originally chose a different set of verses, but had to change them following protests—led by a priest at the Bronx's Fordham University—that the verses insulted religious belief. The offending verse: churches might be "recast, maybe discard them, end them—maybe their work is done, who knows?"

Restorations of the murals in the 1970s have left them in generally good condition.

## 12.2 ★Bronx County Building, 851 Grand Concourse (at West 161st Street) Hausle & Freedlander, 1931–35

The governmental cross between classicism and the modernistic, exemplified by the Post Office, continues in the Bronx County Building (also known as the Bronx County

Courthouse), a ten-story gigantic box of a structure on whose façades grand three-story colonnades merge into unbroken vertical columns of windows. It houses the Bronx courts and the offices of the Bronx borough president, among other borough entities. Its architects, Swiss-born Max Hausle and native New Yorker Joseph Freedlander, apparently worked together only on this one commission.

Like the Post Office, the Bronx County Building includes a sculptural program, but on a much grander scale. Charles Keck's enormous frieze, circling the building at the third story, depicts employment (agriculture, commerce, industry, the arts), while eight huge freestanding groups of figures, carved in pink Georgia marble, celebrate various civic virtues. Adolph Weinman carved two of these, while supervising three other artists—Edward F. Sanford, George H. Snowden, and Joseph Kiselewski—who carved the remainder. The groups—two apiece at each of the building's four entrances—represent *The Song of Achievement* and *Progress* at the Mount Eden Avenue entrance, *Civic Government* and *The Majesty of the Law* at East 161st Street, *Victory and Peace* and *Loyalty, Valor and Sacrifice* at Walton Avenue, and *Triumph of Government* and *Genius of Administration* at 158th Street. The ornamental program continues inside, with four murals by James Monroe Hewlett showing scenes of Bronx history (Hewlett had earlier worked on the painted ceiling, showing the signs of the zodiac, in the main concourse of Grand Central Terminal).

All that over-scale sculpture can overshadow the thoroughly Art Deco window spandrels and entrances—don't miss the wonderful copper (and, in the lower stories, copper and nickel) stylized floral designs that somehow outshine the rest of the building's ornament.

The building's grandeur inspired the *New York Herald Tribune* in March 1934 to hail it as a "Bronx Wonder Building," but the paper also noted a controversy about its style: "The glory that was Greece, the grandeur that was Rome and the splendor that is the Bronx County Building became inextricably involved yesterday. . . . Mayor F. H. La Guardia, on one of his flying excursions two weeks ago, had visited it and said the place reminded him of the palaces of his [Roman] ancestors, Justinian, Augustus Caesar and Nero. Architects, on the other hand, have agreed that the building's predominant note is Grecian." The court's presiding justice, Joseph M. Callahan, apparently took exception to these notions; the newspaper quoted him as insisting, "I rather think that this building is typically American, not only architecturally, in the rugged simplicity and beauty of its lines, but traditionally." The reporter decided to split the difference, and referred to the building as the "Greco-Roman-American courthouse." Nobody thought to call it Moderne. For his part, Mayor La Guardia was so taken with the new building that, to celebrate its dedication, he transferred the seat of city government to the Bronx for three days.

## 12.3 (HD) 888 Grand Concourse Apartments (at East 161st Street) (Plate 13) Emery Roth, 1937

Unlike most of the Bronx Deco apartment houses, No. 888 owes its design to a figure of city-wide significance. Emery Roth (for Roth, see 9.2) brought his unusual—and rarely seen—approach to Deco to this major site opposite the Bronx County Building on the west and, on the north, the Concourse Plaza Hotel—once thought of as the Waldorf of the Bronx. Instead of coming to a standard sharp angle at the corner, Roth's creation meets the intersection with an elegantly prolonged "S" curve in the upper stories, a simpler curve at the first story, and a concave curving entry space—lined with horizontal gold mosaic lines—under a convexly curving canopy. Constance Rosenblum, in her book on the Grand Concourse, memorably describes the overall effect: "a medley of curves, scallops, and concave spaces executed in polished black granite, bronze, stainless steel, marble mosaic, and gold stripes." The only other apartment house entrance remotely like this will be found in Manhattan, at the Normandy Apartments (see 9.2 for a photo comparison)—designed by the same architect in the same year.

Its location opposite the Bronx County Building made No. 888 a logical choice for the politically connected—early residents included Peter Sinnott, described in the *Times* as a "building contractor who is chairman of the Bronx County Democratic Committee of the Fifteenth Assembly District"; County Judge James M. Barrett; and Bernard Hahn, a one-time special assistant to the U.S. Attorney General.

## 12.4 ⋆Park Plaza Apartments, 1005 Jerome Avenue (at East 164th Street) (Plate 14) Horace Ginsbern & Associates, Marvin Fine designer, 1929–31

Directly across the street from the new Yankee Stadium stands one of the very first—possibly *the* first—of the Bronx's Art Deco apartment buildings, and perhaps one of the best designs of the type.

Simon and Louis Bregman, speculative builders active in the borough, hired Horace Ginsbern's firm in 1928 and announced the project in a press release, boasting that the Park Plaza would "be developed in character along Modernistic lines accentuating the simplicity of detail in modernistic architecture—the use of polychrome terra cotta blends harmoniously with the light brick used and a very pleasing effect will be created." The original building would have been ten stories tall—with a rear façade of four stories on Anderson Avenue, which rises steeply just west of Jerome Avenue on the hills of Highbridge—but a fire destroyed the building while still under construction. In a 1981 interview with the author, Marvin Fine recalled hearing about the fire as he ate dinner with his parents, and rushing up to the Bronx to see for himself. The new version rose only eight stories.

Unlike many other Bronx architects of the day, Fine (1904–1981) benefited from a sophisticated architectural education at the University of Pennsylvania, where he came under the influence of Paul Cret's Modern Classic, and landed a job at Cass Gilbert's office—followed by a stint working for George and Edward Blum (for the Blums, see 3.11)—before joining Horace Ginsbern's firm as a designer in 1928. In his interview, Fine spoke of being "imbued with the spirit of the Classics," and described some of his first, classically inspired sketches for the Park Plaza.

What led him to desert the Classical camp in this, his first major design? Fine credited the influence of two major players in the new modernism: Raymond Hood (of the Daily News Building, 5.1) and William Van Alen (of the Chrysler Building, 5.4). Fine heard Van Alen lecture and "decided to follow him." He watched Hood's Daily News Building rise across the street from Ginsbern's East 42nd Street offices, and explained: "I developed

[Hood's] vertical style, and all up the Concourse in all the buildings we designed, the change of brick between the spandrels I got directly from him." Fine recalls telling Ginsbern that the firm should come up with a trademark all its own, "a mark of reference on all our jobs"—and that trademark became the Bronx Art Deco apartment building.

Even though just eight stories tall, Park Plaza has something of the skyscraper to it—and many marks of the new modernism: vertical lines of windows, geometric brick patterns in the spandrels, a three-dimensional presence thanks to the deeply recessed courtyards between its various sections. Most striking is the multicolored terra-cotta banding running across the first and second stories—alternating scenes, separated by a zigzag, of flamingoes and fountains on the one hand, and the sun rising behind a Bronx apartment building on the other.

Most unusual is the terra-cotta scene, one story up, with what appears to be a Roman aqueduct in the background, a representation of the Parthenon on a tall base in the foreground, and a young architect, with a model of his new creation, kneeling in front. Fine explained: "I remember developing this idea of the architect of today, presenting his building to the Acropolis and saying, you know, well, what do you think? Kid, kid's thoughts." The young architect, once "imbued with the spirit of the classics," had thrown it all over for the new modernism—but knelt before the original classical temple and asked for approval.

## 12.5 1001 Jerome Avenue (at East 164th Street) Sugarman & Berger, 1937

The apartment building adjoining Park Plaza on the south shows how much the style had evolved in just half a dozen years from Fine's Deco—and also from the architects' own earlier work (for Sugarman & Berger, see 4.4), for instance the Hotel New Yorker (4.8). White brick, corner windows, horizontal brick speed lines at the first story, and a curving metal hood above the entrance mark No. 1001 as less Deco and more Moderne.

## 12.6 *Noonan Plaza Apartments, 105–149 West 168th Street (at Nelson and Ogden Avenues) Horace Ginsbern & Associates, Marvin Fine designer, 1931

Park Plaza so impressed developer Bernard Noonan, one of Ginsbern's major clients, that he commissioned a much larger version, to be called "Noonan Plaza." Noonan had built many projects in Highbridge, the elevated section just west of Jerome Avenue where he had his office, but considered Noonan Plaza among his best. According to the building's prospectus, "Noonan Plaza, as planned, represents the highest development in the art of the modern apartment house design and construction. The quality of workmanship used in the structure is unquestionably perfect, showing the finest type of craftsmanship possible."

The enormous complex has façades on three sides of its very large block—bounded by West 168th Street and Ogden and Nelson Avenues. Its walls mimic the arrangement of vertical window columns of Park Plaza, but create multiple units mingled with light courts, all wrapped around an interior court. At the corner of Nelson and West 168th, the walls pull back to create a one-story arcade with five entryways on either street, its multicolored brick rippling up and down, while the trees of the garden beckon

from the other side.

In October 1931, the *Times* described the building as "of the garden apartment type," and its interior court as a garden "15,000 square feet in area with a central waterfall and pool crossed by bridges giving access to the five entrance vestibules. The style of architecture is modernistic, with interior decorations to harmonize, including colored marble and indirect lighting. . . . On the roof also is a garden promenade and playground." During the difficult years of the 1970s, Noonan Plaza suffered serious deterioration. The *Times*, returning to the building in January 1976, reported, "Vandalism has destroyed much of the art deco detailing that once made the building . . . one of the prides of the Bronx. And now it is so unprofitable to run that the building's last owner let it fall into receivership last month."

After several false starts, however, Noonan Plaza found new hope in 1982 as a new owner brought in the Ginsbern firm to oversee the building's restoration. Marvin Fine had died a year earlier, and Horace Ginsbern a decade earlier, but Frederick Ginsbern, Horace Ginsbern's son and himself an architect, took delight in undertaking the project. The *Times* reported young Ginsbern's recollection of visiting the complex and its garden with his father: "'Behind the pool was a waterfall,' Mr. Ginsbern said, 'and the water ran down under a Japanese bridge to the pool.'" Today, the restored Noonan Plaza looks splendid once again.

## 12.7 (HD) 1150 Grand Concourse (at McClellan Street) (Plate 15) Horace Ginsbern, 1936–37

No. 1150 is an enormous building—it includes six light courts, three opening onto the street, three hidden The light courts facing the street help break up the unusually long façade, but the architects didn't rely only on light courts. Ginsbern (or more likely his designer, Marvin Fine—for Fine see 12.4) took advantage of the irregular path of the Grand Concourse to create windows angled in from the main façade, making for dramatic effects of light and shadow. These sections project out slightly from the adjoining light courts with their wraparound corner windows. The entire façade seems to be in motion.

The building has lost some of its detail—notably the modernistic metal railing at the roofline, metal grilles on the entrance doors, and the original casement windows. But it still retains its mysterious, magical mosaic around the entrance—enormous, multicolored fish on curving walls—topped by a modernistic metal band and set within a cast-stone base punctuated by inset squares. That mosaic has made No. 1150—"the fish building"—one of the best-known Deco buildings on the Concourse.

## 12.8a (HD) 1166 Grand Concourse (between McClellan and East 167th Streets) Jacob M. Felson, 1938

## 12.8b (HD) 1188 Grand Concourse (between McClellan and East 167th Streets) Jacob M. Felson, 1938

1166 Grand Concourse

1188 Grand Concourse

Unusually for the Concourse, this entire block front is taken up by Art Deco buildings—No. 1150 by Horace Ginsbern, and Nos. 1166 and 1188 by Jacob Felson (for Felson, see 11.2). The wide buildings set on an enormously long block front create the effect of an endless stretch of six-story Deco façades—suggesting what an imaginary, all-Deco Grand Concourse might have looked like.

Though Felson's two buildings, like Ginsbern's No. 1150, have suffered losses, they still show how a talented architect—taking advantage of the winding thoroughfare—could break up the buildings' façades into receding layers, and give every apartment facing the Concourse a fashionable corner window.

## 12.9 (NR HD) 1500 Grand Concourse (at East 172nd Street) Jacob M. Felson, 1935

Felson's design here uses the red and black brick pioneered at the Daily News Building and brought to the Bronx by Marvin Fine and Horace Ginsbern. The white, red, and black checkerboard of a façade might seem somewhat repetitive, but a closer look reveals Felson's sense of ornamental detail. The red and black

geometrically patterned brick window spandrels sprout more elaborate patterns at the roofline, as do the broad uninterrupted columns of white brick—some rising to a curving, red, geometric cast-stone fantasy, others to a square of brick headers (the narrow end of the brick) alternatingly projecting in and out.

Though the original doorway has disappeared, its wonderful cast-stone fantasy of a surround still projects around the entrance, as does the cast-stone ornament marking secondary entrances.

### *Grand Concourse and Fordham Road*

## 12.10 Wagner Building, 2488 Grand Concourse (at Fordham Road) Nathan Rotholz, 1931–32, 1936

Occupying the southeast corner of Fordham Road and the Grand Concourse—perhaps the single most prominent commercial intersection in the Bronx—the four-story Wagner Building represents the scaling back of a much grander, ten-story office building project that most likely succumbed to Depression economics. Constantin Wagner, proprietor of a glassworks factory, intended No. 2488 as a commercial real-estate venture. He expanded his building to the south in 1936, but still dreamed of a taller tower. The *Times* in October of that year described the building and its extension as "of the same modernistic architectural design, being four-story office and store buildings. Mr. Wagner has planned them as ten-story structures with foundations, heating systems and elevators so designed that the extra stories can be added later." Two of the three elevators in the lobby remain dummies—no elevators behind the doors, but with indicator panels that show stories one through ten.

Even in its truncated state, the Wagner Building remains one of the borough's finest surviving Art Deco commercial buildings. Though the first

story has been altered with new storefronts, the Art Deco detail above survives remarkably intact—including at the main-entrance Wagner's symbol of an eagle grasping the tips of a capital "W," and metal detail that could have been lifted from the Chrysler Building.

The polychromatic terra-cotta covering the façade includes columns with zigzag ripples—very few flat surfaces here. The Art Deco lobby survives practically untouched, from floor to ceiling, including scalloped ceiling moldings and patterned flat coffers, a wonderfully geometric railing on a staircase leading up to the first story, staircase shapes on ventilator grilles, and Wagner's eagle on the elevator doors.

## 12.11 **Dollar Savings Bank (later Apple Bank), 2530 Grand Concourse (at Fordham Road) Adolf L. Muller of Halsey, McCormack & Helmer, 1932–33, 1937–38, 1949–52

Visible from miles around, the tall clock tower of the Dollar Savings Bank has long marked the intersection of Fordham Road and the Concourse in a way that the truncated Wagner Building (12.10) never could. Though the bank looks all of a piece, it has a complicated history—initially built in 1932–33 as a tiny building consisting of just what today is the southernmost entrance bay, it expanded a hundred feet to the north in 1937–38, and finally, after the end of World War II, sprouted the ten-story office building and fifty-foot-tall clock tower that make it such a visible landmark.

Dollar opened in 1890, much further south, as the borough's first savings bank. The 1932 building at the Grand Concourse and Fordham Road initially served as one of Dollar's many far-flung branches. By 1948, Dollar had grown to be the sixth-largest mutual savings bank in the country, and, following completion of the new tower, the bank moved its headquarters to this location. Banks, however, generally either swallow or are swallowed by other banks. In 1983 Dollar merged with the Dry Dock Savings Bank, only to be bought up in 1992 by Emigrant Savings Bank, which was in turn absorbed by Apple Bank in 2013. When last heard from, Apple Bank still owned and occupied the complex.

Halsey, McCormack & Helmer specialized in bank buildings—George H. McCormack (1888–1954) began his career as a banker, and his banking connections helped his firm dominate the banking architecture field. The firm's early designs took the classic route of banks-as-Greek-temples. The architects turned to the Modern Classic approach just as Adolf Muller joined the firm—perhaps not coincidentally, Muller had formerly worked in the office of Starrett & Van Vleck, designers of the Art Deco façades of both the American Stock Exchange (2.1) and Bloomingdale's (7.1). No question that Muller designed the Dollar complex—he signed the drawings for all three of its sections.

Typically for the Modern Classic variety, Dollar Savings Bank mimics a Classical temple, but stripped down—its enormous two-story windows suggest a temple's gigantic pillars minus the Classical details (and topped by inscribed savings-bank bromides, such as "If you know how to spend less than you get—you have the philosopher's stone."). Modernistic ornamental detail clusters at the bronze doors—and explodes inside the main banking hall, which survives largely intact, with polished red-marble pilasters lining the walls, wonderful bronze filigree, and five murals illustrating the Bronx's early history.

### *Bronx Zoo*

## 12.12 *Paul J. Rainey Memorial Gates, Bronx Zoo (on East Fordham Road in Bronx Park) (Plate 16) Charles A. Platt, architect, Paul Manship, sculptor, 1929–34

The northern entrance to the Bronx Zoo—an institution founded back in 1895 as the world's first zoological research center—incorporates one of Paul Manship's most remarkable works. Grace Rainey Rogers donated a set of enormous ornamental bronze gates to the Zoo in memory of her late brother Paul Rainey—a zoo supporter and big-game hunter (a combination hard to imagine today).

During the 1930s, Paul Manship (1885–1966) occupied an odd position: one of the country's most prominent classicist sculptors, about to be left behind by modern trends in the arts. His commissions during that decade include the statue of Prometheus at Rockefeller Center (6.10), a medal of President Franklin D. Roosevelt, a set of sculptures at the 1939 World's Fair, and the Rainey Gates.

Manship had spent much time in Europe, first at the American Academy in Rome, and then, from 1921, in Paris—where in 1925 he became one of only two American sculptors to have work displayed at the famous Exposition. According to one account, he spent a fair amount of time visiting the Exposition, which he described as "more than interesting, full of ideas." Manship's biographer, Susan Rather, suggests that Manship "clearly paid attention to the creations of Edgar Brandt" at the fair (for Brandt, see 3.5), and especially the Porte d'Honneur, grand entry to the grounds; she sees the Porte's influence on the Rainey Gates.

The sculptor collaborated on the gates with architect Charles A. Platt (1861–1933), another prominent figure on the conservative end of American arts, who had befriended Manship in the early 1910s. Platt commissioned a number of works from Manship for his own projects, and Manship's obituary quoted Platt as having once said "Mr. Manship's sculpture is known for its rare qualities of humor and grace. The abundance of his creativity energy [sic] is amazing and might be compared to the richness of nature in the spring of the year."

Called "one of the most ambitious undertakings of American sculpture" when first announced, the Rainey Gates combine a sedately modernistic take on architectural form with fantastic images of zoo animals. As recounted by the *Times*: "Mr. Manship is understood to have worked intermittently for five years on this undertaking. The casting of the gates has been in progress a year and is not finished yet. . . . During the years that Mr. Manship has been at work on the gates in both his New York and Paris studios, little or nothing about the undertaking has reached the public."

Manship's gates bear out Platt's words—the sculpted animals combine those "rare qualities of humor and grace." Bears and deer frolic atop the two gates, which in turn are flanked by exotic trees balancing on the shells of giant tortoises, while supporting a variety of birds. The shorter trees on the left and right support a leopard and a monkey, while the central tree supports an enormous seated lion. At the same time, these figures display typically Deco stylization, ranging from the sinuous curves of the trees to zigzag motifs framing the gates.

More than merely imaginary creations, the various animal sculptures represented actual residents of the zoo. As explained by the director, Dr. W. Reid Blair, in a June 1934 *Times* interview, "Paul Manship has faithfully reproduced in immortal bronze our giant Galapagos tortoise, Buster; Jimmy, the shoe-bill stork; Sultan, our great African lion, and other celebrities of the park, all of whom will require no expenditures for bananas, fish or raw beef."

### *Crotona Park area*

## 12.13 *Herman Ridder Junior High School (Public School 98), 1619 Boston Road (at East 173rd Street) Walter C. Martin, Superintendent of School Buildings for the New York City Board of Education, 1929–31

"Modernism in architecture has reached the schools," wrote the *New York Times* in 1929 about Herman Ridder Junior High. "The first thoroughly modernistic school building is being planned by the architects of the Board of Education. . . . Set-back terraces, reminiscent of Babylonian temples, colored enamel tiles borrowed from a later age and flat wall surfaces, exemplified by some recent skyscrapers will be features of the new school, a departure in school construction in the city."

The journal *Architecture and Building* concurred: "This is New York City's first school building to be carried out in modernistic design and the result is both pleasing and interesting."

The Bronx apartment house boom of the 1920s, which culminated in an explosion of Art Deco apartment houses, reflected the borough's huge increase in population, some 72% during that decade alone. That increase included school-age children, and the Bronx consequently saw a boom in school construction. At the same time, New York—like the nation at large—had begun to experiment with the new concept of the junior high school, breaking out those middle grades formerly included in elementary schools. The city began a major construction program for the new junior highs in 1927, and Ridder—built to accommodate three thousand young teenagers—was one of the first new buildings completed.

The schools superintendent and the president of the Board of Education "expressed themselves as pleased with the plans, stressing the educational value of beautiful and expressive [sic] in architecture." That kind of support no doubt helped guarantee that the new building would be an architectural delight.

The building is faced in limestone in the lower stories, and brick and terra-cotta above. Geometrically patterned brickwork in the lower spandrels and terra-cotta panels of stylized floral patterns at the roofline give the building some of its modernistic panache. The design of the corner entrance tower bears a marked resemblance to the Nebraska State Capitol, a much-publicized decade-long project, designed by New York architect Bertram Goodhue, that reached completion in the same years as Ridder. Modeling the entrance tower on a setback skyscraper suggests just how interconnected Art Deco must have been, in the architect's mind, with skyscraper design.

## 12.14 *Crotona Park Play Center, Crotona Park (Fulton Avenue between East 172nd and 174th Streets) Aymar Embury II, consulting architect; Gilmore D. Clarke and others, landscape architects; 1934–36

In the depths of the Great Depression, Mayor Fiorello La Guardia and his Parks Commissioner Robert Moses lassoed federal funds from the Works Progress Administration (WPA) and hired an army of the unemployed to build eleven enormous play centers across the city—each with a vast, if shallow, swimming pool to cool off the depressed citizenry during the blazing-hot summer months. Manhattan and Brooklyn got the lion's share, leaving one Play Center apiece in each of the other three boroughs—in Astoria, Queens (14.1); in St. George on Staten Island (15.1); and here, on the Fulton Street side of Crotona Park, in the middle of the Bronx.

Aymar Embury II (1880–1966) studied engineering before apprenticing with several New York architectural firms, eventually becoming a favored architect for country houses. During the Depression, he served as consulting architect for many New York City public projects—by one count, more than six hundred. Gilmore Clarke (1892–1982), with degrees in landscape architecture and civil engineering, became one of the country's leading landscape architects for public works. Both men, by virtue of their involvement with the city's public agencies, worked closely with Moses on park projects.

Though the designs of the Play Centers differ one from the next, they all share certain characteristics—notably the inexpensive materials of cast-stone and brick, and Moderne styling. The main architectural characteristic of the Crotona Place Center is its blockiness, as in the blocky towers of the brick entrance gate, rising to geometric tops, which support a tall archway. That blockiness is tempered by curving, open brickwork balconies and—appropriately enough, given the setting—playful cast-stone sculptural figures such as the ibis, by Frederick G. R. Roth, on the Center's south façade.

## 12.15 *Orchard Beach Bathhouse, Pelham Bay Park Aymar Embury II, consulting architect; Gilmore D. Clarke and Michael Rapuano, consulting landscape architects; 1934–37

Though not part of the WPA pool and play-center project, the Orchard Beach Bathhouse was designed by the same architects, in the same year, with similar funding, for the same client, and in fact opened officially just one day after the Crotona Park Play Center (12.14).

The Bronx—perhaps more than any other borough—devotes vast swaths of its land to parks, interconnected by a system of parkways. Pelham Bay Park, the city's largest, became on its establishment in 1887 New York's first seaside park, and attracted to its shores a summer bungalow colony known as Orchard Beach. Today's Orchard Beach dates to the mid-1930s, when Mayor La Guardia's new Park Commissioner, Robert Moses, secured federal WPA funds to rebuild the deteriorated and vandalized area. Moses filled in a chunk of the adjoining bay, thereby connecting an island and a peninsula, and trucked in not quite two million cubic yards of sand, to create a one-mile curving beach complete with a public promenade. The *New York Times* in July 1936 described Orchard Beach's grand opening: "The climax of the celebration was reached . . . with a twenty-five-minute

display of fireworks discharged from a barge anchored about 1,500 feet off the beach. About 15,000 persons were present. The display ended with the firing of seventy-nine aerial bombs and a ninety-foot display in which the words 'Orchard Beach' were spelled out in fiery letters."

The two grand curving wings of the bathhouse, in concrete, brick and limestone—each with a colonnade of gigantic square piers—suggest more of a Modern Classic aesthetic than does the Crotona Park Play Center (12.14), but the Bathhouse clearly shares the Play Center's orientation as a modern, publicly funded recreational complex. It has simple but entertaining blue and white tiles in the interior spaces, with a geometric Greek fret design running across the top, and similar tiles outside with circular vents—which vents look rather like portholes, but with wavy lines running across them suggesting ocean motion, very much in the Moderne spirit.

# ITINERARY NO. 13
# BROOKLYN

Until 1898, Brooklyn existed as an independent city—and the nation's third largest at that—with an urban personality noticeably distinct from that of the buzzing commercial giant across the East River. Brooklyn's boosters styled it the City of Homes and the City of Churches—churches, indeed, predominated here, as opposed to the sinful theaters of Gotham. The proposal to link the two cities with the Brooklyn Bridge stirred great opposition among Brooklyn's leaders, who warned that with the bridge in place, New York would swallow Brooklyn whole—as, indeed, it did.

In the early twentieth century, the great, formerly self-sufficient Victorian city evolved into a huge bedroom community for Manhattan. In the years following World War I, large numbers of six-story apartment buildings joined the endless blocks of brownstone row houses that had defined nineteenth-century Brooklyn. In the late 1920s and into the 1930s, Art Deco apartment buildings sprouted all across the borough—not, perhaps, to the same extent as in the Bronx, but certainly enough to change the visual character of newly developing or redeveloping neighborhoods, notably Flatbush in the borough's center and Brighton Beach at its far end on the Atlantic shore.

The list of buildings that follows includes half a dozen of the best examples of the Brooklyn Art Deco apartment house (13.3, 13.4, 13.5, 13.9, 13.10, 13.11)—many dozens more could be added. Besides these, this itinerary includes a small but stunning skyscraper (13.1) by Corbett, Harrison & MacMurray, part of the architecture team at Rockefeller Center (6.10); another telephone-company office building (13.2) by Ralph Walker; a department store (13.6); an elevated subway station (13.7); and the borough's central library (13.8). Though not included because of space limitations, Brooklyn also boasts four WPA pool and play centers, similar to those in the other boroughs, in Greenpoint, Sunset Park, Red Hook, and Brownsville.

## *Downtown and Brooklyn Heights*

### 13.1 *National Title Guaranty Company Building, 185 Montague Street (at Clinton Street) Corbett, Harrison & MacMurray, 1929–30

Brooklyn Heights is geographically as close as the borough gets to Manhattan, and just before beginning work on Rockefeller Center (6.10), the great modernist firm of Corbett, Harrison & MacMurray (for Corbett, see 2.9) brought the latest in Manhattan modernism to the decorous streets of this genteel neighborhood. (Corbett's other Manhattan work includes the Criminal Courthouse, 2.9; Hotel Ten Park Avenue, 3.2; Metropolitan Life North Tower, 3.8; and the Master Apartments, 9.12.) Back in Brooklyn's independent nineteenth-century days, this block of Montague Street had housed the city's great cultural institutions: the Brooklyn Mercantile Library, the Brooklyn Art Association, and the Brooklyn Academy of Music. As the twentieth-century borough expanded, those institutions moved on, and the block developed into a banking center.

According to the *New York Times* in a March 1930 article about the National Title Guaranty Company's new home, "This new building, in its bold modern treatment, is a real architectural addition to the business area of the Heights. . . . The treatment of both the exterior and interior of the building is modern, but not, according to the architects, modernistic"—a sentence suggesting some uncertainty about the meaning of that last word.

Though quite short by Manhattan skyscraper standards, the building reaches skyward with its typical vertical window columns, rising to receding stepped setbacks at the top. Modernistic ornament in the upper stories is set modestly into the window spandrels—layers of patterned brick—but the building's chief Deco glory lies in the first few stories: elaborately handsome but abstract stone grille work designed by that ubiquitous architectural sculptor of the day, Rene Chambellan (see 5.5, 9.10, and 14.10).

The ground floor and lobby disappeared in an unfortunate alteration of 1970, but otherwise the building survives intact. It must have looked splendid back in 1930, when it was bathed in dramatic nighttime lighting—floodlights at the second floor and, as described in the *Times*, a "lighting effect . . . created from behind the stone grille work with two fourteen-foot light standards of black granite surmounted by light sources of gold-plated bronze flanking the building on the street."

## 13.2 ★Long Island Headquarters of the New York and New Jersey Telephone and Telegraph Company Building, 95–105 Willoughby Street (at Bridge Street) Ralph Walker, of Voorhees, Gmelin & Walker, 1929–30

Another in the series of monolithic phone company buildings designed by Ralph Walker, this office building is a fraternal twin to the New York Telephone Company headquarters (2.4), Western Union Building (2.6) and the Long Lines Building (2.10) in lower Manhattan—as well as other relatives up and down the Eastern seaboard. The Brooklyn building's design combines the blocky massing of the Long Lines Building with the rippling brickwork of Western Union and the geometric metalwork at the entrances of both. As described in *Architecture and Building*, December 1931: "A warm reddish-brown brick rising from a red granite base has been used with striking effect in the exterior finish of the building, a slight variation in shades of color with patterned laying giving life to the mass."

Like all three of the Manhattan towers, the building retains a wonderfully dramatic and intact lobby.

## *Flatbush*

Of all Brooklyn's neighborhoods, Flatbush most closely resembles the West Bronx in its development patterns—heavily rebuilt with six-story apartment buildings in the 1920s and 1930s, most in eclectic styles, but with some lively Art Deco additions. Where the West Bronx has the Grand Concourse, Flatbush has Ocean Avenue (and to a lesser extent Ocean Parkway). Brooklyn had its own architectural community, so the architects here are not the architects of the Bronx, but the two groups no doubt knew of each other. As a major commercial center for the borough, Flatbush also attracted a major retailer in the Sears Company.

### 13.3 135 Ocean Avenue (near Lincoln Road)
### Boris W. Dorfman, 1928–29

Boris Dorfman (1881 or '82–1964), though not as well known as some of the other Brooklyn architects of the day, built throughout the borough and designed many apartment buildings on Ocean Avenue, including No. 135, one of Brooklyn's most colorful.

Dorfman's imaginative design here makes use of brick set in half-a-dozen geometric patterns and cast-stone panels with zigzags; with very few flat spots, this façade seems to be in perpetual motion. But what especially catches the eye of passersby is the shiny, colored tile applied at key spots—in abstract vertical panels inserted in the unusual round brick pylons flanking the main entrance, and in light- and dark-blue panels in ziggurat shapes at the top and bottom of the top story. Though a six-story apartment building, not a skyscraper, No. 135 nevertheless sports a skyline, with futuristic brick and cast-stone pergolas at the corners.

### 13.4 832 Ocean Avenue (near Dorchester Road)
### Kavy & Kavovitt, 1931

Morris Kavy (1898–1984) of Kavy & Kavovitt (see 13.9) emerged as one of Brooklyn's most active architects and builders of apartment houses, and his Deco designs rank among the borough's liveliest.

The brickwork at No. 832 Ocean Avenue is as over-the-top as can be found on a Brooklyn Art Deco apartment building.

Almost every inch of brick seems alive and wiggling. Pairs of long, ribbed piers rise uninterrupted from bottom to top, framing the recessed entrance court; projecting and recessed bricks form geometric patterns above, below, and framing the spandrels between the windows; and unusually abstract ornamental cast-stone pieces emphasize the windows' tops and bottoms—including an extraordinary silhouette above the middle window in the third story of either wing of the building that suggests a skyscraper skyline silhouette. In this building, Art Deco is definitely in the details.

## 13.5 855 Ocean Avenue (at Dorchester Road) William T. McCarthy, 1930

Another active Brooklyn architect, William T. McCarthy (1876–1952), had a lively imagination regarding urban issues. He attracted press attention in 1929 with a proposal to relieve congestion in downtown Brooklyn by raising sidewalks to the second-story level, thereby making more room for automobiles on the street. In 1930, representing the Brooklyn Society of Architects, he joined Edward Blum (of Blum & Blum, see 3.11), William Delano (of Delano & Aldrich, see 14.3), and another two dozen appointees to Mayor Walker's committee looking into improvements of the multiple-dwellings law—no doubt his activity as an apartment-house

designer recommended him for the job. McCarthy went on to become well known for large apartment buildings throughout the borough, as well as huge, city-sponsored public housing projects.

McCarthy's design for No. 855 Ocean Avenue is simpler than Kavy & Kavovitt's work just across the street at No. 832 (13.4), but still attractive, and an excellent illustration of how incised lines, alternating colors, patterned brick, and geometrically adorned cast stone can help even a modest building look lively and up-to-date.

## 13.6 ★Sears Roebuck, 2390 Bedford Avenue (at Beverly Road) Nimmons, Carr & Wright, with Alton L. Craft, 1932; expansion along Beverly Road, 1940

In the early twentieth century, two major nineteenth-century catalog companies—Sears Roebuck and Montgomery Ward—entered the retail business, and eventually built large department stores in major markets around the country. Montgomery Ward opened its first New York department store (14.11) in Queens in 1930; Sears—which had built its first retail outlet in Chicago in 1925 and then opened a few smaller stores in New York—followed suit in Brooklyn in 1932, with one of three large metropolitan-area department stores built that year (the other two in Hackensack and Union City, New Jersey). Montgomery Ward chose the dense Queens commercial center of Jamaica, while Sears chose a comparable location near the heart of Flatbush, one of Brooklyn's most densely populated neighborhoods—but on a site just far enough off the beaten commercial path to leave room for a large parking lot targeting newly motorized customers.

With its roots in the Midwest, Sears naturally worked with Chicago architects: George C. Nimmons (1865–1847), George W. Carr (1879–1958), and Clark C. Wright (1880–1948). Nimmons had worked in the office of Burnham & Root before starting his own partnership, and began his association with Sears as early as 1904 (in 1903, Nimmons had designed the Chicago home of Sears executive Julius Rosenwald). In various iterations, the firm designed Sears outlets of one kind or another in some sixty-five cities in twenty-eight states. As out-of-towners in Flatbush, they brought in Alton L. Craft as their local Brooklyn partner.

Sears's first branches tended to the classical, but by the late 1920s Nimmons had settled on an Art Deco look—often including a corner tower with large signs that would catch the eye of passing motorists. Rosenwald became a major supporter of the thoroughly modernistic 1933 "Century of Progress" exposition in Chicago, which included an official Sears Roebuck building—described by the exposition's guidebook as a "building which strikingly carries out the modern architectural scheme of the Fair." As early as 1928 Nimmons and company designed the Art Deco Sears Roebuck on Brookline Avenue in Boston. The Flatbush Sears, built four years later, falls squarely into that same category—lively commercial Art Deco style, prominent tower, parking lot.

Sears's Deco styling is modest but effective. The tower, naturally enough, expresses itself through vertical lines—but so do the low sections along Bedford Avenue and Beverly Road, especially over the Bedford Avenue entrance. There, ribbed limestone piers rise upward, flanking windows with geometrically patterned spandrels (the windows themselves have been covered with plastic panels which try to imitate the spandrel patterns). Still, the tower includes the most eye-catching Deco ornament—three abstract floral cast-stone reliefs above the first story, zigzag and staircase motifs running up the tower, and especially the "Sears Roebuck and Co" spelled out in modernistic cast-stone capital letters—letters which have lured in countless Sears customers over the decades.

*South Brooklyn*

## 13.7 (NR) Fourth Avenue and Ninth Street Subway Station, Independent Line (IND) Squire J. Vickers, opened 1933

Another Art Deco structure for the new Independent subway. Vickers (for Vickers, see also 6.11 and 11.1) wrote later that the announced plans for an elevated station brought protests from the neighborhood, whose residents likely feared a noisy, filthy, overhead eyesore. "But they were persuaded that the structure would adorn rather than desecrate the avenue; then we were directed to make an architectural gesture."

That gesture turned into one of the city's grandest utilitarian Deco designs, an enormous, hulking structure with rippling patterned brickwork set in craggy cliffs of layered levels—not unlike the brickwork at Ralph Walker's Western Union Building (2.6). Cast-stone ornament in abstract patterns suggests an electrical charge from the massive voltage propelling the subways through the system.

Modernistic metallic light fixtures survive at various spots. An enormous steel arch dramatically lifts the tracks over Fourth Avenue, its walls sporting typically geometric metal ornament.

*Eastern Parkway and Grand Army Plaza*

## 13.8 *Brooklyn Public Library, Central Building, Grand Army Plaza (at Eastern Parkway and Flatbush Avenue) Alfred Morton Githens and Francis Keally, 1935–1941; sculptors Paul Jennewein, bas reliefs, and Thomas H. Jones, screen over entry

The Brooklyn Public Library sits in the middle of the borough's major cultural center, not far from the Brooklyn Museum, the triumphal arch in Grand Army Plaza, and Prospect Park. A 1902 merger between the old private Mercantile Library on Montague Street (see 13.1) and the more recently created system of Brooklyn branch libraries (separate then, as now, from the New York Public Library system) led to plans for a grand central Brooklyn library to match, if not exactly rival, the central New York Public Library at 42nd Street and Fifth Avenue. Though the site was selected as early as 1905 and an architect (Raymond F. Almirall) in 1906, with construction beginning in 1911, politics and debates delayed the project—by 1930, it was still just one-third completed. Finally, in 1935 the library scrapped the original plan and hired new architects. Githens and Keally salvaged what they could of the unfinished building, but stripped it of what the *Times* called its "Graeco-Roman ornaments" and designed a deliberately "modern" building. On the library's opening in October 1941, the *Brooklyn Eagle* opined that here was "a swan of a building, so to speak, risen out of an ugly duckling."

The building's enormous central entrance in a blank stone wall facing the plaza, with wings to either side following the adjacent streets, has been likened to an open book. *The New Yorker*'s hard-to-please architecture critic, Lewis Mumford, considered this one of the best library buildings in the city, writing in October 1940, "As . . . one approaches the new building . . . the effect is unexpectedly exhilarating. The bright limestone walls, the handsome, bowed-in front of the central mass glittering with gold, the good proportions, the absence of dreary columns, all create a sense of happy expectation. . . . Thanks to the elemental cubic forms and the clean outlines, the building from a distance has a powerful aesthetic effect."

The building's relatively sparse ornament clusters around the entrance, where it evokes the content of its books. Above the entry doors, an enormous bronze screen, designed by Thomas H. Jones—sculptor of the Tomb of the Unknown Soldier in Arlington National Cemetery—has fifteen squares, each with a gilded relief of a figure from American literature: Tom Sawyer, Moby Dick, even Edgar Allan Poe's Raven.

The enormous pylons to either side—fifty feet tall—illustrate the evolution of science and art in gilded silhouettes designed by Paul

Jennewein. All told, the Library is a splendid monument to the power of the written word—and also of good architecture.

### *Brighton Beach*

Originally developed as a nineteenth-century seaside resort, mixing grand hotels with modest bungalows, Brighton Beach was transformed in the 1920s and 1930s into a year-round neighborhood with apartment blocks designed by many of the same Brooklyn architects working in Flatbush.

## 13.9 Brighton Beach Gardens Apartments, 1120–1130 and 1150–1170 Brighton Beach Avenue (at Brighton 14th Street and Seacoast Terrace) Kavy & Kavovitt, 1935–36

When in April 1936 the *New York Times*—under the heading "Houses of Varied Types Rise In and Near Manhattan"—published a rendering of Kavy & Kavovitt's Brighton Beach Gardens Apartments, the reporter compared it to other new complexes, and described it as in a "more striking modern style, featuring straight lines and broad horizontal bands between floors on the façade."

Built to accommodate 314 families, the complex had apartments "ranging in size from one and one-half to four and one-half rooms," and, according to the article, "the bathrooms will be supplied with salt water." Salt-water taps were a mark of luxury in the enormous Newport seaside "cottages" built for the likes of the Vanderbilts—but Brighton Beach apartment houses? Who knew? Ads for the complex in the *Times,* in September 1936, picked up on that detail, as well as other luxury amenities: "When you move this fall—MOVE AHEAD! Not just from one apartment to another but to a better, more healthful kind of living right in New York City. . . . AIR-CONDITIONED BY THE ATLANTIC OCEAN. Come down today and see with your own eyes the Extra Large Rooms, Huge Closets, Cross Ventilation, Modern Refrigeration, Beautiful Tiled Bathrooms (salt water as well as fresh), Roof Garden, Lockers in Basement. . . . 30 minutes from downtown Manhattan, by 5c express subway."

Kavy & Kavovitt's design relies on lively brick patterns. Horizontal brick bands, with projecting courses in a slightly different color, zip around the façade and wrap around curving corners, while brick panels rise above the roofline, with futuristic metal railings, to create a skyline effect. The architects add bursts of color including an almost cartoonlike sun rising behind a mountaintop in a panel above the main doorway, set in a projecting circular porch, flanked by colored glass windows set between panels of wild terra-cotta fantasy foliage.

## 13.10 Brighton Beach Apartments, 1159 Brighton Beach Avenue (at Brighton 15th Street) Kavy & Kavovitt? 1934

Though this building's architect appears to be unknown, it seems likely to be the firm of Kavy & Kavovitt. No. 1159 bears some resemblance to Kavy & Kavovitt's work a year later, at Brighton Beach Gardens (13.9) across the street, but, more to the point, its brickwork and small ornamental cast-stone detailing are practically identical to the brickwork and cast-stone detailing at 832 Ocean Avenue (13.4), which the firm built in 1931. Take a close look at the lighter-colored brick—it seems two-toned.

Each brick has been roughened in the center—part of a thoroughly inventive approach to a material that more often seems quite plain.

## 13.11 711 Brightwater Court (at Coney Island Avenue) Martyn N. Weinstein, 1934

Martyn N. Weinstein (later Weston; 1895–1972) studied at the Hebrew Technical Institute, Pratt Institute, and Columbia University, and spent two years with the firm of George B. Post & Sons before hanging out a shingle, first in a 1920s partnership, but by the 1930s strictly on his own. A thoroughly Brooklyn-based architect, Weinstein was a charter member of the Brooklyn Society of Architects, later serving as its president, and eventually also served as president of the Brooklyn chapter of the American Institute of Architects. Weinstein's output included large apartment houses in Brooklyn and Queens, built from the 1930s through the 1960s, and several Brooklyn synagogues.

No. 711 Brightwater Court has one of the most colorful and imaginative Art Deco façades anywhere in Brooklyn, the color provided partly by alternating shades of brick—like the endless repeating upside-down "V"s above the first-story windows, or the zigzag red and black brick panels beneath the windows at the building's edges—but especially by wildly ornamental, glazed terra-cotta panels. The panels beneath the windows above the main entrance pulsate in abstract asymmetrical floral designs in bright red and blue, almost like a paisley—except at the top story where they take on more orderly leafy patterns in more sedate shades.

The roofline at either end of the building is capped by a parapet of red semicircles against a blue background. But most stunning of all is the main entrance. The doors are surrounded by yellow and black triangles, which are in turn flanked by undulating black panels, while the whole is topped with a jungle pattern in green, yellow, and black glazed terra-cotta that makes this the most eye-popping front door of any Brooklyn Art Deco apartment house.

# ITINERARY NO. 14
# QUEENS

In 1898, New York City absorbed the western half of the once much larger Queens County, leaving the eastern half renamed Nassau County. Even then, Queens was less a recognizable geographic entity and more a collection of towns and villages, which for the most part survive today as distinct neighborhoods.

Queens is remarkable in its collection of Deco structures—they are few, but choice. They include two rare Art Deco churches (14.2, 14.4), the Marine Air Terminal at LaGuardia Airport (14.3), a gorgeously ornamental bank in Forest Hills (14.5), a late Moderne theater (14.6), two department stores (14.8 and 14.11), an office building (14.10), and an unusual surviving nightclub (14.9) in downtown Jamaica. They are arranged here by neighborhood.

### *Astoria and Long Island City*

### 14.1 ★Astoria Park Pool and Play Center, Astoria Park, 19th Street between 22nd Drive and Hoyt Avenue North John M. Hatton and others, architect; Aymar Embury II, consulting architect; Gilmore D. Clarke and others, landscape architects, 1934–36

This is one of the eleven giant swimming pools and recreation centers—and the only one in Queens—built by Robert Moses with Federal WPA funding (for the pools, see Crotona Park Play Center, 12.14). The Astoria Pool and Play Center has perhaps the most impressive setting of them all—in the middle of a park sloping down to the East River, set between two hugely dramatic bridges, the RFK (formerly Triboro) and the Hellgate. The enormous pool, capable of holding sixty-two hundred

people, was large enough to host the final trials for the 1936 Summer Olympics.

Architect John Hatton apparently had a predilection for glass block, which he employed liberally both here and in his play center at Betsy Head in Brooklyn, along with the usual brick and concrete. The "classic" of Modern Classic shows up in the huge brick piers surrounding the pool, while the "modern" shows up in the geometric brick patterns. Particularly nice details include the round brick piers and glass-block windows of the "girls" and "boys" restrooms, and the brick filter house topped by a flying saucer in concrete.

## 14.2 Church of the Most Precious Blood, 32–23 36th Street and 32–40 37th Street (between Broadway and 34th Avenue) Henry J. McGill and Talbot Hamlin, 1931

Talbot Hamlin (1889–1956) may be better known for his history of Greek Revival architecture, or his Pulitzer Prize–winning biography of architect Benjamin Latrobe—as well as his distinguished career at Columbia University's School of Architecture—but, until the Depression forced him into academia, Hamlin also practiced as an architect. McGill (1890–1953), his partner from 1920 to about 1930, had strong connections to the Catholic Church. The firm designed churches in Brooklyn and Queens, as well as Nassau County, New Jersey and beyond, many of them Art Deco or Moderne—including elsewhere in Queens the Church of the Blessed Sacrament in Jackson Heights (14.4). McGill also designed the remarkable Deco Crucifixion Tower for the National Shrine of the Little Flower Catholic Church in Royal Oak, Michigan (1929–31)—with carved reliefs by Rene Chambellan—as well as a memorial to New York's Cardinal Hayes in the Bronx in 1939. On August 5th of that year, the *Brooklyn Eagle* called McGill the "foremost liturgist of Catholic architects in the country."

The Church of the Most Precious Blood has been called the firm's masterpiece. As Robert A.M. Stern described it in *New York: 1930*, the design "somehow succeeded in marrying references to Celtic architecture, the Jazz Age, fin-de-siècle Vienna, and the elemental medievalism of Sir Edwin Lutyens's Castle Drogo." An article in *Architecture and Building* in February 1932 called out the church as an excellent example of modernism in church design, noting that "it is hard to break away from" precedence in church design, with the result that "we mostly adhere to ancient types in design which do not fit the modern" church structure. But at the Church of the Most Precious Blood, which represents "the best type of present day construction . . . the further step was taken. The design is modern too." "Modern," of course, meaning "Art Deco."

The church complex runs through the block, and, despite the official address, the main façade is on 37th Street, where Deco detailing shows up in the remarkable stone arch over the main entrance, in the geometric stone grilles to either side of it, and in the symbols of the four evangelists surrounding a cruciform window above the entrance—though look carefully and you'll find geometric patterns worked into the very stone of the façade, and in the metalwork atop the octagonal bell tower. Typically Deco geometric patterning also adorns the 36th Street façade.

### *Jackson Heights and East Elmhurst*

## 14.3 ★★Marine Air Terminal, LaGuardia Airport Delano & Aldrich, 1939

Off to one side of LaGuardia Airport stands one of the country's earliest surviving airport buildings, which began life as the terminus for the world's first trans-Atlantic passenger airline service.

Just one decade after Charles "Lucky" Lindbergh's 1927 solo flight from New York to Paris, Mayor Fiorello La Guardia proposed a new "New York City Municipal Airport" on the site of an abandoned private airfield in an area then called North Beach. La Guardia himself had taken flying lessons as early as 1913, and served as a pilot during World War I. As mayor, he pushed hard for federal money to build his new airport. President Roosevelt approved WPA funding in September 1937, and La Guardia had the pleasure of presiding over the groundbreaking a few days later for what became what *Fortune Magazine* called the WPA's "single greatest undertaking."

The Marine Air Terminal—just one part of the original complex, but the only survivor—owed its name to the original Pan Am "Yankee Clippers" making the first trans-Atlantic flights: "flying boats"—airplanes with pontoons—arriving and departing from Flushing Bay, just beyond the Terminal. The early airplane designers believed that such seaplanes offered extra safety for long flights over the Atlantic. The Clippers also offered luxury comparable to first-class train travel, with private dining rooms and sleeping bunks. Clare Boothe wrote in *Life* magazine: "Fifty years from now, people will look back on a Clipper flight of today as the most romantic voyage of history."

William A. Delano (1874–1960) and Chester H. Aldrich (1871–1940) both studied in Paris at the École des Beaux-Arts, both taught architecture, and both worked for the prominent New York City firm of Carrére & Hastings, where they met. Delano & Aldrich went on to design homes and estates for wealthy clients, including oil baron John D. Rockefeller, financier Otto Kahn, and, perhaps most appropriately, "Lucky Lindy" himself.

Delano & Aldrich's design is all about geometry—a massive rectangle forming the entrance to a large circular space. Typically for the late date, but also logically for a low building, its windows run horizontally rather than vertically. Its simple materials play off against each other, mostly buff and black brick with a horizontal band of stainless steel separating the first and second stories. The somewhat austere composition takes off with a very Deco flight of fancy just below the roofline: a glazed terra-cotta band of golden flying fish (they've also been called dolphins) against a blue background. Peter Pennoyer and Anne Walker, in their monograph on Delano & Aldrich, point out that Delano used this motif on many other buildings—but surely nowhere more appropriately than here.

Inside, the terminal's central rotunda boasts what has been called the largest and last of the nation's WPA murals, a history of flight—from birds to the Wright Brothers to the 1930s—by James Brooks. Though they'd been painted over in 1952, a major campaign in the late 1970s—thankfully—restored the murals to their original state, and Brooks lived to see it happen.

## 14.4 Blessed Sacrament Church complex, 35th Avenue from 93rd to 94th Streets Henry J. McGill: School 1932, convent 1936, rectory 1937, church designed 1941, built 1948–50

Who builds a new church complex in the middle of the Depression? A new parish serving a new population with children in need of proper schooling, that's who. In the first decade of the twentieth century, Jackson Heights consisted largely of wheat fields. With the opening of the Queensboro Bridge connecting to Manhattan and the pressure of returning World War I veterans, the neighborhood began developing quickly, and attracted, among other people, an upwardly mobile Irish Catholic community (so says the church's fiftieth anniversary booklet). The new parish of the Blessed Sacrament, established in June of 1929—barely four months before the great Crash—provided parishioners a modest frame church for worship. Despite the worsening Depression, the community grew, and its children needed a school—hence the 1932 school building (now used as a New York City public school) at the corner of 94th Street. Before long, however, the Sisters who taught at the school needed proper housing, hence the new convent building of 1936 next door. A new rectory followed in 1937. Finally, the old wooden church, on the corner of 93rd Street, could no longer accommodate church-goers, who were spilling over into the school auditorium on Sundays. Following a groundbreaking in August 1948, and a cornerstone laying in January 1949, Thomas E. Molloy, archbishop of Brooklyn, dedicated the new church in June 1950.

School

Convent

The three main buildings line up on 35th Avenue from 93rd Street (on the west) to 94th Street (on the east) in reverse chronological order. The school has a long, low façade, stretching along 94th Street, that seems to jump forward a few feet toward the street every couple of windows. Patterned brickwork abounds, and the cast-stone trim takes on interesting geometric forms—but it's on the 37th Avenue façade that

Rectory

Church

Church entrance detail

McGill fully indulges his taste for the modernistic, with a round-arched entrance that has a tall shaft running up through its middle to a patterned cast-stone top and a staircase motif topping the arch. The Convent next door offers a contrast in its curving apse of a façade—but always with Deco flourishes in the brick patterning and cast-stone ornament. The church at the corner of 93rd Street starts off at the bottom with wide red brick stripes and narrow light stone stripes—but gradually the brick stripes become thinner and the stone stripes thicker until the tower at the top is faced entirely in stone.

The design creates that typically Deco effect of color growing lighter toward the top, and taking our eyes with it. The sculpted figures at the top—and the shape of the tower generally—recall McGill's 1931 Crucifixion Tower in Royal Oak, Michigan. The church complex continues further north along 93rd Street with the rectory, which mixes modestly interesting geometric brick patterns with a memory of older styles.

If 1950 seems like a very late date for such a 1930s-style church design, there's a good reason—the design dates back a decade before construction. As reported by the press at the dedication: "Henry J. McGill . . . has described the structure as reflecting an ageless quality even though the design and details were completed in 1941. The building blends modern line with the classical tradition and is essentially American in its expression."

### *Forest Hills*

## 14.5 ⋆Ridgewood Savings Bank, 107–55 Queens Boulevard (at 108th Street)<br>Halsey, McCormack & Helmer, 1939–1940

Bank specialists Halsey, McCormack & Helmer (for the firm, see 12.11) designed this Ridgewood Savings Bank branch—the bank's first—to serve the fast-growing neighborhood of Forest Hills. The location on Queens

Boulevard, near a major subway stop, offered the Queens version of the location of the firm's Dollar Savings Bank (12.11) in the Bronx built a few years earlier.

The unusual design for the Ridgewood Savings Bank—a rectangle with projecting semicircular ends—won a Queens Chamber of Commerce building award for excellence. Taking advantage of its traffic-island site, the architects lavished attention on every one of the building's façades. Typically Moderne ornament includes decorative bronze grilles and stylized eagles. At either curving end, the roofline above the inscription of the bank's name sports a pair of wavy lines enclosing a contrasting curve, sectioned off by flame-like stone crowns every few feet. Below, the clock surmounting the entrance (above the inscription "FOREST HILLS OFFICE") sits atop curving triple speed lines. But it's not just the lines that wave—the window bays around the side, perhaps taking a cue from One Wall Street (1.3), curve concavely, so that the entire building seems in motion. The overall design depends less on decorative details than on the contrast between the curving window bays and the neighboring broad flat stone surfaces.

The large open interior, surrounded by 360 degrees' worth of enormous windows, enjoys wonderful daylight. Particularly handsome details include the ceiling plasterwork and the original Moderne chandeliers suspended high overhead. Both the exterior and interior of the bank have changed little over the past seventy-five years.

## 14.6 RKO Midway Theater, 108–22 Queens Boulevard (at 71st Road) Thomas Lamb Associates, 1941–42

Catty-corner across Queens Boulevard from the Ridgewood Savings Bank, the RKO Midway Theater took its name from the Battle of Midway in World War II—as described in its opening brochure, which imagined the theater speaking to its new patrons: "June 4th and the thrilling news of the great victory at Midway Island proved not only an inspiration to the world, but also to my bosses. They were unanimous in their decision that there

could be but one name for me. And so—in respectful tribute to those gallant and brave Americans, I was named the MIDWAY. It is a great and illustrious name—and I am mighty proud of it." The theater's opening night gala included a newsreel describing its namesake victory.

In chatty mode in the brochure, the Midway went on to describe its architectural style, and pay tribute to its architect: "I am what you would call modernistic—with all the newest wrinkles and latest gadgets. Here and now I want to give thanks to the late Thomas Lamb, one of the greatest of theatrical architects. In me, his last theatre, you will find the best example of his genius."

One of New York's—and the country's—most prolific theater architects, Thomas Lamb (1871–1942) designed hundreds of theaters for cities around the world. His grand eclectic movie palaces of the 1920s, seating many thousands, eventually gave way in the Depression years to much smaller Moderne houses, of which the Midway appears to be the last. Its interior, sadly, is no more, but its white granite façade still ripples along Queens Boulevard, marked by its modernistic vertical sign. Typically for theaters of the period, it includes related storefronts in a wing that turns the corner in a streamlined curve.

### *Elmhurst*

## 14.7 Mathews Houses, Grand Avenue, Calamus Avenue, Ankener Avenue, Elks Road, 79th to 82nd Streets Curtis X. Mathews, 1931–1942

Though housing construction—and construction generally—slowed to a crawl during the 1930s, one builder saw only endless potential and pent-up demand for new houses. Gustave X. Mathews (1871–1958), founder of the G. X. Mathews Company, a major builder of Queens housing, was quoted at length in the *Long Island Daily Star* in April 1933—near the lowest point of the Great Depression—on what he saw as "a shortage of desirable up-to-date housing space, newly built." Mathews declared "it is safe to predict that the first revival of activity will be in popular-priced one-family houses." Moreover, he continued, "Home seekers . . . want new houses—the same as they want new shoes and new clothes."

Mathews knew quite a bit about house construction. Starting in the first decade of the twentieth century, his company built well over a thousand houses, flats, and tenements across the borough. The "Mathews Model Flats" still dominate the streets of Ridgewood. In 1915, New York City's Tenement House Department chose the Mathews Flats as "the most up-to-date method of housing for the masses at a minimum of cost."

From Ridgewood, the company branched out to other Queens neighborhoods. In September 1931, the Mathews Company brought housing for the masses to Elmhurst, with plans to build "forty two-story one-family brick dwellings" on the blocks of Ankener Avenue, Elks Road, Calamus Avenue, and 79th Street in Elmhurst, on land formerly part of a Long Island Railroad station. In November of that year, the company filed plans for another thirteen houses on Calamus Avenue south of Elks Road; in 1932, ten more, now on the west side of Grand Avenue west of Calamus Avenue, in 1933, a seventeen-family tenement at the corner of Ankemus and Calamus, and four thirteen-family tenements on the corner of Calamus and Grand, plus another forty-nine houses at Ankener, Calamus, Grand, and 79th Street; and so on in 1935, 1936, 1938, 1939, and 1940. In August 1942, the *New York Sun* could report that the Mathews company had "completed the last of 400 two-family attached homes of the garden type in Elmhurst," dwellings containing "three and four-room suites with garages and garden areas."

Each filing listed Mathews's son, Curtis X. Mathews, as "owner and architect," though there's no available indication that Curtis was a licensed architect rather than a builder. In Ridgewood, Louis Allmendinger had served as architect for almost all the Mathews flats. Allmendinger's designs moved in modernistic directions after 1930—he designed the Art Deco Kurtz Brothers Store (14.8) in Jamaica in 1931, the same year that the Mathews operation in Elmhurst got underway—and perhaps Allmendinger had some initial involvement with the project (though he died in 1937, five years before completion of the final batch of houses).

In any case, the resulting development includes some of the very few Art Deco houses anywhere in the city. The company advertised them in the *Times* in March 1933 as "Mathews new style homes." In August 1942, the *Times* wrote: "Each block in the project is a self-contained community with gardens and garages" and "all the houses have a modernistic type of exterior architecture." The earlier houses use red and yellow brick and a very simple geometry—including projecting red brick verticals, where the houses meet, that rise above the roof to provide a modest skyline; the last batch, from 1942, continue the geometry, but the yellow brick has disappeared.

### *Jamaica*

## 14.8 *Kurtz Brothers Store, 162–24 Jamaica Avenue (at Guy Brewer Boulevard, near 163rd Street) Allmendinger & Schlendorf, 1931

On the south side of Jamaica Avenue, in the heart of the borough's major urban center, stands a six-story neighborhood furniture store that somehow manages to suggest the pizzazz of a 1930s Midtown skyscraper. Jacob Kurtz founded his company in 1870, and by 1931 it had expanded to four retail stores, including this one, which the Kurtz firm operated until 1978. In the 1930s, Jamaica Avenue still had an elevated train rumbling overhead; the Kurtz family asked their architects to design an up-to-the-minute modern structure that would catch the eye of passing train passengers.

Louis Allmendinger (1876–1937) and M. Allen Schlendorf (1902–?), both New York–trained, worked together out of a Brooklyn office from 1926 until Allmendinger's death. Their work tended to conservative styles, making the Kurtz Brothers store an unusual project for the firm. Half a century later, in a letter to the Landmarks Commission, Schlendorf explained that his clients specifically requested a "modern and colorful" design to match the style of the modern furniture on display in the store. Though Schlendorf also cited the influence of Frank Lloyd Wright on his design, "modern and colorful" in 1931—the year of the Chrysler Building's completion—could mean only one thing: Art Deco.

Comparing the humble Kurtz store to the mighty Chrysler Building (5.4) might seem a stretch, but consider: a combination of vertical columns of windows playing off horizontal windows at the corners, a black stone base with white brick above, a silhouette of receding verticals (the Chrysler

Building's own profile, the Kurtz store's four-story window bays). There's something about the choice of materials—black and white glazed tile, cast aluminum bands, even skyscraper silhouettes in silver once painted across the windows—that conjures Manhattan towers. The only, perhaps unexpected, contrast comes from the top corners with panels of golden foliage in glazed terra-cotta.

## 14.9 ★La Casina, 90–33 160th Street (between Jamaica Avenue and 90th Avenue) c. 1933

The little building with the big Moderne roof—and tall central sign with letters spelling out "Jamaica Dental"—once played home, according to ads in the *Long Island Daily Press*, to "Bert Voegel and Marie Lawson gyrating rhumba rhythm to the tune of 'Ma She's Making Eyes at Me'" and such lineups as "Bobbie Trotter, Chubby Stanley, Gladys Cross, Bill M'Donald, La Casina Swing Band and Bevy of Beautiful Girls. 3 shows nightly." That was back in the mid-1930s, following the conversion of a small office building into La Casino (the original spelling, later changed to La Casina), a nightclub in downtown Jamaica that styled itself the "Show Place of Long Island." Barely a decade later, the nightclub gave way to a church, provoking this reminiscence in the April 17, 1943 *Long Island Daily Press*: "La Casina, a former Jamaica night club, has been converted into a church. Recently, a funeral was held there. As the casket was being carried in, a bystander remarked, 'I've seen a lot of guys being carried out of that place in the old days, but this is the first time I've seen anybody carried IN!'"

Aside from the stuccoed first floor—including wall segments stepping into the entrance—the design is all about the extraordinary roofline: a streamlined ziggurat sheathed in aluminum (which replaced the original galvanized sheet metal).

Subsequent changes of use for the building led to its embalming in aluminum siding, but a preservation effort in 1995 brought the façade back to its original condition, minus only the vertical neon sign—hidden within the aluminum projection—that once lured revelers from nearby Jamaica Avenue.

## 14.10 ★Suffolk Title and Guarantee Company Building, 90–04 161st Street (at 90th Avenue) Dennison & Hirons, 1929; terra-cotta panels by Rene Chambellan

Bank specialists Dennison & Hirons (for the firm, see 5.2) designed this modest office building for a Long Island–based company—with the slogan, "A Title Company that Knows Long Island"—just a year after winning the competition for the Beaux-Arts Institute of Design (5.2) in Midtown. Suffolk's offices once filled the entire building.

The architects gave the Title Company's new home a very straightforward Deco design (the original announcement of the project in the *New York Times* in September 1928 described it as "a modernized treatment of the Gothic"), with the typical vertical columns of windows and setbacks, and nicely handled brickwork at the very top, ending in blocky piers in setback upon setback. But it's the highly ornamental metalwork and wonderful, brightly colored glazed terra-cotta panels that distinguish this building from so many other small office buildings.

The elaborate, stunning metalwork around the double-height entrance—including a pair of gryphons over the doorway, and typically Deco images of vividly stylized foliage—would be sufficiently distinguishing, but they are joined by second-story window spandrels with glazed colored terra-cotta images of fountains superimposed over fabulous abstract geometric patterning, apparently the work of Rene Chambellan, and not unlike the terra-cotta panels adorning Dennison & Hirons's State Bank Building in Midtown (5.10) designed a year earlier.

## 14.11 Montgomery Ward Department Store, 151–14 Jamaica Avenue (at 153rd Street) Montgomery Ward staff architects, 1930–31

The old Montgomery Ward building on Jamaica Avenue offers a counterpart to the Sears Roebuck store in Flatbush (13.6) built the following year—Flatbush being to Brooklyn what Jamaica is to Queens, a large and centrally located residential and commercial district. Founded in Chicago in 1872, Montgomery Ward became the country's largest mail-order operation, but decided to branch out into retail stores as well. In 1930, the company announced the construction in Jamaica of their largest department store east of their Chicago headquarters. It was planned, according to the *Daily Press* in January 1931, to "cater to Greater New York and Long Island. It will carry a complete line of women's, men's, and children's wearing apparel, and jewelry, household furnishings, furniture, automobile parts, electrical equipment, plumbing and paint supplies, stationery, sporting goods, farm implements and delicacies."

On March 19, 1931, just days before the grand opening, Montgomery Ward invited all of Jamaica to an inspection—and some twenty-eight thousand people accepted. As reported in the *Long Island Daily Press*: "The store wore its brightest air last night as formally dressed executives and department heads received the guests at the Jamaica Avenue doors, just opposite King Park. . . . The cold rain failed to dampen the ardor of the thousands who waited in long lines last night to enter the store."

The *Daily Press* went into some detail describing the building's design, which it characterized as displaying a

> conservative modernistic trend. . . . The customer is given beauty with utility and hidden comfort. The big surfaced building is

kept from taking on a squatty appearance . . . by slender white terra cotta pilasters set along its façade. Lancing strips of chromium decorating the outer walls glint black [sic] the light and help create the illusion of slenderness in a big building. Slabs of black stone give contrast to the grey brilliance of the metal. The modern decoration is carried out in the interior. The elevators shine with chromium. The floor indicators and push button[s] are chromium and bronze. Doorways are decorated with the flat angularity which makes for utility and beauty at once. Throughout the building the wood fittings maintain the soft luster of honey colored maple finish. . . . Lights never glare; they're deftly hidden in the newest of indirect effects—even in showcases, and window displays. . . . The new Montgomery Ward building is big and it is built for shopping comfort. A lot of planning has gone into Jamaica's newest and largest store.

Long since converted to other uses, the building still retains much of its "conservative modernistic" exterior detail, especially the "slender white terra-cotta pilasters" (more likely cast stone) flanking the entrance, carved with floral fantasies. But the "strips of chromium" seem to have disappeared.

# ITINERARY NO. 15
# STATEN ISLAND

Though geographically large, Staten Island has by far the smallest population of the city's five boroughs—perhaps one-tenth the population of Brooklyn. Many new neighborhoods that have grown up in recent decades reflect earlier towns and villages. The borough has very little Deco, but definitely some buildings of interest.

## 15.1 *Tompkinsville (Joseph H. Lyons) Pool, Victory Boulevard (at Murray Hulbert Avenue) Joseph L. Hautman and others, architects; Aymar Embury II, consulting architect; 1934–36

The Lyons Pool is part of the same set of eleven giant swimming pools and recreation centers—the only one in Staten Island, and the only one not part of a larger park—built by Robert Moses with federal funding; see Crotona Park Play Center (12.14) for details. The entrance to the Lyons Pool is through a domed rotunda with narrow windows.

## 15.2 Paramount Theater, 560 Bay Street (at Union Place), Stapleton Rapp & Rapp, 1930

Most Staten Island movie theaters were built by the local Moses family, including the Art Deco Lane Theater in New Dorp (15.5) in 1937–38. But in 1930, the big national corporation of Paramount brought in Rapp & Rapp to design this small theater on Bay Street in Stapleton.

Better known for their four- and five-thousand-seat eclectically designed 1920s movie palaces in Chicago, and the skyscraping Paramount

Building (5.9) in Times Square, in the early 1930s Rapp & Rapp turned to small Moderne theaters, including the Warner Theater (1930) in West Chester, and the Erie Theater (1931) in Erie, both in Pennsylvania, and the Paramount (1931) in Aurora, Illinois.

Rapp & Rapp's design for the Staten Island Paramount exaggerates its size with what amounts to a monumental false front faced in two colors of brick set in geometric patterns; tall cast-stone geometric piers run vertically up the façade. At the base on either side of the entrance, the Rapps included a tall panel with a typically modernistic stylized floral pattern inscribed in an oval and surrounded with a honeycomb full of fleurs-de-lis—a reminder perhaps of their 1920s French-inspired extravaganzas.

The design of this tiny building seems to suggest a skyscraper—precisely the architects' intention. In the April 1930 issue of *Exhibitors Herald-World*, the Rapps' chief designer, Arthur Frederick Adams, described the theater's façade as "emphasizing the domination of 'skyscraper lines' and the depth of the reveals. Note the participation of light in the general effect of this modernistic exterior. If the sun is friend to Stapleton, the actual effect cannot be far different from that got by the artist." Adams went on to note that "[t]he spirit of modern art which has influenced quite a great deal of our commercial work . . . is gradually finding its place in the designing of theatres. . . . The new, or modernistic art, is beginning to assert itself prominently, especially in smaller theatres."

Adams's idea of what "modernistic" should look like seems clear from his description of the interior: "While the subject is romantic, the rendering is in the modern manner, with direct lines and sharp surfaces carrying the outline of the figures."

## 15.3 Ambassador Apartments, 30 Daniel Low Terrace (at Crescent Avenue) Lucian Pisciotta, 1931–32

Staten Island's only Art Deco apartment house—which looks like it got lost on its way to the Bronx—is also one of the city's most inventively

ornamental. Though just six and seven stories tall (thanks to the sloping site), it occupies its entire block front—giving it three façades—and towers over neighboring houses. Pisciotta, though less well known than some of his contemporaries, had already designed apartment houses in the Bronx, but the Ambassador must be his best-known work.

As reported in the *Times*, "The equipment includes many of the refinements which have come to be associated with tall modern apartment buildings. The lobby is modernistic in design. The bathrooms are finished in colored tile, with built-in clothes hampers." Pisciotta's design includes all the standard elements of Art Deco apartment buildings: light and dark alternating brick courses, vertical columns of windows, abstract geometric spandrels between the windows. What stands out, however, is the terra-cotta ornament that shows up all over the building, most notably at the entrance, where, in the words of Susan Tunick, of the Friends of Terra Cotta, "[t]he metallic finish in combination with brilliant glaze colors creates a stunning entry." Most of the building's ornament survives, with the unfortunate exception of a pair of six-foot, nickel-plated wrought-iron sculptures of peacocks that once graced the front doors—sold, it is said, by a prior owner to an antique dealer.

The building's convenience to the Staten Island ferry made it a viable option for young actors—Paul Newman and Martin Sheen once lived here.

## 15.4 Public Health Service Hospital (now Bayley Seton Hospital), 75 Vanderbilt Avenue (at Bay Street) Kenneth Murchison et al., 1933–36

Bayley Seton Hospital occupies the grounds of the old Seamen's Retreat, established back in 1831 to provide hospital care for sailors. Several of the buildings here date to the 1840s, but the main building facing the entrance from Vanderbilt Avenue is a tall, wide Art Deco hospital built a century later as part of a New Deal program, the National Recovery Administration (NRA). Indeed, in September 1933, the *Times* reported the hospital's groundbreaking as the program's very first project: "While Representative Anning S. Prall was breaking ground yesterday for the new $2,000,000 Public Health Service Hospital at Stapleton, S.I., a telegram was received from Assistant Secretary of the Treasury Lawrence W. Robert. It read: 'This project will be the first under the NRA program. The people of Staten Island are to be commended on their effort to see that this work was approved.'" The "people of Staten Island" in question included the twenty thousand islanders who had signed a petition, from the Staten Island Chamber of Commerce, in favor of the project.

Kenneth Murchison's broad, low pavilioned design—with a central tower and projecting wings at either end—kept to a modest brick ornamental scheme. Only at the roofline and the entrance did he (or the federal budget) allow cast-stone ornament in typically modernistic patterns. Stylized floral panels top all the windows at the uppermost story, while at the entrance geometrically patterned metal grilles support cast-stone reliefs of oddly metallic-looking American eagles (representing the federal government), flanking an image of a sailing ship (presumably representing the original Seamen's Retreat)—the whole entrance flanked by tall stone pylons with geometric metal light fixtures.

## 15.5 ★★★Lane Theater, 168 New Dorp Lane (at 8th Street), New Dorp John Eberson, 1937–38

Another rare survivor of New York's small, Depression-era Moderne movie theaters (like the Midtown in Manhattan, 9.9, the Midway in Queens, 14.6, or the Paramount on Bay Street, 15.2), the Lane Theater is among the last surviving pre-World War II theaters on Staten Island, and the last built by the island's dominant theater family, the Moses brothers. To design the Lane, Charles Moses hired John Eberson, one of the country's top movie-palace architects. The grand, so-called atmospheric theaters, seating thousands, that made Eberson's name in the 1920s no longer made economic sense in the 1930s, so instead Eberson turned out a number of much smaller neighborhood houses, like the Lane, in the newly fashionable Moderne style.

Outside, the Lane occupies part of a one-story row of storefronts. Though small, its entrance dominates the street with its chrome trim marquee and, above, the letters "Lane" spelled out in modernistic typeface and tucked into a curving speed line—like no other theater entrance in New York.

Inside, Eberson designed the auditorium as an ellipse—a decidedly modernistic shape—adorned with geometric bands zooming across the ceiling and running down the sides, and abstract ceiling murals on astronomical themes (similar murals on the walls disappeared some time ago). Originally lit indirectly from the banding, the murals were later described as some of "the first fluorescent murals utilizing black light." In Eberson's famous 1920s atmospheric theaters, he painted the auditorium's sides and ceilings to suggest the illusion of an outdoor scene, under an evening sky, in a far-away exotic locale. At the Lane, Eberson updated that concept to a modern, astronomical evening sky—a concept reflected in some of the names Eberson initially suggested for the theater: the Globe, the Astro, or the Novo. In later years converted for use as a nightclub, and as of this writing a church, the Lane's landmark interior nevertheless survives intact.

# A NOTE ON SOURCES

This book is, strictly, a guidebook, not a work of scholarship. The definitive history of New York City architecture in the 1920s and 1930s has yet to be written. The research behind this guidebook comes from many sources. By far the largest source: the dozens of designation reports prepared by my colleagues, past and present, at the New York City Landmarks Preservation Commission. These include solid work by Janet Adams (6.10, 7.7), Betsy Bradley (2.6, 9.12, 12.13), Christopher D. Brazee (12.1), David Breiner (2.10), Michael Caratzas (5.6), Andrew S. Dolkart (8.1, 8.9, 14.9), Nancy Goeschel (14.3), Gale Harris (1.4, 6.1a), Tara Harrison (15.1), Virginia Kurshan (1.1a and b, 1.3, 3.4, 3.5, 13.2, 14.5, 14.8, 14.10), Lynne Marthey (9.9), Jennifer Most (12.14), Marjorie Pearson (5.4), Margaret Pickart (2.4), Matthew Postal (1.6, 2.1, 6.12, 13.6, 13.8), Donald Presa (12.15, 14 1), Gina Santucci (7.9), Charles Savage (6.4/6.6, 6.9, 12.11), Jay Shockley (1.5, 9.10, 12.6), William Stargard (5.11), and Elisa Urbanelli (5.2, 5.3, 5.9), as well as by the author (3.3/3.6, 5.1, 5.8/5.12, 6.5/6.7, 12.4, 15.5). Some of the early reports are anonymous; some reports, especially historic district reports, are the collective work of the staff. All the reports are available online and make for excellent additional reading. The author also wrote several National Register nominations for buildings not also designated as local landmarks (4.6, 10.2, 10.7, 11.3, and for historic districts in Murray Hill, the Wall Street Financial District, and the Garment District that include Art Deco buildings). Links to all these reports are available on a web page (http://tinyurl.com/NYCDeco).

A second major source—both for the reports just mentioned and also for new information included in this book—is the *New York Times*, which covered the New York real-estate market in extraordinary detail during the 1920s and 1930s (and also ran some very interesting ads), as well as a variety of local newspapers.

Excellent biographies or monographs cover the work of several major architects from the period. Particularly helpful: Jewel Stern's book on Ely Jacques Kahn (Jewel Stern and John A. Stuart, *Ely Jacques Kahn, Architect: Beaux-Arts to Modernism in New York*, W.W. Norton & Co., 2006); Andrew

Dolkart and Susan Tunick's study of George and Edward Blum (Andrew S. Dolkart, Susan Tunick, *George & Edward Blum*, Princeton Architectural Press, 1996); Steve Ruttenbaum's work on Emery Roth (Steven Ruttenbaum, *Mansions in the Clouds: The Skyscraper Palazzi of Emery Roth*, Balsalm Press, 1986); Peter Pennoyer and Anne Walker's book on Delano & Aldrich (Peter Pennoyer and Anne Walker, *The Architecture of Delano & Aldrich*, W.W. Norton & Co., 2003); and Annice Alt's study of Boak & Paris (Annice M. Alt, *Boak & Paris/Boak & Raad: New York Architects*, XLIBRIS, 2014). Ralph Walker's office produced a monograph on that architect's work (Ralph Walker, *Ralph Walker: Architect*, Henahan House, 1957). Walter Kilham, who worked in Raymond Hood's office, later wrote a biography of his employer (Walter H. Kilham, Jr., *Raymond Hood Architect: Form Through Function in the American Skyscraper*, Architectural Book Publishing Co., 1973). Joan Kahr wrote the definitive book on ironworker Edgar Brandt (Joan Kahr, *Edgar Brandt: Master of Art Deco Ironwork*, Harry N. Abrams, 1999). The murals and mosaics of Hildreth Meière now have their own book, by Catherine Coleman Brawer and Kathleen Murphy Skolnik (Catherine Coleman Brawer and Kathleen Murphy Skolnik, *The Art Deco Murals of Hildreth Meière*, Andrea Monfried Editions, 2014). And one massive complex, Rockefeller Center, is the subject of several excellent books, notably those by Alan Balfour (Alan H. Balfour, *Rockefeller Center: Architecture as Theatre*, McGraw-Hill, 1978) and Carole Krinsky (Carole Herselle Krinsky, *Rockefeller Center*, Oxford University Press, 1978).

Other works cover more general topics. Robert A. M. Stern's enormous compendium, *New York 1930*, is a treasure-trove of information and research resources (Robert A. M. Stern, Gregory F. Gilmartin, and Thomas Mellins, *New York 1930: Architecture and Urbanism Between the Two World Wars*, Rizzoli, 2009). *Terra-Cotta Skyline* by Susan Tunick—founder of the Friends of Terra Cotta—is a must for any building adorned with that material (Susan Tunick, *Terra-Cotta Skyline: New York's Architectural Ornament*, Princeton Architectural Press, 1997). The Bronx's Grand Concourse has found its biographer in Constance Rosenblum (Constance Rosenblum, *Boulevard of Dreams: Heady Times, Heartbreak, and Hope along the Grand Concourse*, New York University Press, 2009). Jules Stewart offers a broad survey of life in New York during the 1930s (Jules Stewart, *Gotham Rising: New York in the 1930s*, I.B. Tauris, 2016). And David Garrard Lowe looks at Art Deco architecture in its wider cultural setting (David Garrard Lowe, *Art Deco New York*, Watson-Guptill, 2004).

# REFERENCES

## Introduction

Skyscrapers, World Series, tabloids, radio, movies: Martin Weyrich, editor at the *New York Graphic.*

"entirely too much talk": *New York Tines Magazine*, November 1, 1931, p. 81.

"Beauty is utility": *Liberty*, December 7, 1929, p. 66.

"brilliant bad boy": *The New Yorker*, April 11, 1931, p. 26.

"Ziegfeld of his profession": *American Architect*, September 1930, p. 24.

"rising in sheer exultation": *Lippincott's Magazine*, March 1896.

"Do you realize we are living through the second time people got tired of Art Deco?": *The New Yorker*, October 1, 1984, p. 41.

## Itinerary No. 1

Introduction "probably at no previous time": *Wall Street Journal*, June 12, 1930, p. 5.

1.2 "modern expression of classic motifs": *New York Times*, November 20, 1929, p. 58.

1.3 "the building does relate well to Trinity Church": *Ralph Walker Architect*, p. 36.

1.5 "modernized French Gothic": *Wall Street Journal*, April 10, 1929, p. 19.

1.6 "we really get a thrill": *Metalcraft*, July 1932, p. 4.

"elevator flirtations": *The Citizen Advertiser*, Auburn, New York, October 24, 1931; cited in the Landmarks Preservation Commission's designation report.

1.7 "one of the dominating structures": *New York Times*, April 26, 1931, p. RE6.

1.8 "evidence of the demand for office space": *New York Times*, February 23, 1930, p. 161.

1.9 "the best points of the Empire State Building": Lewis Mumford, "The Sky Line: Skyscrapers and Tenements," *The New Yorker*, June 3, 1933, p. 36 (cited by Andrew S. Dolkart in the National Register nomination for 99 John Street).

1.11 "Our Skyscrapers Take Simple Forms": *New York Times*, May 2, 1926, p. SM11.
"If there is any pessimism": *New York Times*, April 14, 1928, p. 35.

## Itinerary No. 2

2.1 "the volume of business transacted": *Wall Street Journal*, March 16, 1931, p. 18.

2.2 "Erect Taxpayer on $3,000,000 Plot": *New York Times*, June 3, 1934, p. RE1.

2.4 "as modern in conception as the telephone": *Ralph Walker Architect*, p. 15.

2.6 "the heart of a nerve system of wires and cables": Cited in the Landmarks Preservation Commission's designation report.

2.7 "the largest architectural program in the United States": *New York Times*, February 14, 1928, p. 22.
"monumental in character": *New York Times*, March 5, 1927, p. 1.

2.8 "probably the foremost metal craftsman": *Iron Age*, April 6, 1939.

2.9 "the oldest criminal tribunal in the country," *New York Times*, August 30, 1941, p. 15.
"The new building assumes for the first time": *New York Times*, June 29, 1941, p. X7.

## Itinerary No. 3

3.1 "shining through transparent panels": *New York Times*, August 24, 1930, p. RE2.

3.4 "the nation's leading authority": Jewel Stern, *Ely Jacques Kahn*, p. 104.
Contemporary interview in *The New York World*: Robert A. M. Stern, *New York 1930*, p. 105.
"a permanent showcase": Jewel Stern, *Ely Jacques Kahn*, p. 109.

3.5 "I saw his work in Paris": Joan Kahr, *Edgar Brandt, Master of Art Deco Iron-work*, p. 168.
"thirty designs inspired by Edgar Brandt's work": *New York Times*, February 16, 1925, p. 4.

3.8 "The building is not fashioned": *New York Times*, November 3, 1929, p. N6.

3.10 "The building is simple in design": *New York Times*, December 7, 1937, p. 26.
"If our predecessors": *Christian Science Monitor*, June 29, 1939, p. 19.

3.11 "exhibit some of the most notable Art Deco terra cotta": Dolkart and Tunick, *George & Edward Blum*, p. 44.

## Itinerary No. 4

Murray Sices: *Seventh Avenue in the city of New York* (Fairchild Publications, 1953), p. 3.

4.1 "New York seldom has witnessed": *New York Times*, July 21, 1929, p. 140.

"1441 Broadway gives new distinction": *New York Times*, January 7, 1930, p. 57.

4.2 "one of the last of the famous old hostelries": *New York Times*, March 9, 1930, p. 169.

"the idea of a terrace just outside your office": *Architecture and Building*, April 1931, p. 86.

4.3 "With [Abraham] Bricken tearing down the old Casino": *World*, February 9, 1930.

"coming into the drafting room to announce": Jewel Stern, *Ely Jacques Kahn*, p. 160.

4.4 "This shift of the cloak and suit trade": *New York Times*, December 7, 1919, p. S5.

"The building exhibits the modern tendency": *New York Times*, April 22, 1928, p. RE1.

"thirty-seven years ago . . . sold candy for a living": *New York Times*, February 1, 1930, p. 36.

"Artistic Banking Office": *New York Times*, February 9, 1930, p. RE2.

4.5 "To many people, the towers standing side by side": *New York Times*, December 5, 1984, p. B6.

4.6 "his firm started to build six twenty-five-story buildings": *New York Times*, July 18, 1943, p. 35.

4.7 "If you lived in New York anytime from the 1930s": *New York Times*, December 10, 2000, p. CY1.

4.8 "Hotel New Yorker Open": *New York Times*, January 3, 1930, p. 41.

4.10 "while the structure is being prepared": *New York Times*, January 18, 1930, p. 32.

## Itinerary No. 5

5.1 "In Kilham's telling": Walter H. Kilham, Jr., *Raymond Hood, Architect*, p. 19.

"A contemporary critic": Douglas Haskell, "The Stripes of the News," *The Nation*, December 24, 1930, p. 713.

5.3 "When the new building of the Beaux-Arts Institute of Design": *New York Times*, February 10, 1929, p. 50.

"Café Bonaparte": *New York Times*, January 6, 1930, p. 35.

5.4 "to give his son something to be responsible for": Walter P. Chrysler, *Life of an American Workman* (New York: Dodd, Mead & Co., 1950), p. 197.

"from the top of the dome like a butterfly from its cocoon": William Van Alen, "The Structure and Metal Work of the Chrysler Building," *Architectural Forum*, October 1930.

5.5 "an impressive realization of the most hopeful predictions": Matlack Price, "The Chanin Building," *Architectural Forum* 50, May 1929, p. 699.

"an individual . . . may rise from a humble beginning": Cited in Donald L. Miller, *Supreme City: How Jazz Age Manhattan Gave Birth to Modern America* (New York: Simon & Schuster, 2014), p. 246.

5.6 "has avoided entablatures, architraves, pediments": *New York Times*, December 21, 1930, p. 141.

5.7 "Unlike any office building in the country": *New York Times*, January 20, 1924, p. RE1.

"the most daring experiment in color in modern buildings": Cited in the Landmarks Preservation Commission's designation report.

"blocking traffic as they stand to contemplate": *The American Architect and the Architectural Review*, November 19, 1924, p. 487.

5.10 "the marked increase in banking facilities": *New York Times*, December 9, 1928, p. RE1.

5.12 "Dutch blue at the base": Raymond Hood, "Comfort, Daylight & Air Architect's Aim—Raymond Hood Tells How He Designed New Building," *McGraw-Hill News*, August 1931, p. 4.

"lacquered like the body of a motor car": Frank Gale, "New West Side Tower Already Well Occupied," *New York Herald Tribune*, January 31, 1932, p. C8.

"simonized, just like the old car": *McGraw-Hill News*, August 1931, p. 3.

## Itinerary No. 6

6.1a "The Verticality of the Skyscraper": John Mead Howells "The Verticality of the Skyscraper," *American Architect* 134, Dec. 20, 1928, pp. 787–810.

"John Mead Howells . . . has scored what seems to be another knockout": "New Apartments," *The New Yorker*, September 22, 1928, p. 57.

"Towering above the East River, the Panhellenic House": *New York Times*, December 30, 1928, p. 66.

6.1b "enjoys all the charm of this exclusive old neighborhood": *New York Times*, May 12, 1931, p. 30.

6.2 "With the construction of these two houses": *New York Times*, April 12, 1931, p. RE2.

"The trend is toward the river": *The New Yorker*, June 8, 1935, p. 91.

"Two to five rooms . . . some with river view": *The New Yorker*, May 27, 1933, p. 35.

"You might like a studio apartment": *The New Yorker*, September 23, 1933, p. 40.

6.3 "private homes in a skyscraper": *The New Yorker*, September 12, 1931, p. 36.

"many prominent men and women": *New York Times*, April 30, 1930, p. 3.

6.6 "Romantic though radio may be": *Real Estate Record and Guide*, May 30, 1931, p. 8.

"an aura of colored light at night": *New York Times*, March 1, 1930, p. 18.

"downward at a thousand angles": *Real Estate Record and Guide*, May 30, 1931, p. 8.

6.7 "to incorporate in the future Waldorf-Astoria": *New York Times*, March 9, 1929, p. 1.

"smart contemporary effects and beautiful period interpretations": *New York Times*, September 27, 1931, p. SM8.

"Modernism, revivalism, eclecticism": *The New Yorker*, February 13, 1932, p. 48.

## Itinerary No. 7

7.1 "No store is more conveniently located": *New-York Tribune*, October 30, 1904, p. 5.

"Specialists in art, literature, politics": *New York Times*, April 22, 1930, p. 57.

7.2 "It is in the belief that the street presents": *New York Times*, February 24, 1929, p. 50.

"vertical shops": *New York Times*, December 16, 1928, p. RE2.

"the first high-class multiple-purpose skyscraper": *New York Times*, December 2, 1928, p. 191.

7.3 "the advantages of freedom from noise": *New York Times*, July 9, 1929, p. 58.

7.4 "whether engaged in the ART of BUSINESS or the BUSINESS of ART" and "The Barbizon has proximity to art galleries": W. Parker Chase, *New York: The Wonder City* (Wonder City Publishing, 1932), p. 139.

"the first fully equipped music-art residence": *New York Times*, May 12, 1930, p. 43.

"a semi-philanthropic hotel chain": Henry Collins Brown, *The Story of Old New York* (E. P. Dutton, 1934), p. 121.

7.5 "an adaptation to the modern tall building of the Georgian style": *New York Times*, March 25, 1931, p. 49.

"boarded up and left to the mercy of the elements": *New York Times*, June 1, 193, p. 37.

"a traditional London town home": *New York Times*, May 13, 1937, p. 47.

7.8 "newsreels are edited for release": Federal Writers Project, American Guide Series, *New York City Guide* (Random House 1939), p. 158.

Information on Furman supplied by his grandson, Richard Furman, the third generation to work in the firm.

7.9 "The customer drives into the garage": *New York Times*, June 29, 1927, p. 44.

## Itinerary No. 8

Introduction"Central Park West seems to have only one future": *Real Estate Record and Builders Guide*, December 20, 1890, Supplement, p. 29.

"The benefits of the multiple-dwelling act": *New York Times*, July 27, 1930, p. 131.

8.1 "While Europe is the motherland": *New York Times*, September 22, 1929, p. RE1.

"modern American": *New York Times*, January 3, 1932, p. RE1.

"Towers, roofs and terraces make the building": Century Apartments, sales brochure, cited in *A Romance with the City: Irwin S. Chanin* (Cooper Union Press, 1982) p. 80.

8.3 "Chanin told historian Andrew Dolkart": Interview with Andrew Dolkart, June 6, 1985, cited in the Landmarks Preservation Commission's Majestic Apartments designation report.

"large dining rooms, a grand ball room": *New York Times*, April 26, 1929, p. 1.

"a large solarium on the roof": *New York Times*, July 20, 1930, p. RE7.

8.5 "Much of the charm of the Living Room": *New York Times*, April 1, 1931, p. 27.

8.7 "a modern house of study": *New York Times*, March 22, 1925, p. 4.

8.10 "Architecture at all periods and at all times": *New York Sun*, May 5, 1931, p. 47.

## Itinerary No. 9

9.1 "a system of exterior and interior illumination": *New York Times*, November 30, 1930, p. RE1.

"Modern Uptown Eating Place": *New York Times*, October 20, 1931, p. 39.

9.2 "It will be definitely 1939": *New York Sun*, August 7, 1938 (cited in the Landmarks Preservation Commission's designation report).

9.3 "Much of the success in renting suites": *New York Times*, October 10, 1937, p. 198.

9.5 "West Eighty-sixth Street has undergone a rapid transition": *New York Times*, April 9, 1929, p. 61.

9.6 "touch off the first dynamite explosion": *New York Times*, October 9, 1939, page 17.

"Known as the 'skyscraper' school": *New York Times*, November 27, 1940, p. 17.

9.8 "the largest individual operation": *New York Times*, August 18, 1940, p. 123.

9.11 "dropped living rooms": *New York Times*, July 26, 1931, p. RE5.

9.12 "copy of a Tibetan monastery library": *The New Yorker*, July 14, 1934, p. 12.

"For the first time in the history of steel and brick": *New York Times*, September 15, 1929, p. RE1.

## Itinerary No. 10

10.1 "The building at 3–5 East 84th Street": *New York Times*, March 3, 1929, p. RE9.

10.2 "The house is designed in a modernistic spirit": *New York Times*, February 9, 1930, p. RE1.

"This is a materialistic, scientific and practical age": *New York Times*, November 30, 1930, p. RE2.

10.3 "freedom from drudgery": *New York Times*, December 7, 1930, p. 172.

"the English residential plan": *New York Times*, October 26, 1930, p. RE1.

10.4 "a modern adaptation of classical motifs": *New York Times*, December 29, 1929, p. RE2.

10.8 "People are tired of the monotonously colorless façades": *Buildings*, August 13, 1928, p. 38.

"the architect the opportunity to bring out whatever lines": *New York Times*, October 28, 1928, p. 179.

"Gradually our architects are able to convince": Bertram Hartman, Letter to Henry McBride (January 6,1926); cited in Martha Gage Elton, *Bertram Hartman (1882–1960), An Early Modernist from Kansas*, PhD dissertation, History of Art, University of Kansas.

## Itinerary No. 11

11.2 "A Barkin Apartment": *New York Times*, September 13, 1936, p. RE15.

11.3 "a very modernistic building, beautifully lighted": "Historical Sketch of Fourth Church of Christ, Scientist, New York City," typescript, 1933; held by the Mary Baker Eddy Library in Boston.

"believed to be the first such church": *New York Times*, May 23, 1932, p. 13.

11.12 "present to the eye the simple vernacular of our period": *The New Yorker*, October 28, 1939, p. 61.

11.14 "George Grey Barnard's old Cloisters, museum, home and studio": *New York Times*, December 30, 1943, p. 29.

11.15 "While Fort Tryon Park was under construction": *New York Times*, October 26, 1938, p. 42.

## Itinerary No. 12

12.1 "excellent example": *Architectural Forum*, June 1938, cited in the Landmarks Preservation Commission's designation report.

"My idea": *Magazine of Art*, April 1944, p. 140.

12.2 "Bronx Wonder Building": *New York Herald Tribune*, March 6, 1934, p. 2.

12.3 "a medley of curves": Constance Rosenblum, *Boulevard of Dreams*, p. 66.

"building contractor who is chairman": *New York Times*, August 16, 1938, p. 19.

12.4 "be developed in character along Modernistic lines": Ginsbern press release, copy formerly in the office of Horace Ginsbern & Associates, 205 E.42nd Street, New York City. The press release was quoted in part in the *New York Sunday Times* Real Estate Section, January 27, 1929, XII, 11:3.

12.6 "15,000 square feet in area": *New York Times*, October 11, 1931, p. RE11.

"Vandalism has destroyed much of the art deco": *New York Times*, January 15, 1976, p. 37.

"Behind the pool was a waterfall": *New York Times*, February 7, 1982, p. 49.

12.10 "of the same modernistic architectural design": *New York Times*, October 4, 1936, p. RE 10.

12.12 "more than interesting, full of ideas": Isabel Manship, in John Manship, *Paul Manship*, cited by Susan Rather, *Archaism, Modernism, and the Art of Paul Manship* (University of Texas Press, 1993), p. 158.

"clearly paid attention to the creations of Edgar Brandt": Susan Rather, *Archaism*, p. 158.

"Mr. Manship's sculpture is known for its rare qualities": *New York Times*, February 1, 1966, p. 31.

"Mr. Manship is understood to have worked intermittently": *New York Times*, March 14, 1933, p. 17.

"Paul Manship has faithfully reproduced": *New York Times*, June 15, 1934, p. 3.

12.13 "Modernism in architecture has reached the schools": *New York Times*, September 3, 1929, p. 3.

"This is New York City's first school building": *Architecture and Building*, March, 1932, pp. 12–13.

12.15 "The climax of the celebration was reached": *New York Times*, July 26, 1936, p. N1.

## Itinerary No. 13

13.1 "This new building, in its bold modern treatment": *New York Times*, March 30, 1930, p. RE1.

13.2 "A warm reddish-brown brick": *Architecture and Building*, December 1931, p. 161.

13.6 "building which strikingly carries out the modern architectural scheme": "Century of Progress" exposition guidebook, p. 100.

13.7 "But they were persuaded": *Municipal Engineers Journal*, 1933, v. 19, first quarterly issue.

13.8 "Graeco-Roman ornaments": *New York Times*, June 6, 1938, p. 16.

"a swan of a building, so to speak": *Brooklyn Eagle*, October 26, 1941, p. G5.

"As . . . one approaches the new building": *The New Yorker*, October 19, 1940, p. 57.

13.9 "more striking modern style": *New York Times*, April 12, 1936, p. RE1.

"When you move this fall—MOVE AHEAD!": *New York Times*, September 1, 1936, p. 16.

## Itinerary No. 14

14.2 "foremost liturgist of Catholic architects": *Brooklyn Eagle*, August 5, 1939, p. 10.

"somehow succeeded in marrying references": Robert A. M. Stern, *New York: 1930*, p. 167.

"it is hard to break away from": *Architecture and Building*, February 1932, p. 18.

14.3 "single greatest undertaking": *Fortune*, August, 1940. p. 41.

"Fifty years from now": *Life Magazine*, November 3, 1941, p. 99.

14.4 "Henry J. McGill . . . has described the structure": *Long Island Star-Journal*, June 10, 1950, p. 5.

14.7 "a shortage of desirable up-to-date housing space": *Long Island Daily Star*, April 8, 1933, p. 7.

"the most up-to-date method of housing": *Ridgewood Times*, December 31, 1914, p. 2.

"completed the last of 400 two-family attached homes": *New York Sun*, August 28, 1942, p. 30.

"Mathews new style homes": *New York Times*, March 26, 1933, p. RE3.

"Each block in the project is a self-contained community": *New York Times*, August 30, 1942, p. RE2.

14.9 "Bert Voegel and Marie Lawson gyrating": *Long Island Daily Press*, December 29, 1937, p. 14.

"Show Place of Long Island": *Long Island Daily Press*, August 14, 1936, p. 20.

"La Casina, a former Jamaica night club": *Long Island Daily Press*, April 17, 1943, p. 16.

14.10 "a modernized treatment of the Gothic": *New York Times*, September 2, 1928, p. 139.

14.11 "cater to Greater New York and Long Island": *Long Island Daily Press*, January 24, 1931, p. 3.

"The store wore its brightest air": *Long Island Daily Press*, March 20, 1931, pp. 1-2.

## Itinerary No. 15

15.2 "emphasizing the domination": *Exhibitors Herald-World*, April 1930.

15.3 "The equipment includes many": *New York Times*, November 8, 1931, p. RE2.

"metallic finish in combination with": Susan Tunick, *Terra-Cotta Skyline*, p. 108.

15.4 "While Representative Anning S. Prall": *New York Times*, September 19, 1933, p. 6.

15.5 "the first fluorescent murals": Theatre catalogue, Philadelphia, 1948.

# INDEX

Note: "Plate x" refers to an image in the color plate section following page 136.

# ABOUT THE AUTHOR

*Photo: Joyce Ravid*

A native New Yorker and twenty-year veteran of the New York City Landmarks Commission, Anthony W. Robins is the author of books on Grand Central Terminal, the World Trade Center, and the art and architecture of the New York subway system. He teaches about New York City architecture at New York University and Columbia University, and lectures nationally and internationally. A popular leader of New York City walking tours (for details please visit www.AnthonyWRobins.com), he is best known for Art Deco. He organized the city's first regularly scheduled series of Art Deco tours, sponsored by the Art Deco Society of New York. The Guides Association of New York City has honored him with the 2017 Guiding Spirit Award.

Robins lives on the Upper West Side with his wife and two cats.